On spiders, cyborgs and being scared

MANCHESTER
UNIVERSITY PRESS

On spiders, cyborgs and being scared

The feminine and the sublime

JOANNA ZYLINSKA

Manchester University Press

MANCHESTER AND NEW YORK

distributed exclusively in the USA by Palgrave

Published by Manchester University Press
Oxford Road, Manchester M13 9NR, UK
and Room 400, 175 Fifth Avenue, New York, NY 10010, USA
http://www.manchesteruniversitypress.co.uk

Distributed exclusively in the USA by
Palgrave, 175 Fifth Avenue, New York, NY 10010, USA

Distributed exclusively in Canada by
UBC Press, University of British Columbia, 2029 West Mall, Vancouver, BC, Canada V6T 1Z2

British Library Cataloguing-in-Publication Data
A catalogue record for this book is available from the British Library

Library of Congress Cataloging-in-Publication Data applied for

ISBN 0 7190 5823 6 *hardback*

First published 2001

10 09 08 07 06 05 04 03 02 01   10 9 8 7 6 5 4 3 2 1

Typeset in Stone fonts
by Koinonia, Manchester
Printed in Great Britain
by Bookcraft (Bath) Ltd, Midsomer Norton

To Krzysiek

Contents

Acknowledgements

This book would be unimaginable without the inspiration and support I have received over the years from Professor Tadeusz Sławek, my first supervisor and mentor.

I would like to thank Tempus-Phare, the Foundation for the Development of the Education System, for providing me with an Individual Mobility Grant in 1996 which allowed me to visit the University of Teesside, where this project first took shape. I am also grateful to my colleagues in the School of Law, Arts and Humanities at Teesside, in particular to Su Reid, Ben Knights, Dave Boothroyd and Mark Dooley, for inviting me and for providing such a stimulating research environment. My thanks also go to the British Council in Poland for awarding me an individual grant which allowed me to visit the University of East Anglia in 1997/98 and conduct the further research into the sublime that eventually resulted in this book. I am particularly indebted to Lorna Sage for her support and encouragement. I am also grateful to the English Department at the University of Wrocław, Poland for providing me with prolonged periods of study leave, without which the completion of this book would not have been possible. My heartfelt thanks go to my friends and colleagues from Wrocław: James Lynn, Ela Klimek, Dorota Kołodziejczyk and Patrycja Poniatowska. I am extremely grateful for the support I received from Bath Spa University College during the final stages of my work on this book. I also want to record my gratitude to my students at the Universities of Wrocław and Teesside, and at Bath Spa University College.

I am grateful to the three anonymous readers at Manchester University Press who commented on the manuscript at its different stages and provided some extremely helpful suggestions. I also want to thank the editors at Manchester University Press for their interest in this project and their help in its publication.

Thanks also to Gary Hall for his suggestions, advice and much more.

The earlier version of the first part of chapter 2 was originally published in *Women: A Cultural Review* in 1998. Selected parts of chapters 1 and 2 were published as 'Sublime Speculations: the Economy of the Gift in Feminist Ethics' in *j_spot: The Journal of Social and Political Thought* in June 2001. I am grateful to Routledge and *j_spot* for permission to use them here.

Introduction: 'a point of view'

> Without trying too much to *verify*, my sights always set on convincing you, I will tell you a story and describe for you a point of view. Indeed the point of view will be my theme. (Jacques Derrida, *Memoirs of the Blind*)

The experience of writing a book on the sublime itself creates a certain sublime feeling, a feeling of negative pleasure which mixes fear with delight. Exposed to an overabundance of thought on the subject, one has to find one's own way of managing its vertiginous excess. First of all, a sense of academic duty, which prompts me to provide a historical presentation of the body of knowledge on the sublime, has to be reconciled with a desire to develop my own 'extension' to that tradition. However, numerous analyses of the concept of the sublime, from that of Longinus through eighteenth-century aesthetics and the Romantics to the present, have already been conducted: I am thinking here of Samuel H. Monk's *The Sublime*, Paul Crowther's *The Kantian Sublime*, Thomas Weiskel's *The Romantic Sublime* or Peter de Bolla's *The Discourse of the Sublime*, to name but a few. This is why I have opted for a more contemporary reading of the sublime, a reading which, nevertheless, draws heavily on the historical tradition of sublimity.

Why the sublime?

> What has 'the sublime' to do with us? In common parlance, 'sublime' is one of those diminished words (like 'fantastic' or 'terrific') used to exclaim at anything from the delights of a certain kind of ice cream to the skills of a foreign footballer. It seems, banally, just to mean 'much better than usual'. But if we can rescue its older, deeper meanings, 'the sublime' catches an experience that we still recognise in a postmodern world, glimpsed in the dizzying reaches of interplanetary space or the vertiginous spirals of the human genome. (John Mullan, 'A Terrible Beauty', *The Guardian*, 19 August 2000)

This book is not only intended for those who have systematically traced recent developments in the areas of aesthetics, art and sublimity. By orientating my argument around the concept of the sublime, a concept which has undergone something of a renaissance in contemporary theoretical debates, I intend to introduce readers to a number of current events and issues. The sublime refers here to what Edward Rothstein describes in his 1997 contribution to *The American Scholar* as a 'relationship between disorder and order'. It is the effect that this relationship between order and disorder has on the mind, which is trying to create one out of the other, that sums up the experience of sublimity. As Rothstein puts it, 'the sublime provides an important model, an extreme case, of how we come to understand the world'.[1] The sublime is thus a particularly useful concept when it comes to describing the fears, anxieties and fascinations connected with the technological age. This sense of simultaneous confusion and enlightenment, the contradictory feeling of frailty and elevation, is associated with the broadly conceptualised condition of postmodernity.

Although I am reluctant to rely on 'postmodernity' as my reference point, precisely because of a somewhat frivolous use this term has enjoyed in both academic and non-academic discourses, I want to focus on the feeling of saturation, or excess, that characterises our everyday experience of being-in-the-world. Put crudely, for me the sublime names a certain sense of confusion, which is caused by what David Harvey calls 'space–time compression', resulting from progressing globalisation, increased communication and general acceleration of life.[2] I do not argue that we all experience these phenomena in the same way or with the same intensity, but rather that changes in the world economy, including the transformation of the cultural domain and the commodification of knowledge, are affecting our sense of identity, belonging and 'connectedness' in one way or another. As well as depicting the emergence of new, multiple, but also fragmented, identities, the sublime represents the waning of knowledge about what is going to happen: it is a sign of opening oneself to the future, which, in Derrida's words, 'is necessarily monstrous'[3] and thus unpredictable and perhaps also scary. However, like a good horror story, the sublime combines the conflicting feelings of terror and delight: it both frightens and offers a promise of relief.

One aspect I am particularly interested in when it comes to managing what I term the excess of the everyday is the possibility of making judgements. And even though the sublime was traditionally associated with aesthetics and art, it is not only judgements regarding artistic value that I want to investigate in this book. I am more concerned about the ethical dimension of the everyday, recognising at the same time that everyday life is not ultimately prescribed by any authority, be it divine or political. The sublime is therefore a term which is useful in bringing aesthetics, with its canons of perfection, and ethics, with its postulates of what it means to live a good life, together. It allows me to foreground the tension between pleasure and pain, or jubilation and horror, which is evident in every act of making a decision about value. But it also indicates that it is impossible *not* to choose, even if we are deprived of the ultimate guarantee regarding the rightness of our choice. I am thus interested in developing an ethical proposal outside a strictly delineated domain of philosophy, a proposal which responds to the (re)awakening of an ethical impulse in contemporary cultural studies and cultural theory. But I hope to do more than merely expound my 'theory'. Inspired by the spider's work, I want to weave my text together from a web of seemingly heterogeneous discourses – Orlan's carnal art, philosophies of the everyday, the French feminism of Hélène Cixous and Luce Irigaray, as well as the gender theory of Judith Butler, the European philosophy of Emmanuel Levinas, Jean-François Lyotard and Jacques Derrida, and the music of Laurie Anderson. Through the actual 'performance' of my argument (with all its accompanying first-night nerves, stage fright and fear of forgetting my lines), I hope to go some way towards blurring the boundaries between cultural theory and textual practice.

The feminine and the sublime

What I have found particularly fascinating when it has come to writing my own study of the sublime is the discovery that most theorists of the sublime attempt to control or even annul the discursive excess evoked by sublimity. This excess is often described in sexual terms, usually through images of disempowered and feeble femininity. As a consequence of this shrewd management of gains and losses, the self-reflexive theoretical excess of the discourse of sublimity is converted to produce the idea of a self-sufficient universal subject. The sublime thus serves as a means of strengthening the precarious foundations of modern subjectivity, whose universality is acclaimed at the cost of the suppression of sexual difference. As a response to this systemic restrictiveness of the aesthetic tradition of

sublimity, I want to propose in this book a new discursive arrangement, which I term 'the feminine sublime'. Embracing that excess
which is restrained and controlled in the sublime of Edmund Burke
and Immanuel Kant, for example, the feminine sublime opens itself to
an incalculable difference which threatens the stability and self-
sufficiency of the modern subject. I am particularly interested in
exploring a number of gender-specific mechanisms which many
earlier theorists of the sublime shared and which they employed to
achieve a certain sense of self-preservation or self-aggrandisement.
The feminine sublime which I delineate here does not, in turn,
capitalise on difference in order to enhance modern selfhood with its
founding institutions and economies; instead, it constitutes an
ethical moment in which an absolute and indescribable otherness is
welcomed. My understanding of ethics as a 'calling into question of
my spontaneity' by 'the strangeness of the Other' is derived from
Emmanuel Levinas, for whom ethics is the first philosophy, even
preceding ontology.[4] The feminine sublime I develop here is thus not
only a new aesthetic arrangement but, first of all, an ethical proposal.[5]

Situating my sublime investigations in an ethical realm allows me
to introduce a new set of questions regarding identity and difference
(including sexual difference). It is in this sense that my project of the
feminine sublime can be perceived as feminist. But what I call 'the
feminine sublime' is by no means another grand narrative of feminist
ethics or feminist politics. As the French philosopher Jean-François
Lyotard observes, the sublime does not necessarily have to involve
grandeur. When pointing to the legacy of the sublime which for him
is 'perhaps the only mode of artistic sensibility to characterise the
modern',[6] Lyotard abandons the traditional search for the sublime in
celestial heights. Instead, he argues in *The Inhuman* – a book which
constitutes a decisive moment for contemporary studies on sublimity
– that 'What is sublime is the feeling that something will happen,
despite everything, within this threatening void, that something will
take "place" and announce that everything is not over. That place is
mere "here", the most minimal occurrence'.[7] In his other writings,
including *The Differend* and *Lessons on the Analytic of the Sublime*,
Lyotard explains how the concept of sublimity can be seen as a
(somewhat unsteady) bridge between the domains of aesthetics, ethics
and politics.[8] By displacing it from its elevated position, he awards the
sublime a new validity in contemporary debates on culture and
philosophy. Now, the uniqueness of the sublime event does not

spring from its scale, but rather from the recognition of the fact that something is actually taking place in the world, no matter how inconspicuous this event might be.

The feminine sublime I develop here responds to this 'displacement' initiated by Lyotard, allowing me to conceptualise aesthetics beyond grandeur and might, and to search for wonder in the most minuscule spaces of the quotidian. This experience of wonder – for Burke, the first condition of the sublime – underlies the amorous encounter which I see as a paradigm for the ethics of the feminine sublime. It is this *possibility* of an encounter with the alterity of the other, which for a moment suspends Burke's fear of nothingness and death, that gives the feminine sublime an ethical character.

Desperately seeking novelty

A desire to come up with an entirely 'new' discourse, a discourse taking issue with the past but also distancing itself entirely from the past's achievements, has always been an ambition of Western logocentric philosophy. As this book is intended to take issue with what Derrida calls the logocentrism, or even phallogocentrism,[9] of Western thought, any attempt to think of a new discourse of the sublime has to acknowledge the problematic status of 'novelty'. The discourse of the feminine sublime I elaborate here can therefore be seen as a 'point of view', or a different way of looking at the sublime, rather than as a new 'corrected' tradition of aesthetics and ethics. The 'novelty' of this discourse lies in its rewriting of an aesthetic tradition which is nearly two thousand years old. Indeed, as Lyotard explains in *The Inhuman*, the act of rewriting is always aimed at discovering some hidden, 'forgotten' aspects of the area in question, i.e. of acknowledging the things that are already there but will only become visible when looked at from a different angle:

> Essentially linked with writing in this sense, the 're-' in no way signifies a return to the beginning but rather what Freud called a 'working through', *Durcharbeitung*, i.e. a working attached to a thought of what is constitutively hidden from us in the event and the meaning of the event. … Rewriting … concerns the anamnesis of the Thing. Not only that Thing that starts off a supposedly 'individual' singularity, but of the Thing that haunts the 'language', the tradition and the material with, against and in which one writes. In this way rewriting comes under a problematic of the sublime.[10]

As we can see, this method of working through a tradition of thought (in this case, the tradition of the sublime), leads to the experience of sublimity. We seem to find ourselves on a dangerous precipice: the area of investigation – the discourse of the sublime – itself has a sublime character, offering us the promise of 'what is constitutively hidden from us in the event' but also haunting us with the horror of nothingness. And yet there is no end to this ordeal. As Lyotard recognises, *Durcharbeitung*, the process of rewriting, must be inter-minable, always open to the possibility of new associations and unexpected connections. The newness of the discourse I weave from the threads of the past is therefore both provisional and tentative: 'It is "new" in so far as it is felt as new'.[11] The discourse of the feminine sublime is constituted by an open-ended sequence of occurrences, or *events*, which take place in my encounter with what I describe, somewhat tentatively, as 'the masculine tradition of sublimity'. In this project, I acknowledge my debt to both earlier theorists of sublimity, including Longinus, Burke and Kant, and the feminist critics of this tradition, among them Barbara Claire Freeman and Patricia Yaeger. As a result, the discourse of the feminine sublime I expound in this book can perhaps best be described in Derrida's words as 'the invention of an other inscription, *one very old and very new*'.[12]

On the brink of feminism and deconstruction

I want to embark upon this process of rewriting the tradition of the sublime by drawing on two discourses that have been, in a somewhat sublime way, particularly alert to the incommensurability of ideas, faculties and meanings, namely: feminism and deconstruction. As Hugh J. Silverman observes, 'The sublime is that which marginalises the literary text, takes it out of what it literally says and gives it another dimension, renders it more than "literary"'.[13] What makes feminism and deconstruction such propitious figures for the explora-tion of the sublime is a kind of excess – this 'more than' Silverman mentions – which they produce not only in their encounter with each other but first of all in any textual intervention they are engaged in. As Diane Elam points out in *Feminism and Deconstruction* – one of the first books in critical and cultural theory that proposed such a straight-forward alliance between the two 'approaches' – 'The political effectiveness of feminism and deconstruction, their critical force as *events*, has most readily been understood through narration, through the possibility of linking events'.[14] Clearly, then, the idea of the event is a defining moment for both the sublime and deconstructive feminism. Indeed, Lyotard has drawn our attention to the possibility of the sublime occurring in the most minuscule perspective: it is the fact that something (rather that nothing) *is* actually *taking place* that for him is the source of sublime feeling. Similarly, feminism and deconstruction cannot be described as coherent 'theories': they can only be grasped in an infinite number of events or interventions, which in turn produce the discursive excess that is also associated with the sublime. It is through these multiple and indeterminate interventions that I want to revisit the magisterial tradition of the sublime in an attempt to look for what Lyotard identifies as 'the Thing that haunts the "language"'.

Unweaving the spider's web, or, a summary of chapters

The spider's web is one source of inspiration for this book. It allows me to open the linearity of the argument to a certain circular, or perhaps spiral, movement. My three main chapters are thus linked with, but also separated by, two parts I call '*Webwords*', a term which corresponds to both the spider's activity of spinning and the modern technologies of networking. The ideas presented in the main chapters are expanded upon in the *Webwords* and tested against the web of theoretical, literary and artistic discourses and practices. The spiders and cyborgs of my title can be seen as harbingers of unprecedented couplings and unwanted connections. In this sense, the spider and the cyborg are next of kin, inhabiting both the natural and the technological world and transgressing the distance between human and inhuman. The respective feelings of arachnophobia and technophobia they evoke reflect a broader anxiety at the heart of the modern world, which both bemoans the loss of the natural and passionately yearns for the alien. We can see these anxieties in recent controversies over genetically modified food, organ transplants, plastic surgery, cloning and 'foetus personhood', to name but a few of the aspects of the battle for (or against) the control of Nature. These fears and desires, often formulated in clearly polarised, dialectical terms, seem to me to be also representative of the negative pleasure that is associated with the sublime, i.e. 'a strong and equivocal emotion [which] carries with it both pleasure and pain'.[15] By constructing the book around the metaphors of spiders and cyborgs, I want to draw attention to what Lyotard calls the 'incommensurability' of feelings about the modern world, in which ideas, identities and spaces can no longer be seen to constitute a totality.

In chapter 1 I discuss the aesthetics of the sublime, its organising principles and silences. I start by looking at the similarities between traditional theories of the sublime as worked out by, among others, Longinus, Burke and Kant. Demonstrating that the traditional discourse of the sublime depended on capitalisation, I then introduce the notion of the feminine sublime, which is born from the excess that the earlier theorists of the sublime attempted to tame or annul. I am not interested, however, in determining whether or not there *is* a sublime which is specific to women. Instead, I use this term to explore instances in which absolute and incalculable alterity can no longer be housed by the discursive restraints of traditional aesthetics, leading, as a consequence, to the eruption of affect and the weakening of the idea of the universal subject. What starts in this chapter as an elaboration of the practice of *écriture féminine* collapses the traditional opposition between affect and thought, and supports the possibility of thinking through affect and suffering. Open to sexual difference, the discourse of the feminine sublime I propose can be perceived as a certain (per)version of eighteenth-century aesthetics. This mutation 'from within' is also an attempt to preserve the tradition of the sublime, a tradition which, paradoxically, can only perhaps survive by revealing its weaknesses and limitations. My sublime speculations are thus intended as a non-lamenting funeral rite. If death is the ultimate source of fear in the experience of the sublime, the feminine sublime can be interpreted as a recognition, rather than denial, of mortality and finitude to which the self is exposed in its encounter with absolute difference. In the light of the gravity of the affairs happening under its aegis, the feminine sublime takes responsibility for the inaccommodable otherness that many theorists of the sublime have attempted in one way or another to deny or tame. Thus it situates itself in an ethical, rather than aesthetic, realm.

However, chapter 2 traces the impossibility of the exact separation between the realms of aesthetics and ethics in British political history. This is why, instead of attempting to accomplish a decisive shift from an allegedly disinterested aesthetics to an engaged ethics, I postulate that the sublime, at least since Kant, has *always* had ethical underpinnings. Referring to the writings of Emmanuel Levinas and Luce Irigaray, and emphasising the need for the recognition of sexual difference in an encounter with the other, I position the feminine sublime as an exploration of an ethical dimension in the discourse of sublimity. One of the ways in which the alterity of the other can be appreciated is by applying a principle of the gift, which transgresses the rules of capitalist exchange and the equal calculation of gains and losses, to the relationship between the sexes. In this way, the ethics of the feminine sublime can be justified through a-rational acts of infinite expenditure. According to Derrida, 'Only infinite love can renounce itself and, in order to become finite, become incarnated in order to love the other, to love the other as a finite other'.[16] Rather than as a cultural universal, I perceive 'love' here as an enactment of the principle of infinite spending in numerous encounters between two singularities, encounters which I see as paradigmatic of the ethics of the feminine sublime. Tracing the emergence of the discourses of friendship and love in Western philosophy, from Plato and Aristotle through Bacon and Nietzsche to Derrida, I investigate the possibility of the overcoming of the economy of proportion in relationships between the sexes. Amorous spending threatens to disrupt the progress and development of a sexuate encounter – i.e. towards matrimony, child-bearing and family genealogy – with its demand for absolute consummation. This leads me to question the traditional concept of the 'consummating gaze' which was the foundation for ideas of selfhood and difference in our culture. Unlike the traditional sublime, the feminine sublime does not accept the gaze with its active/passive dichotomy as the principle of the perception of otherness. Instead, it opts for a less fixating interaction, allowing for a form of 'visual caress' which involves more than the eyes. Revealing the masculine bias inherent in the Enlightenment 'ocularcentric' discourse on the sublime, I then go on to propose an 'ethics of blindness' (which is inspired by the writings of Derrida, Cixous and Irigaray). Blindness here is understood not as a disability or anomaly but rather as a choice. The ethics of blindness does not denigrate sight as opposed to the other senses, but rather creatively explores the crevices and gaps resulting from the imperfection of representation.

Since I maintain throughout my work that the feminine sublime should not be perceived as a grand project of redemption, I devote chapter 3 to the problem of the minimal perspective in which this 'new' discourse of the sublime can be situated. The minimal perspective guarantees that the ethical event taking place under the aegis of the feminine sublime will not be judged according to a pre-established, general moral code. Inspired by Wittgenstein's philosophy of ordinary language and the attitude of 'Critical Regionalism' in postmodern architecture, I follow architectural metaphors to trace the limits of sublime micro-spaces. Mapping them on to the versions of the spider's web represented by the postmodern metropolis and the technological information network, I use the concept of the cybercity as an example of a space in which the singular ethics of hospitality and respect towards the other can best be explained. The experiments of the Australian performance artist Stelarc, which I discuss in this chapter, illustrate new ways of establishing connections between the self and its surroundings.

The two linking, but also disjoining, chapters entitled 'Webwords', provide a space where the feminine sublime, discussed in the three main chapters, can be encountered, contested and expanded in the network of artistic practices such as literature (Lisa St Aubin de Terán), music (Laurie Anderson) and art (Orlan). I hope in this way to have composed a web of discourses which will serve as both an illustration and a germinating ground for the working of the feminine sublime. By looking closely at selected artistic examples, I want to expose the traditional discourse of subjectivity underpinning the sublime to a new politics of self-fashioning and self-fragmentation. Informed by different strands of feminist and gender theory, the Webwords explore the possibility of developing alternative forms of identity and identification.

Notes

1 Edward Rothstein, 'Contemplating the Sublime', *The American Scholar*, 1.09.1997.
2 David Harvey, 'The Time and Space of the Enlightenment Project', in *The Condition of Postmodernity* (Oxford: Blackwell, 1989).
3 Jacques Derrida, 'Passages – from Traumatism to Promise', in *Points ... Interviews, 1974–1994*, ed. Elizabeth Weber (Stanford: Stanford University Press, 1995), 386.
4 Emmanuel Levinas, *Totality and Infinity*, trans. Alphonso Lingis (Dordrecht, Boston, London: Kluwers Academic Publishers, 1969), 43.
5 As I will demonstrate in chapters 1 and 2, the sublime has always had ethical implications. Therefore, rather than propose a straightforward shift 'from aesthetics to ethics', I am interested in rethinking the ethical principles upon which the sublime was traditionally based.
6 Jean-François Lyotard, *The Inhuman*, trans. Geoffrey Bennington and Rachel Bowlby (Cambridge: Polity Press, 1991), 93.
7 Ibid., 84.

8   See Jean-François Lyotard, *The Differend*, trans. Georges Van Den Abbeele (Manchester: Manchester University Press, 1988) and Jean-François Lyotard, *Lessons on the Analytic of the Sublime, Sections 23–29: Kant's Critique of Judgement*, trans. Elizabeth Rottenberg (Stanford: Stanford University Press, 1994).

9   This is how Derrida defines 'phallogocentrism' and the possible ways of overcoming it: 'The truth value (that is, Woman as the major allegory of truth in Western discourse) and its correlative, Femininity (the essence or truth of Woman), are there to assuage such hermeneutic anxiety. These are the places that one should acknowledge, at least that is if one is interested in doing so; they are the foundations or anchorings of Western rationality (of what I have called "phallogocentrism" [as the complicity of Western metaphysics with a notion of male firstness]). Such recognition should not make of either the truth value or femininity an object of knowledge (at stake are the norms of knowledge and knowledge as norm); still less should it make of them a place to inhabit, a home. It should rather permit the invention of an other inscription, one very old and very new, a displacement of bodies and places that is quite different'. Jacques Derrida and Christie V. McDonald, 'Choreographies: interview', *Diacritics*, 12: Summer (1982), 69–70.

10   Lyotard, *The Inhuman*, 26–33.

11   Ibid., 31.

12   Derrida and McDonald, 'Choreographies: interview', 70, emphasis added.

13   Hugh J. Silverman, *The Textual Sublime: Deconstruction and Its Differences* (New York: State University of New York Press, 1989), xii.

14   Diane Elam, *Feminism and Deconstruction* (London and New York: Routledge: 1994), 13, emphasis added.

15   Jean-François Lyotard, *The Postmodern Condition: A Report on Knowledge*, trans. Geoff Bennington and Brian Massumi (Manchester: Manchester University Press, 1986), 77.

16   Jacques Derrida, *The Gift of Death*, trans. David Wills (Chicago and London: University of Chicago Press, 1995), 50–1.

1 *Décriture féminine*: the discourse of the feminine sublime

Preambles

In this chapter I intend to demonstrate that capitalisation was the underlying principle of the eighteenth-century discourse of the sublime. As a result of this capitalisation, the self-reflexive theoretical 'excess' of sublimity – whose emergence I will discuss below – produced the cornerstone of modernity: a self-sufficient universal subject. But the rigid gendering of the discourse of the sublime and the repression of incalculable alterity from this discourse resulted in the simultaneous weakening of both capitalism (as a system that calculates precisely all gains and losses) and the modern subject.[1] Against the sublime annulling any form of excess so as to enhance modern subjectivity, I therefore want to set the notion of the *feminine* sublime, born out of the excess that the defensive principles of decorum ruled out of eighteenth-century aesthetics. Challenging the two main aspects of the traditional sublime – i.e. the capitalisation of excess and the fear of eruption – the feminine sublime will also allow me to trace a *feminist ethics*, an ethics which springs from the aporias of the logic of capitalisation and the precarious foundations of modern subjectivity.

Even though it is inscribed in the paradigm of 'femininity', the feminine sublime I speak of does not reflect traditional gender binaries. Instead, 'femininity' is to be read as a marker of irreducible difference, represented here as it is for Luce Irigaray, whose thought has strongly influenced my sublime adventures, through the figure of sexual difference. Drawing on the economy which denounces 'the spirit of capitalisation which is purely artificial and produces nothing but death',[2] I do not intend to master the feminine sublime, although this term serves as a (necessarily precarious) foundation of the feminist ethics I develop here. The discussion of the feminine sublime will thus be more spiral than linear, and will consist of a number of illustrations, probings and shifts in meaning. This does not mean that my argument will be unfounded: but it will be based on an economy 'that upsets the linearity of a project, undermines the goal-object of a desire, diffuses the polarisation toward a single pleasure, disconcerts fidelity to a single discourse.'[3]

And yet the notion of 'discourse' is important for my analysis, even though the 'discourse of the feminine sublime' I propose here should be seen as non-linear and dispersed. When discussing the evolution of the notion 'discourse' in structuralist theory, Ernesto Laclau contends that discourse does 'not refer to a particular set of objects, but to a viewpoint from which it [is] possible to redescribe the totality of social life'.[4] Taking into account the post-structuralist critique of language as a meaningful totality, Laclau explains that 'The post-structuralist trend has been to experiment in the logic of subversion of discursive identities which follow from the logical impossibility of constituting a closed system'.[5] It should therefore come as no surprise that the 'discourse of the feminine sublime' I am referring to here cannot be described as a closed entity. Rather, it should be seen as a text which is, to use Jacques Derrida's phrase, always already 'overflowed'.[6] In my attempts to trace the fluid contours of this discourse of the feminine sublime, with its affective rhetoric of pleasure and pain, I intend to draw on the concept of *écriture féminine*, developed in the early 1970s. As Rosi Braidotti concludes in *Patterns of Dissonance*, the feminine can be seen as a useful proposition for rethinking the old notions centred around the masculine, disembodied notion of Reason.[7] Warning against any subsequent metaphorisation of women for the sake simply of the construction of new, alternative discourses, Braidotti argues that opening a debate about sexual difference – a difference which is defined as a sign of the corporeal, the affective, the irrational and the multiple – is only possible from the position of 'woman', whose active movement within the man/woman dyad destabilises any system based on the equivalence of the male and the universal.

Woman does not believe in truth

Because, indeed, if woman *is* truth, *she* at least knows that there is no truth, that truth has no place here and that no one has a place for truth. And she is woman precisely because she herself does not believe in truth itself, because she does not believe in what she is, in what she is believed to be, in what she thus is not. (Jacques Derrida, *Spurs: Nietzsche's Styles*)

My use of the term 'woman' does not refer to some alleged feminine essence which acts as a thread linking all women, irrespective of their background, age and experience. Instead, 'woman' here stands for the representation of femininity in Western thought, but also for the potential disruption that is inherent in this figure of representation. This is one of the 'nodal points' in which the two main strands informing my project of the feminine sublime – i.e. Derridean decon-struction and non-essentialist feminism – come together. I would like to dwell for a moment on Jacques Derrida's encounter with 'woman', which I see as an important intervention into debates on both femin-ism and femininity. This encounter seems to me to be symptomatic of a larger battle for the 'ownership of woman' that has been going on for a while now, not only between male and female thinkers, but also among feminist theorists, all of them trying to establish who has the ultimate access to the truth of 'woman' and the right to speak in the most political and ethical way about her. Derrida has often been accused by feminists of conforming to stereotypes of femininity. By reducing 'woman' to distance itself, or confining her to the position of non-identity, he has been said to replicate patriarchal oppression for the sake of displaying his linguistic mastery. However, by tracing the 'origin' of 'woman' through the history of Western metaphysics Derrida reveals the precarious foundations upon which this tradition has rested. Driven by the authority of truth, metaphysics has taken recourse to the figure of femininity to construct this truth, and then to veil its constructedness, as Derrida illustrates in his reading of Nietzsche's depiction of 'woman as truth' in his 1971 book *Spurs: Nietzsche's Styles*:

> There is no such thing as the essence of woman because woman averts, she is averted of herself. Out of the depths, endless and unfathomable, she engulfs and distorts all vestige of essentiality, of identity, of property. And the philosophical discourse, blinded, founders on these shoals and is hurled down these depthless depths to its ruin. There is no such thing as the truth of woman, but it is because of that abyssal divergence of the truth, because that untruth is «truth». Woman is but one name for that untruth of truth.[8]

But Derrida does not stop at tearing the veil off 'truth' disguised as woman: he goes on to expose the power of 'what goes under the name «woman»' to subvert and destroy the discursive certainty of Western philosophy. (Let me just remark in passing that the quoted excerpt mimes the discourse of the sublime with its constituting fears of both depthless abyss and 'woman', something I want to come back to a little further in this chapter.) Looking beyond oppositions between concept and matter, and truth and falsehood, Derrida recognises the enormous power of femininity – perceived as distance, abyss or simulacrum – to contest the master discourse of philosophy and work its way through it.

All this allows me to read *Spurs* as an important feminist text, opening up the concept of 'woman' to a plurality that is not reduced to the politically vital markers of identity, such as class, sexuality and age. What distinguishes Derrida's feminism from an essentialist-feminist standpoint, then, is the way in which he thinks about identity.[9] As Alice Jardine puts it, 'For Derrida, the questions of how women might accede to subjecthood, write surviving texts, or acquire a signature of their own, are the wrong questions – eminently phallogo-centric questions'.[10] If, for Derrida, identity 'comes only from alterity called by the other',[11] femininity must be seen as always different/ deferred and never reduced to the politically significant markers of presence. This, I believe, is both a political and an ethical way of speaking of 'woman'. My project of the feminine sublime is therefore not going to be free from political or emotional involvement (even if I disclaim the presence of any stable identity): I am speaking here as a feminist who cannot resist the seductive charm of deconstruction.

The vertigo of deconstruction

[W]oman is always, via Derrida, that which calls out to Man, that which puts him into question. (Alice A. Jardine, *Gynesis*)

It goes without saying that Derrida shares this perception of 'identity as difference' with a number of women theorists: Luce Irigaray's ethics of sexual difference and Hélène Cixous' *écriture féminine* are only two examples of what we might call 'the feminism of difference' to which I will be referring in this chapter. But non-essentialist feminism does not need to rely on the biological identity of its theorists to make its point, which allows me to position Derrida's *Spurs* as a significant text on a feminist agenda. I am not trying to determine here whether Derrida *is* or *is not* a feminist, but rather to indicate that his decon-structive thinking creates a radical space for a feminist project of 'working through' the premises and foundations of Western meta-physics. Derrida's work is important for me because it challenges and opens up accepted ideas and concepts (such as 'woman', 'man', 'reason', 'aesthetics', 'politics', or 'sublimity', to name but a few), without naïvely attempting to get rid of them altogether. Derridean deconstruction exposes the logic of oppositions organising Western philosophy, a logic which, in Derrida's words, is 'violent' because it depends on the suppression and denigration of one term for the sake of the elevation of the other (thus the autonomy of the concept 'man' depends on the suppression of 'woman'; the privileging of 'speech' as the source of truth and presence relies on the subordination of 'writing', etc.). Revisiting a number of the canonical texts of Western philosophy, Derrida forces 'these same old texts to say something quite different from what they had always seemed to say',[12] thus collapsing the old and simultaneously constructing the new from exactly the same material. This is why 'the undoing, decomposing, and desedimenting of structures', as Derrida explains, is not 'a negative operation. Rather than destroying, it [is] also necessary to understand how an "ensemble" was constituted and to reconstruct it to this end'.[13] Derrida has warned many times that deconstruction should not, however, be described as a method or a critique; instead, it can only be perceived as an open-ended series of events, occurring in every act of reading (against) a text.

It is not really surprising that deconstruction, or at least that form of deconstruction represented by Derrida, should be treated with suspicion by some cultural theorists, since it questions (even if not negates) the safe orientational categories that they have relied on, including oppression, inequality, power, politics and, indeed, feminism. Robert Scholes described his fear of deconstructive manoeuvres as follows: 'From the heights of deconstruction we are given a glimpse into the bottomless abyss of textuality, a vertiginous perspective in which constructs are erected upon constructs, without foundation and without end'.[14] Significantly, deconstruction is described here as leading to the feeling associated with the sublime. Reason's victory, a victory which springs from the conceptual grasp of the vastness of 'theory', is suspended because of the impossibility of the feat the critic is faced with: deconstruction and a desire for mastery simply cannot be reconciled. Indeed, both deconstruction and the sublime deny the possibility of reconciliation, their *raison d'être* being the constant reopening of difference, or incommensurability, resulting in what Scholes perceives as 'horrified fascination'. It is precisely at this point that for me deconstruction, feminism and sublimity come together.

Men on sublimity

> Under a great variety of titles, a great variety of men at one time or
> other composed an essay or a book or a poem on taste or beauty or
> sublimity or the pleasures of the imagination or the art of poetry, of
> painting, or of music. Not everyone who wrote had something to say.
> (Samuel H. Monk, *The Sublime*)

There has been a resurgence of interest in the sublime of late, mainly
connected with debates over postmodernity. But I do not intend to
present yet another history of the sublime, since many excellent
scholars have carried out this project before me.[15] Instead, I want to
draw on a number of accounts of this tradition, including Peter de
Bolla's study of eighteenth-century aesthetics, *The Discourse of the
Sublime*, Paul Crowther's discussion of the Kantian sublime, and
Barbara Claire Freeman's analysis of the canonical theories of the
sublime and their dominant ideology of misogyny, *The Feminine
Sublime*, to cast a light on *the ethical dimension of sublimity*.

When starting my sublime investigations I have to acknowledge
the excessive fecundity of the term 'sublime', something David B.
Morris describes as follows:

> We should begin by accepting an uncomfortable fact: the sublime ...
> embraces such a variety of historical practices and of theoretical
> accounts that the quest for a single, unchanging feature or essence is
> futile. There is no essence of the sublime. Instead, what we encounter
> is (in Wittgenstein's phrase) shared 'family resemblances' which link
> the countless, related discussions of sublimity with Longinus, who
> first described the irresistible power of great writing to seize control of
> the reader, to take us outside of ourselves with the sudden, startling
> intensity of a thunderbolt (*Peri Hupsous* §1). As we know, these
> discussions abruptly multiplied and intensified in the early decades
> of the eighteenth century, following Boileau's French translation of
> Longinus in 1674.[16]

Let me now briefly outline these 'family resemblances' and connections that emerged between early theorists of sublimity. My intention
in doing so is to demonstrate how the authors of the sublime seem to
have been seduced by the discourse they tried to elaborate and master.
This 'seduction' can perhaps account for their attempts to annul the
power of the sublime by either describing it in feminine terms or,
contrarily, protecting it against femininity at all cost.

The first theorist of sublimity, Longinus, draws attention to the sublime's element of unexpectedness resulting in violence and turmoil, but also evoking ecstasy in the hearer. In his first-century treatise on the sublime he writes: 'Sublimity ... produced at the right moment tears everything up like a whirlwind and exhibits the orator's whole power at a single blow'.[17] What we are experiencing here is a form of 'controlled excess', staged by the orator for his astounded audience, who are transported beyond themselves as a result of his rhetorical skills. But it is not until the eighteenth century that the sublime becomes a prominent concept in debates on art, aesthetics and experience, debates that shape, to a large extent, the newly emergent, modern discourse of subjectivity. In his *Philosophical Enquiry into the Origin of our Ideas of the Sublime and the Beautiful* first published in 1757, Edmund Burke, one of the most prominent theorists of the sublime, focuses on the reception of sublime phenomena by the bewildered self, whose peace of mind is threatened by the excess of power and terror it cannot master. 'The passion caused by the great and sublime in nature, when those causes operate most powerfully, is Astonishment; and astonishment is that state of the soul, in which all its motions are suspended, with some degree of horror.'[18] However, the sublime does not describe the moment of the arrival of danger, but rather the permanent withdrawal, or deferral, of this danger. Exposed to the terror of annihilation and death, the self is nevertheless able to rejoice in its survival, in having escaped what seemed to be inevitable perdition and being able to reassert its security and integrity. In fact, the awaited danger can *never* actually arrive: to stay within the bounds of the experience of the sublime, it has to be constantly deferred, striking what might seem like a secret pact with the self that participates in this theatre of terror and darkness on the unspoken assumption that its safety is always already assured. The element of control and regulation is the organising principle of the Burkean sublime. As Crowther points out, for Burke 'the sublime is essentially *a passion of modified terror* or pain and pertains, thereby, to the instinct for self-preservation'.[19] Even though death is the greatest threat in the sublime, it is the self's survival and the restoration of 'life and health' that provide a necessary counterbalance to the feeling of pain, and that complete the experience of sublimity. Indeed, Burke goes to great lengths to emphasise the necessary element of moderation in the sublime: 'When danger or pain press too nearly, they are incapable of giving any delight, and are simply terrible; but *at certain distances*, and *with certain modifications*, they may be, and they are delightful, as we every day experience'.[20] Ending one's life 'in the torments' would preclude the possibility of drawing satisfaction from self-preservation and the overcoming of danger. This is to say, the self needs to experience great terror in order to be plucked out of the indifference of existence – be it by 'serpents and poisonous animals', 'incomprehensible darkness' or the wisdom, justice and goodness of God – and to appreciate life, but the sublime is ultimately the experience of overcoming this terror and thus celebrating one's invincibility in the face of what *seemed* to be a greater power. The sublime, of which Burke presents himself as an objective and disinterested spectator, is in fact prescribed by him a priori, a move which allows him to eliminate any potential disruption to subjectivity.

While Burke focuses on the removal of danger for the sake of maintaining the self's security, for Immanuel Kant the sublime does not necessarily need to involve a threat to our physical well-being. Rather than emphasise the withdrawal of danger resulting in the self's survival, Kant points to the control that the human mind can exert over sublimity. The mind's supremacy manifests itself in its ability to always think the infinity which imagination fails to grasp. As Kant argues in *The Critique of Judgement*, pleasure, resulting from the correspondence of the sublime feeling to the law of reason, clashes with pain caused by the impossibility of balancing the judgement of different faculties. Insisting that '[t]he point of capital importance is that the mere ability even to think it as a whole indicates a faculty of mind transcending every standard of sense',[21] he allows reason to triumph over senses, thus claiming the self's power over the insurmountable and the unlimited.

But the attainment of the Kantian sublime depends on a sacrifice. Kant makes it clear that imagination has to collapse when facing the infinitely great for the sake of an achievement of a higher goal – i.e. 'the awakening of a feeling of a supersensible faculty within us'.[22] When it attempts to overcome 'principally distracting feelings and desires',[23] the self realises its rational and autonomous dimension, something which Kant takes as a given. Premised on the sacrifice of imagination, the sublime is ultimately a state of moral consciousness.[24] We have to remember that moral law, according to Kant, is binding on us absolutely. He formulates the main principle of this law in his universal categorical imperative: 'Act only on that maxim through which you can at the same time will that it should become a universal law'.[25] This moral consciousness can, as Crowther argues, be described as sublime 'because it manifests the ultimate authority and transcendence of our rational over our sensible being'.[26] The pain element of the sublime elevates us with a sense of our rational vocation. The sacrifice of imagination is for Kant inevitable, given that we are ultimately ruled by our supersensible faculty. The Kantian sublime, spanning a bridge between the singular and the universal, is thus an ethical predicate. And yet this elevation towards ethics instantiated by the sublime is not unconditional. As Kant explains:

> [W]ithout the development of moral ideas, that which, thanks to preparatory culture, we call sublime, merely strikes the untutored man as terrifying. ... But the fact that culture is requisite for the judgement upon the sublime in nature (more than for that upon the beautiful) does not involve its being an original product of culture and something introduced in a more or less conventional way into society. Rather is it in human nature that its foundations are laid, and, in fact, in that which, at once with common understanding, we may expect every one to possess and may require of him, namely, a native capacity for the feeling for (practical) ideas, i.e. for moral feeling.[27]

We can see from the above that moral feeling, innate in humans, is not operative at all times. This 'native capacity' for morality has to be developed by means of tutoring, or cultivation; otherwise 'the untutored man', deterred by the terror of the experience of sublimity, will not be able to resort to the faculty of reason and move on from the singular to the universal. This logic is reminiscent of Rousseau's (il)logic of the supplement which Derrida outlines in *Of Grammatology*. There Derrida focuses on the ambiguity of the word 'supplement' in Rousseau's texts, which stands for both addition and replacement. Rousseau, 'the natural man', perceives all evil as external, and as threatening the perfection of the human being. At the same time, Rousseau sees education as a necessary 'supplement' to the child's weakness, which testifies to a certain imperfection, or fallibility, of the human he otherwise denies. Since for Rousseau 'the supplement is *exterior*, outside of the positivity to which it is super-added',[28] Derrida concludes that it must undermine the alleged completeness of Nature:

> Nature does not supplement *itself* at all; Nature's supplement does not proceed from Nature, it is not inferior to but other than Nature. Yet all education, the keystone of Rousseauist thought, will be described or presented as a system of substitution [*suppléance*]

destined to reconstitute Nature's edifice in the most natural way possible. ... It is indeed culture or cultivation that must supplement a deficient nature, a deficiency that cannot by definition be anything but an accident and a deviation from Nature.[29]

Even though in Rousseau nature is seen as originary perfection, while for Kant it is the site of raw passions which need to be overcome if one is to be elevated towards moral feeling, the contaminating logic of the supplement Derrida exposes as operative in Rousseau's *Confessions* can also, I believe, be detected in Kant's 'Analytic of the Sublime'. For Kant, the ethical evaluation of the sublime sentiment depends on the development of the innate capacity of the mind. When hindered, this capacity will lead to nothing but misery and distress. Unconsoled by the properties of his mind, which is unable to theorise the danger it faces and thus enhance the self's identity, 'the untutored man' is left in the darkness of the pre-ethical. The cultivation of the mind, in turn, leads to the overcoming of the natural and the elevation of the mind towards morality. 'The simple-minded peasant' is unable to see beyond the moral sensitivity of mountain lovers, whose daring adventures produce 'soul-stirring sensations'. His lack of cultivation makes him reduce the vast scale of nature, which defies imagination but enhances the mind, to 'misery, peril, and distress'. The untrained mind is unable to achieve the degree of the moral sentiment, which, even though 'innate', needs to be appropriately developed. In this sense, education (or 'tutoring') functions as a supplement, whose 'naturalness' has to be activated if the self is not to be overcome by sheer terror. Education thus supplements the mind, constituting the cornerstone of Kant's ethics, and yet 'lacking in nature' because 'It feels only itself'.[30] While in Rousseau it is the self-sufficiency of nature that is eventually exposed as fictitious, in Kant we are facing the dethronement of practical reason which is revealed as lacking, i.e. as being not-nature, or not-imagination. As Lyotard puts it, 'The *Geistesgefühl*, the sentiment of the mind, signifies that the mind is lacking in nature, that nature is lacking for it. It feels only itself. In this way the sublime is none other that the sacrificial announcement of the ethical in the aesthetic field'.[31] Lyotard points out that imagination has to be sacrificed in the interest of practical reason, which replaces the horror and agony of the self exposed to the sublime.

This inevitability of the sacrifice of imagination indicates that Kant's moral law is in fact based on violence. In *Lessons on the Analytic of the Sublime* Lyotard describes the struggle between imagination and reason in terms of sexual dynamics, with reason usurping the masculine role of both a legislator and a violator. As Lyotard puts it:

> The law (the father) is so authoritarian, so unconditional, and the regard the law requires so exclusive that he, the father, will do nothing to obtain consent, even through a delicious rivalry with the imagination. ... He pushes forms aside, or, rather, forms part before his presence, tear themselves apart, extend themselves to inordinate proportions. He fertilises the virgin who has devoted herself to forms, without regard for her favour. He demands regard only for himself, for the law and its realisation. He has no need for a beautiful nature. He desperately needs an imagination that is violated, exceeded, exhausted. She will die in giving birth to the sublime.[32]

The Kantian Reason, personified in this tug-of-war with imagination, is seen here as a rapist. Even if the self does regain its autonomy after the momentary arrest of the faculties, a sacrificial, violent aspect of this transaction creates serious problems for the self's integrity. Kant's universal subject is not 'universal' at all: it is dependent on the disavowal of both alterity and what we might call 'participatory' sexuality. Lyotard's 'fable' on the tyrannical authority of masculine reason does not seem too far-fetched if we consider, for example, Kant's description of war presented in the third *Critique*. The grandeur of war reasserts the traditional ideology of masculinity and is thus intended to protect subjectivity against its two most prominent threats, weakness and effeminacy:

> War itself, provided it is conducted with order and a sacred respect for the rights of civilians, has something sublime about it, and gives nations that carry it on in such a manner a stamp of mind only the more sublime the more numerous the dangers to which they are exposed, and which they are able to meet with fortitude. On the other hand, a prolonged peace favours the predominance of a mere commercial spirit, and with it a debasing self-interest, cowardice and effeminacy, and tends to degrade the character of the nation.[33]

For Kant here, then, the dangers inherent in the experience of sublimity are overcome for the purpose of shaping a national character. Thus what, due to its formlessness and immediacy, poses a threat to the individual subject, also reasserts the formation of the nation. The fear of the sublime can be overcome in the face of a greater danger: that of a commercial exchange with the other conducted without the desire to liquidate this otherness. The spirit of commerce, with its principle of capitalisation and its interest in the accumulation of wealth, introduces an economy of speculation which threatens subjectivity based on the equation between the masculine and the universal. The economy of exchange always generates a surplus, which can be a blow to the unified subjectivity of the nation Kant wants to defend against weakening, dispersal and effeminacy. The Kantian self, elevated in the experience of the sublime, is protected against the potential excesses of its phenomenal side (with all its accompanying feelings and corporeality) by being described as both rational and masculine. It is in this sense that '[v]iolence and courage ... are necessary to the sublime'.[34]

As we can see from the above overview, the principal theorists of the sublime rely on a number of protective mechanisms (verbal control; maintaining a proper distance; overcoming – or even 'raping' – imagination; warding off weakness and effeminacy, etc.), whose underlying aim seems to be the construction of the autonomous subject. But I have to admit here that the coherence of this brief 'history of the sublime' I have just presented, usually demarcated by the names of Longinus, Burke and Kant, is problematic. As I mentioned before, David B. Morris criticises such 'holistic' interpretations of the 'history of the sublime'. Emphasising the lack of an 'essence' of the sublime, he insists instead on 'family resemblances' between particular definitions and theories. Morris's claim challenges the more traditional view promoted by Samuel H. Monk, author of the seminal book on the 'history of sublimity', *The Sublime*, which was first published in 1935. Monk's 'organic theory of the sublime' presents the development of thought on the subject in teleological terms, eliminating any potential disparity and postulating that the Romantic sublime is a continuation of the theories of Burke and Kant, who, in turn, are supposed to have inherited the immaculate Longinian thread: 'The study of the sublime is of interest because it permits one to observe from a fresh point of view the gradual coming to domination of such standards as characterise the romantic age of English literature'.[35] And yet ambiguity creeps into Monk's theory under the guise of femininity – unmasked, deprived of its seductive veil and thus giving itself for 'truth': 'Theories of beauty are relatively trim and respectable; but in theories of the sublime one catches the century somewhat off its guard, sees it, as it were, without powder and pomatum, whalebone and patches'.[36] Clearly, then, what we have here is yet another trick of a lascivious woman who is using her skills of masquerade to undermine man's conceptual mastery of the world. While Monk conveys the feeling of ambiguity and anxiety he experiences in his encounter with eighteenth-century discourse of the sublime, the origins of this feeling are ascribed to woman's lasciviousness. If it can be represented only by the figure of a woman without disguise, the theoretical excess produced by the discourse of the sublime cannot be taken seriously. However, Derrida has pointed out in *Spurs* – an extremely thought-provoking intervention into the debates over sexual difference – that to resort to the figure of a naked feminine body, and thus to attempt to unveil femininity, is to disclose that the truth of feminine identity is merely a ruse, a product of the wishful thinking of the philosopher who believes woman gives herself to him willingly. Such rhetorical manoeuvres are usually employed by male theorists who are not fully in control of the material they are working on and who feel threatened by its discursive excess. In what could be perceived as an act of both bravado and self-mutilation, Derrida undresses this truth of femininity which is only the philosopher's truth, and which eventually leaves him bare, trembling and exposed to his greatest fear of physico-intellectual castration. This is how he explains the paradoxical (non)essence of femininity:

> Since [woman] is a model for truth she is able to display the gifts of her seductive power, which rules over dogmatism, and disorients and routs those credulous men, the philosophers. And because she does not believe in the truth (still, she does find that uninteresting truth in her interest) woman remains a model, only this time a good model. But because she is a good model she is in fact a bad model. She plays at dissimulation, at ornamentation, deceit, artifice, at an artist's philosophy.[37]

Monk's attempts to ignore the seductive power of the discourse of the sublime by inscribing it in an orderly historical narrative follow the footsteps of his predecessors. The figure of the feminine dominates and overpowers sublimity, but it is used by its theorists with a view to controlling the discursive excess this theory produces (something Longinus already defined as the main feature of the sublime). Commenting on Monk's textual possession of the femininity he resents and clearly fears, Freeman points to the defensive mechanisms some authors come up with to reassert their own identity when threatened by the encounter with sublime grandeur: 'Speculation about the sublime becomes the obstacle the scholar needs to overcome in order to construct its definitive study and, appropriately enough, a woman unfit to be seen presents herself as the appropriate symbol for this inhibiting, yet necessary, force'.[38] If femininity in fact foregrounds the mimicking of femininity, if woman's identity can only be reasserted at one remove, and if the philosopher needs this image of 'woman' to reassert his own position, then dissimulation, artifice and masquerade constitute the very foundations of eighteenth-century aesthetics and its theories of the subject.[39]

Peter de Bolla's sublime vortex

As we can see, the discourse of the sublime itself has fallen prey to numerous attempts to eradicate alterity and formlessness by imposing a coherent, linear structure on it. Challenging what he perceives to be the unfounded unity of theoretical speculations on the sublime, Peter de Bolla, in his book *The Discourse of the Sublime*, insists on the recognition of the historical specificity of this concept. Working in the liminal space between what he terms the discourses *on* and *of* the sublime, de Bolla investigates the discursive excess produced by the discourse on sublimity. In other words, in his study he sets himself the ambitious task of 'theorising theory', that is demonstrating how *the discourse on the sublime* (i.e. descriptions of the sublime) resulted in the production of another discourse, *the discourse of the sublime*, which was a critical reflection not only on the issue of sublimity but also on the whole question of self-reflexivity, or theorisation, as such. De Bolla introduces here one of the most disturbing and subversive ideas in contemporary critical and cultural theory, i.e. reflexivity. N. Katherine Hayles defines reflexivity as 'the movement whereby that which has been used to generate a system is made, through a changed perspective, to become part of the system it generates'.[40] The American Constitution, the founding document of the United States, is quoted by her as an example of the application of the principle of reflexivity: the Constitution is said to produce the very people whose existence it presupposes. De Bolla reveals a similar logic in his exploration of the idea of modern subjectivity in the context of the sublime. His study 'begins with the assumption that the human subject is not the same through history, and that, furthermore, the modern subject, the subject generated in, by and through the age of reason, is the result or product of a particular discursive network not uniquely present to the years 1756–63, but largely initiated and substantiated during this period.'[41] This is the strongest, perhaps even most important, claim in his book: the discourse of the sublime is not, for de Bolla, confined to the realm of aesthetics. Its theoretical self-reflexivity gives rise to a discursive excess, which is then regulated to produce one of the cornerstones of the modern age: the idea of the rational, self-reflexive subject.

De Bolla's analysis of how the discourses on debt and on the sublime generated the discursive milieu within which the autonomous subject became apparent (i.e. the subject was both a producer and a product of its own discursive formation) is extremely scholarly and rigorous. He is wary not to commit the mistake of his predecessors, who ignored the specificity of the concept of the sublime in the eighteenth century and applied it freely to cross-historical debates on aesthetics and art. De Bolla does not want to fall prey to a similar methodological fallacy, which is why he delineates his research strategy in great detail, making sure his project cannot be accused of the sort of a-historical and 'organic' theorisation he locates in writers such as the aforementioned Samuel H. Monk or Thomas Weiskel, author of *The Romantic Sublime* (1976). This is why he feels compelled to make the following reservation: 'In order to stabilise the discourse for analysis, then, the working method I have used is to isolate a discrete discourse when it appears to operate the principle of exclusion (even though we know that this never was, nor is possible), when it proclaims itself as a discourse on something'.[42]

By giving us an opportunity to progress with an academic argument, de Bolla – himself an expert on discourses of debt and expenditure – is probably aware that something gets lost in his discursive ordering of texts on sublimity. Introducing the separation between the discourses *on* and *of* the sublime, the latter itself being made of a number of 'disparate' discourses, de Bolla realises that his 'analytical method' is 'no more than one momentarily stabilised account'.[43] He must thus be also aware that such an act of pre-describing the discourse on the sublime, which allows us to decide then which discourses conform with the category and which do not, itself curbs the productive excess that sublimity opens up.

Perhaps de Bolla wants to brace himself in advance against the sense of confusion and loss Burke experienced when attempting to give an account of sublimity? The discursive paths he traces in the field of the sublime suddenly seem extremely tangled:

> This discourse [of the sublime], it seems to me, is distinguished from any of its neighbours by the fact that it has, effectively, no boundary.

It is a discourse which produces, from within itself, what is habitually termed the category of the sublime and in doing so it becomes a self-transforming discourse. The only way in which it is possible to identify this newly mutated discursive form is via its propensity to produce to excess. This production to excess might be expected as the 'natural' result of the discourse on the sublime: enquiries into the nature and causes of sublime experience were necessarily led to an investigation of the 'transport' of the sublime experience. The experience was itself defined as one which broke through a boundary, which was, in some sense at least, excessive. Hence the discourse on the sublime, in its function as an analytic discourse on excessive experience, became increasingly preoccupied with the discursive production of the excess: once it had begun to describe how an experience is sublime and what caused it, it began to create a discourse which not only explained the effect or demonstrated the mechanism by which it is produced, but also created the experiential possibility for sublime sensations. There is, then, a natural tendency for the discourse on the sublime to produce the conditions necessary for the construction of the discourse of the sublime, a discourse which produces from within itself sublime experience.[44]

If the discourse of the sublime has, effectively, 'no boundary', what we seem to have arrived at is a dangerous abysmal land. The discourse of the sublime *is itself sublime*: it stands for the unpresentability of the Thing, foregrounding this unpresentability, or 'unboundedness', in presentation itself.[45] If excess is seen as an intrinsic feature of the sublime, something that results in the enormous productivity of this discourse, it should come as no surprise that the discourse *on* the sublime must eventually collapse into its theoretical, self-reflexive other. De Bolla admits that 'in time' the sublime as a topic or object of enquiry (i.e. the discourse *of* the sublime) replaces an empirical investigation into the forms, causes and effects of the sublime. This process is explained as follows: as a result of the inevitable contamination of the discourse *on* the sublime by neighbouring discourses there emerges a discourse organised upon the recognition that the enquiry has no object.

[T]he discourse of the sublime effectively describes and analyses itself, it explains how sublime sensation arises in the individual by recourse to the workings of the discourse of analysis. ... it is self-reflexive in the first instance, making reference to itself as discourse in its explanatory procedures rather than to adjacent or prior discourses, objects in the world or human subjectivity.[46]

But how does this process of discursive transmutation occur? Does something really happen to the discursive network de Bolla recognises, or is it perhaps his own attitude to textual alignments that undergoes a transformation? How can what seems to be a 'narrower' discourse (i.e. the discourse *on* the sublime) produce a discourse 'without boundaries', which itself then produces the experience of the sublime? What economy underlies these transactions?

For de Bolla, the boundary between the discourses *on* and *of* the sublime is permeable. Even what he terms 'a commentary upon a sublime sensation' has to draw from a discursive network which is not confined by these two discourses. However, if the discourse of the sublime has, in fact, 'no boundary', the process of arranging a discursive network is at the same time an act of its destabilisation. This is why it is not possible ultimately to separate the discourse *on* the sublime from the discourse *of* the sublime, especially as both of them seem to be able to produce a sublime discourse. But de Bolla probably needed to choose such a laborious method of erecting discursive boundaries and barriers in order to demonstrate that his initial distinction between the allegedly disparate discourses was unsustainable. The principle of self-reflexivity on which his argument is based can only be justified through an exposition of what may appear to be illogical couplings and transformations. Hayles claims that 'reflexivity has subversive effects because it confuses and entangles the boundaries we impose on the world in order to make sense of that world. Reflexivity tends notoriously toward infinite regress'.[47] As reflexivity is performative, it cannot really be stated 'in advance', or 'outside' the discursive network to which it applies. The principle of reflexivity explains in what way the discourse of theory, which for de Bolla is a historically marked product of the reflection *on* the sublime, can itself be a site of sublime vertigo: the discourse on the sublime simultaneously produces the sublimity it describes. The discourse of the sublime can be said to describe this discursive vortex which regresses *ad infinitum*, embracing both the subject of analysis and the analytical discourse employed.

Sublime overflow

It is thus understandable that the discourse of the feminine sublime I develop in the book should be marked with the possibility of overflowing. However, even though I am wary of its disappearance in the vortex of critical reflexivity, I do not intend to abandon the use of the term 'discourse' altogether. Instead, I follow Derrida's suggestion that we borrow 'an old word from philosophy in order to immediately demarcate it'.[48] The discourse of the feminine sublime is not, therefore, an entirely new discourse, but rather an attempt to trace this discursive overflowing in the traditional discourse of the sublime. By focusing on the two main aspects of the traditional sublime, i.e. the capitalisation of excess and the fear of eruption, I hope to investigate the possible intrusion of the incalculable and the untamed into this discourse.

As I mentioned before, this fear of eruption and 'overflow' poses a threat not only to the newly emergent subjectivity but also, it seems, to the selfhood of the predominantly male theorists of the sublime. This is probably the reason why the discourse of the sublime relies on the idea of 'woman' as its cornerstone and reference point. 'Woman' is usually disempowered in this discourse (i.e. reduced to the images of weakness, submission and beauty), a manoeuvre which allows its practitioners to reassert their masculinity. Significantly, Barbara Claire Freeman defines the sublime as an 'allegory of the construction of the patriarchal (but not necessarily male) subject, a self that maintains its borders by subordinating difference and by appropriating rather than identifying with that which presents itself as other'.[49] In a similar vein, de Bolla concludes,

> [T]he discourse on the sublime produces and examines subjectivity in gender-specific terms, thereby signalling its participation within the larger set of discourses determining sexuality for the period. ... [This discourse] is faced with the product of its own analysis, which we will here label as the sexed subject, with which it is both uncomfortable – an unwanted product – and hopelessly drawn to, fascinated by. The discourse on the sublime recognises this sexed subject, but refuses to theorise it, refuses its distances.[50]

It is interesting that the figure of distance, which Derrida interprets as standing for, but also protecting against, femininity in Western thought, is mentioned here in a similar context. The gendering of the sublime, manifesting itself as an emphasis on the indubitable difference between masculinity and femininity, allows the male subject to maintain a distance from 'woman', i.e. from distance itself, which occludes, as well as presents, the instability and arbitrariness of the truth of gender polarity. De Bolla explains further that even though the discourse on the sublime eventually turns towards the examination of subjectivity, it 'continually forecloses on the possibility of the subject; it constantly sees it in terms of an unlegislatable, an unthinkable'.[51] The subject matter of this discourse – the experience of the sublime – 'leaks', however, into the subject position, whose very constitution is always threatened by the eruption of the difference it tries to tame and annul. The discourse of the sublime thus seems to foreclose on the possibility of the subject because of the fear of *sexual difference*. Subjectivity is a terrifying concept precisely due to its links with sexuality and femininity, which in the gendered theories of the sublime are reduced to sameness, obedience and beauty. If identity cannot be thought outside difference, the theories of the sublime construct a male subject position which is to be a defence mechanism against the irreducible difference of the other. In this way subjectivity is both asserted and denied, which explains the reluctance to acknowledge the excess of the subject de Bolla detects in what he terms 'the discourse of the sublime'.

The feminine sublime

[H]e can sustain himself only by bouncing back off some objectiveness, some objective. If there is no more 'earth' to press down/repress, to work, to represent, but also and always to desire (for one's own), no opaque matter which in theory does not know itself, then what pedestal remains for the ex-sistence of the 'subject'? If the earth turned and more especially turned upon herself, the erection of the subject might thereby be disconcerted and risk losing its elevation and penetration. For what would there be to rise up from and exercise his power over? And in? (Luce Irigaray, *Speculum of the Other Woman*)

The discursive excess produced by the sublime is described as power, a term which serves as 'as a deflection for the name of the subject'.[52] In Burke's theory the subject cannot be named; it does not yield to conceptualisation, because the available discursive framework within which this theorisation occurs is constructed upon the negation of absolute difference and the assertion of binary logic. As long as an appropriate distance from the threatening object is maintained, the self's weakness is turned into strength, which results from the mind's ability to grasp the nature of the fear and thus guarantee the self's protection. Similarly, in Kant, subjectivity is encoded as might. As a result, the excess of representation is absorbed by the mind, leading to the enhancement of the self which is initially threatened by the unpresentable. 'The astonishment amounting almost to terror, the awe and thrill of devout feeling ... – all this, when we are assured of our own safety, is not actually fear. ... [I]t is a might enabling us to assert our independence as against the influences of nature, to degrade what is great in respect of the latter to the level of what is little, and thus to locate the absolutely great only in the proper estate of the Subject.'[53] Consistent with the tradition which separates reason from affect, culture from nature, and masculinity from femininity, the elevating moral aspect of Kant's sublime does not apply to women (even though 'woman' constitutes an unspoken foundation of this discourse). As a consequence of this way of thinking, women, as Christine Battersby observes, 'have traditionally been confined to the stage of consciousness that post-Kantian philosophers termed "the aesthetic"'.[54] Situated outside the ethical sphere, women have been excluded from the universal concept of 'personhood'.

It is, however, possible to conceptualise subjectivity *beyond* identity and sameness. As part of her feminist ethical project, Luce Irigaray contends we should open up another era in our culture, 'an era in which the subject is no longer *one*, solipsistic, egocentric and potentially imperialistic, but which rather respects differences, and particularly the difference inscribed in nature and subjectivity them-selves: sexual difference'.[55] I believe the feminine sublime I am pro-posing can be seen as one possible realisation of Irigaray's project. The feminine sublime does not domesticate the object that might be a source of threat but rather accepts the amorous relationship of pleasure and pain, and life and death, and the potential dispersal of the self. This mode of encountering difference takes up 'a position of respect in response to incalculable otherness'[56] and thus situates itself in the realm of ethics, defined after Levinas as 'respect for the alterity of the other', rather than impersonal, subject–object-orientated aes-thetics. Interestingly, in *The Feminine Sublime* Freeman argues that the traditional aesthetics of sublimity has always had ethical implications: 'To invoke the non-demonstrable – not as a familiar feature of aesthetics but rather in the context of the incommensurable – is to situate the sublime as a site of resistance to aestheticism and also to underscore its political and ethical dimensions'.[57]

Freeman's book, however, stops short of exploring the conse-quences of this shift of analytical perspective. I hope my project, indebted to but also parallel with her investigation of 'the dominant ideology of misogyny that haunts canonical theories of the sublime',[58] will situate the *feminist* discourse of the *feminine* sublime, with its multiple historical and theoretical affiliations, or what Morris calls 'family resemblances', along the politico-ethical axis. Instead of merely looking for examples of 'subversive sublimity' in the selected novels by women writers (which is what Freeman does in her book), I want to explore the more ambiguous relationship between political discourses and literary genres. I am particularly interested in the collapsing of the discourse of the sublime into a sublime discourse, or, to put it another way, in the production of sublimity in and by the theoretical discourse of the sublime. If femininity is understood as a marker of difference which can open up the rigid boundaries of the discourse of Western philosophy, ethics as the recognition of and respect for difference can facilitate what Irigaray has envisaged as the arrival of 'a new era'. What I will further call 'the ethics of the feminine sublime' springs from the respectful recognition of the power of the sublime, and from the acknowledgement that the traditional sublime was constructed upon the suppression of excess and the negation of sexual difference. Thus, even though the sublime has always been 'feminine', the excess of difference the theorists of sublimity feared was strictly controlled.

Revisiting *écriture féminine*

> There is no action, even in the classical sense of the word, no political or ethical action which could be simply dissociated from, or opposed to, discourse. There is no politics without discourse, there is no politics without the book in our culture. (Jacques Derrida, 'Hospitality, Justice and Responsibility')

The *feminine* sublime I propose here should not be seen as only a women's practice, even though certain aspects of both feminism and women's art might be its driving force. I cannot agree with Patricia Yaeger when in her article 'Toward a Female Sublime' she claims that 'women write in the sublime mode'.[59] Such an assumption would, on the one hand, leave the power structure unchanged, and, on the other, turn my project into a 'women's thing' (a mere trifle). By insisting on the adjective 'feminine', I want instead to draw attention to the problem of sexual difference and to open the alleged neutrality of the previous concepts of the sublime to the recognition of incalculable otherness. But the feminine sublime is not to be limited to linguistic experimentation, though I accept the post-structuralist contention that experience is always already coded – and thus available to us – as textual. This is why in my search for the possible modes of the functioning of the feminine sublime I want to engage with the concept of *écriture féminine*, which describes a subversive literary practice. To acknowledge that experience cannot be accessed or conceptualised outside signifying structures does not mean that the feminine sublime is not able to transgress the textual principles of phallogocentric discourses and masculinist decorum. My engagement with *écriture féminine* will eventually lead to the development of an *ethical* proposal, one which recognises both the materiality of experience and its describability in textual terms, and which focuses on the little events of the everyday. The shift from aesthetics to ethics should not, however, be seen as absolute, as an exact separation between the two realms has never been possible.

In the 1970s, *écriture féminine* ('feminine writing') as developed by the French writer Hélène Cixous offered an alternative to the systemic discourse of Western philosophy by bringing together poetry and thought, body and mind. Cixous delineated the principles of *écriture féminine* in her celebrated 1975 essay 'The Laugh of the Medusa' as well as her book *The Newly Born Woman*, which she wrote with Catherine Clément in the same year. Cixous describes writing as a liberating practice for women who are otherwise gagged, silenced and sentenced to both intellectual and emotional exile in society. Women's writing can thus be seen as an existential act, helping them to assert their identity and reclaim their voice; it is the place where desire, body and intelligence can 'flow to the limits of the universe'.[60] Having rejected Freud's and Lacan's perception of 'woman as lack', Cixous calls for a recognition of the fact that the female body is marked with a positive value of plenitude. Speaking for the linguistically dispossessed, she announces proudly: '[W]e labyrinths, the ladders, the trampled spaces, the bevies. … We're stormy, and that which is ours breaks loose from us without our fearing any debilitation. Our glances, our smiles, are spent; laughs exude from all our mouths; our blood flows and we extend ourselves without ever reaching an end'.[61] In her rhetoric of infinity there can be heard an echo of Burke's and Kant's fearsome landscapes and terrifying oceans, which allow the lone traveller to face the omnipotence of nature and still show resistance. Thanks to the power of his senses, Man does not question the positioning of the sublime in the realm of the dangerous, and instead keeps away from what might otherwise threaten his peace of mind. Cixous's sublime does not offer such consolation. Here the infinite abyss which is the source of both fascination and fear is to be found within woman's self, in the heart of her labyrinth. Cixous describes this feeling as follows: 'Time and again I, too, have felt so full of luminous torrents that I could burst – burst with forms much more beautiful that those which are put up in frames and sold for a stinking fortune'.[62] Acting like a thunderstorm, the feminine calls for an abandonment of Burke's safe distance and Kant's secure position and for a confrontation with 'the fantastic tumult of her drives'. Exposed to the tectonics of the feminine sublime, language recoils back on itself, a state of affairs which results in the restructuring of the phallic landscape. After the sublime earthquake, 'The sky isn't up there: it's between us'.[63]

Écriture féminine was a non-militant but nevertheless active way of asserting women's right to and need for self-expression. By no means built on flat emotionalism or radical biologism for which it was sometimes criticised, it contested the rigidity of the discourse of Enlightenment rationality by proposing another mode of thinking. Écriture féminine allowed for the presence of the other, for an incongruity that would not slip away from discursive roughness or fissure but would willingly explore the liminalities, thicknesses and crevices of the linguistic texture.[64] In this sense, the 'femininity' of this mode of writing stood for a radical alterity which should not be identified with the absolute and essentialist difference of the feminine body, but which rather spoke about the link between rationality and corporeality, and which exposed the sexual dimension of the process of writing. Even though it was intended as a feminist practice of linguistic liberation from the constraints of phallogocentrism, écriture féminine was not restricted to 'biological women': Cixous quoted Jean Genet as one of the practitioners of this type of writing. This so called 'feminine element' was thus not to be a consequence of the writer's sex or gender but should rather be perceived as a mode of insubordination towards master discourses and an attempt to open thought to feeling. The signifier 'feminine' (which in the French language stands for both 'femaleness' and 'femininity') should not be reduced to either gender polarity or radical biologism. As Claire Joubert argues in her article, 'The "Feminine": A Critical Angle for Poetics', the concept of feminine writing can instead be seen as a 'corrosive act within language':

Clearly, 'Woman' is only one of those paradoxical figures of the
literary effect, which inscribes itself in language at the very place
where it marks out language's constitutive lack. The themes and
tropes of sexual difference in these texts do not so much aim at
recovering a woman's view of womanhood. Rather, the 'feminine'
character of these texts functions as one of the figures of the
'identical neutrality of the abyss' which is also the nucleus of
Mallarmé's poetics, for instance. It is one way to avoid speaking in
the Name-of-the-Father, one of the deconstructive forces which
encourages the *différance* of meaning and brings language to its
critical edge. It may be that feminine writing is not so much that
which tries to establish a woman's voice, but that which proposes to
use sexion [i.e. the law of division that rules both sexual identity and
language] as an instrument in the literary critique of the symbolic
order.[65]

Therefore, though the 'feminine' sublime takes the material experience of femininity as a starting point, it is not to be an exclusive
practice reserved just for women. If, as Joubert argues, '"Woman"
retains its force as a critical sign, as abrasive device for the critical
exploration of the *Logos*, within which it indicates a point of semiotic
turbulence',[66] women's entry into the world of the male sublime
exposes the silencing of sexual difference in this discourse. In consequence, a space is opened for writing immersed in the materiality of
the everyday, but not limited to *women's* writing. In insurgent texts
written 'like a woman'[67] and spun from 'lights, colours, vegetation,
heat, air, slender explosion of noises, scant cries of birds, children's
voices from over on the other side, passages, gestures, clothes of
inhabitants near or far away',[68] one can feel their texture, see pores
and touch knots. They are possessed by other texts, haunted by the
multilingual demon, introducing themselves as 'Legion'. As Roland
Barthes blasphemously announces, the plurality of such texts is against
the law: 'it reads without the inscription of the Father'.[69]

If we take into account the productivity of signs that construct
'reality', the notion of *écriture féminine* may be extended to relate not
only to the actual practice of literary writing but also to some other
discourses, or better (to refer to Laclau's use of the term 'discourse')
'viewpoints', which describe the world around us. The 'feminine'
inscription in these discourses is a sign of the recognition of the excess
and irreducibility which are experienced in the self's encounter with
otherness. This mode of thinking gives credit to the expelled affective
element which has been suppressed in the discourse of Western

philosophy. In *The Republic*, Plato, having sent poets behind the city walls, and thus separating philosophers' reason from *pathos* and *techne*, has initiated the scission between thought and affect. But, since the principles of exclusion often turn back against themselves, the tight and erect discourse of *logos* has always been haunted by its excluded 'other'. Thus this proposition for a 'new' discourse of the sublime – a discourse of thinking through suffering and affect – is an attempt to liquidate the imposed sterility of thought and accept its waste products: the abject, the maternal and the corporeal.

Décriture féminine: an ethical proposal

That political change must begin in language has been the contention of numerous feminists who have undermined the rigidity of the symbolic discourse. Julia Kristeva, for example, has described language as regulated by the exclusive, even deadly, economy of the Father. The possibility of language recoiling back on itself and revealing its precarious foundations was associated with the sublime by its first theorist, Longinus: 'Sublimity ... produced at the right moment tears everything up like a whirlwind and exhibits the orator's whole power at a single blow'.[70] Significantly, Longinus ascribes the force of linguistic transport to the skilful mastery of the orator, for whom language is a powerful but nevertheless controllable tool. It is only the listeners who are plunged into horror and awe by the orator's linguistic manoeuvres. (As we should be aware by now, eighteenth-century theorists of the sublime, when faced with an indescribable and thus frightening phenomenon, also resorted to the power of mind, which allowed them to theorise danger and thus keep it at bay.)

Drawing on the rhetoric of the sublime, Lyotard's *The Inhuman* constitutes an attempt to rethink some of the discursive frameworks which were forged in the 'old world of the human'. Lyotard here appears to pick up a Longinian thread in order to expose the link between language and violence. '[H]ow could we capture the breath of wind that sweeps the mind into the void when the landscape arrives', asks Lyotard, 'if not in the texture of the written word?'.[71] Lyotard's definition of landscape is extremely broad: it transcends the topography of physical spaces to embrace the most minuscule territories one encounters in one's linguistic wanderings: from a busy city corner to the temple of the other's body. His landscape is sensuous, inviting a lone traveller to savour its flesh. But what is at stake in Lyotard's wanderings is the difficulty of giving account of one's experience: he is trying to work out how the excess of the everyday can be expressed in words. Lyotard is aware of the potential failure, even 'explosion', of language when faced with the excess of FORM, as well as of the 'horrifying presence' of the LACK inherent in the system of signification which is available to us. This difficulty is elsewhere described as the differend, i.e. a moment 'when something "asks" to be put into phrases, and suffers from the wrong of not being able to be put into phrases right away', leading, as a consequence, to the conflicting feeling of pleasure and pain.[72] But rather than resort to hysteria or silence (traditionally, the two routes of escape which were available to women who felt entrapped in phallogocentric language), Lyotard explores poetry as one possible way of dealing with the sublime of the everyday. This situation of linguistic impasse, 'wherein something which must be able to be put into phrases cannot yet be',[73] gives rise to a political moment, understood here as a need to engage in a polemic between at least two heterogeneous discourses 'that cannot be equitably resolved for lack of a rule of judgement applicable to both arguments'.[74] Defying the solace of good form, or decorum, the acceptance of the impurity and heterogeneity of language constitutes for Lyotard a necessary condition of poetico-political action:[75]

> Poetry arises out of this understanding of wretchedness; otherwise it is merely a staging [*mise en scène*] and a mobilisation [*mise en ouvre*] of the powers of language. It is the writing [*écriture*] of the impossible description; DESCRIPTURE [DÉCRITURE]. And the difference between describing and recounting should not be confused with deferring, which is the fate that awaits the mind when it tries to grasp itself through logic, theory of knowledge or literature, narrative or essays. It is a matter of landscape that is at stake in poetic descripture, and not the forms in which it can be inscribed.[76]

Lyotard's insistence on the link with wretchedness and abjection foregrounds the material/maternal aspect of the experience with language. Instead of relying on fixed rules of decorum, Lyotard retreats to metaphor, declaring that poetry 'is a matter of landscape'. This way of theorising poetry – something Lyotard shares, for example, with Julia Kristeva or Hélène Cixous – invites a comparison between his concept of *décriture* as 'writing of an impossible description' and Cixous' notion of *écriture féminine*. Both these concepts draw to a large extent on the rhetoric of the sublime with its residues of passion and its terror of death. The exploration of this coupling is particularly important in my search for the conditions of the functioning of this old–new discourse which I term 'the feminine sublime'. Since poetry can be seen not only as a discrete literary genre but also as an insurgent discursive strategy which challenges the tightness of *logos* by embracing both thought and affect, I propose that the feminine sublime be read as a reworking of the concept of *écriture féminine*, initially referring to poetic writing attuned to woman's bodily space. Entering the territory of Lyotard's *décriture*, I would like to coin the term *décriture féminine*, naming a politico-ethical discourse which winds itself along the paths of the bodily landscape and always defers the possibility of ultimate arrival. This 'new' discourse is by no means another grand narrative, intent upon replenishing the old bottles with new wine. If the concept of *décriture féminine* is to be at least temporarily retained, it will always refer to a microspace, a singular event or a fragment. It does not aim at reinstating the belief in presence or the possibility of overcoming what Lyotard calls 'the implosion of forms' in language. An instance of presence will be momentary, always suspended before the moment of arrival. To illustrate this, we could use the metaphor of the guest who is just about to appear, and whose visit has been long awaited, but who may have been delayed by the unexpected. This waiting and belief in his or her coming, culminating in the opening of the door and our triumphant '*Voilà!*' (to the guest but also to those who have tried to undermine our hope), is what Lyotard portrays as the sublime. The visitor may still be on the pathway; we do not even actually get to see him or her at all. In fact, there is always a chance that *nothing will happen*. And yet in his account of the sublime Lyotard shifts the perspective towards a positive belief in the occurrence of the event. Thus the feminine sublime I develop on the basis of his ideas can be understood as an occurrence, a flash, or a permanent beginning, which undermines the continuity of being with its immediacy and its constant return to a zero point. 'What is sublime is the feeling that something will happen, despite everything, within this threatening void, that something will take "place" and will announce that every-thing is not over.'[77] The phrase 'despite everything' points to the irrationality of this belief, in the sense that it does not receive any confirmation. It is an utterly counter-logical thought, which ignores the warnings of reason. Indeed, as Lyotard concludes in *The Differend*, the constant re-enactment of the sublime by leaving the key question *Is it happening?* open is a guarantee of the survival of philosophy (or what he also calls 'philosophical politics'), whereas 'economic calculation seems fatal to it'.[78]

Décriture féminine can thus designate a discourse which does not capitalise on difference, and which embraces femininity as a mark of non-binary difference. In this discourse the theoretical excess is not to be controlled or prescribed. If, as Peter de Bolla argues, the broadly defined discipline of theory is the product of the discourse of the sublime, *décriture féminine* can be seen as a reversal of thinking in terms of origin: produced by the sublime, it can itself give way to sublimity, thus allowing for an illogical process of intergeneration and grafting which breaks with the logic of primacy and parenthood. For me *décriture féminine* also serves as a useful concept for analysing the transformations within the extensive field of feminist discourses. As a 'writing of impossible description', it challenges the ideas of clarity, mastery and presence. Celebrating an event, immersion or plunge, it collapses the distinctions between theory and practice, or primary and secondary texts. It questions not only the phallogocentric discourses of Western philosophy, but also certain forms of 'phallogocentric feminism' which silences indeterminacy for the sake of arriving at clearly defined feminist politics and feminist ethics. In what I perceive to be the most political and most revolutionary of manoeuvres, *décriture féminine* is always deferred, 'which is the fate that awaits the mind when it tries to grasp itself through logic, theory of knowledge or literature, narrative or essays'. Deferral does not need to stand for the refusal of feminist action, but it does involve the radical questioning of the concepts of both action and feminism, thus opening a conceptual abyss which evokes the incommensurate feelings of fascination and horror.

Contradictory, insubordinate and a-rational, *décriture féminine* is also a discourse of transgression, crossing over the boundaries drawn for the maintenance of the self's identity. Through the recognition of the particularity of the landscape in which the sublime event is taking place and of the alterity of the other who is participating in it, an attempt to master this alterity gives way to proximity and engagement. Opening oneself to the arrival of the other is a highly significant gesture. The self no longer remains 'at certain distances' from its source of enticement and fascination, but rather embarks on a fearful encounter with the other who poses a threat to its integrity but who also offers a promise of bliss (*jouissance*). Ultimate responsibility for this event rests with its participants. As Emmanuel Levinas states in

Totality and Infinity, an individual has an ethical choice to either welcome the stranger and speak to him or her, or to remain in isolation and seclusion. But when the encounter eventually does happen, it collapses the subject–object division maintained in traditional encounters with sublime grandeur. It is precisely the uncertain arrival of the other – who has 'all the traits of the *Is it happening?*'[79] – that allows Lyotard to interpret Levinasian ethics in the context of the sublime. For Lyotard sublimity does not have an essence but rather consists in an acknowledgement that something is taking place, almost against all odds. The withdrawal of knowledge about both the other who will be arriving and the character of this encounter deprives the self of conceptual mastery. Wounded and bare, it can only wait for the uncertain arrival of the other who puts the self in question. But, as Levinas notices, when I open myself to the infinite alterity of the other, 'the proximity of the neighbour in its *trauma* does not only *strike up against me* but *exalts and elevates me*, and, in the literal sense of the term, inspires me'.[80] Levinas's description of this encounter is embedded in the rhetoric of the sublime, emphasising pain mixed with pleasure, elevation and greatness. The ethical relation with the other transforms the everyday and the commonplace into a most significant event, whose importance is stressed by the upward movement the self experiences when confronted with the other's alterity. However, as elevation goes hand-in-hand, or rather, to quote Levinas, face-to-face, with proximity, the self needs to risk and reveal its vulnerability for the sake of experiencing the infinite *jouissance*, a feeling which results from a direct contact with otherness.

Resituating the sublime within the context of Levinasian ethics, defined as 'respect for the alterity of the other', allows me to propose a different way of encountering, and engaging with, alterity and excess. As I argued before, the Kantian sublime is intrinsically ethical, but it is also based on the sacrifice of imagination and the overcoming of the self's phenomenal (i.e. 'natural') side. This is not to undermine the extreme importance of Kant's moral thinking: we have to remember it was one of the first ethical systems in Western philosophy to be freed of the need for a positive metaphysical foundation. For Kant, morality has to come from our reason, rather than from any external concept of the good, and it does not involve any non-universalisable principles. His categorical, universal imperative is developed into the so-called 'Formula of the End in Itself', which demands that we treat 'humanity in your own person or in the person of any other never

simply as a means but always at the same time as an end'.[81] Postulating respect for other persons, Kant's ethics stems from the self. As
Crowther explains, moral consciousness in Kant does not arise out of
love or respect towards human beings which is then universalised in
to a moral principle; 'we find instead that moral feeling (i.e. 'respect')
is the outcome of our recognition that the will is necessarily subject to
the moral law. It arises, in other words, *from* our self-transcendence
towards the universal'.[82] The Kantian sublime, in the last instance,
aggrandises the self. Even though Kant professes that 'The feeling of
our incapacity to attain to an idea *that is a law for us*, is RESPECT',[83] it
is reason that is ultimately respected because of its ability to transcend
the limits of imagination. Excess resulting from an encounter with the
unpresentable and the threatening is absorbed by the mind, which
wards off the danger of encountering alterity in the self. The moral
sentiment is thus awakened as a response to the break-up of
imagination.

Lyotard is a less sympathetic reader of Kant's sublime than, for
example, Derrida or Crowther. He emphasises numerous times, as I
mentioned before, that Kantian thinking abuses and violates nature,
an attitude that for Lyotard is clearly counter-ethical, even if conducted in the name of obedience to a higher principle. In fact, it is the
premises of Kant's ethical imperative that Lyotard questions when
stating: 'in the sublime feeling thinking becomes impatient, despair-
ing, disinterested in attaining the ends of freedom by means of
nature'.[84]

My discussion of Kant's ethics is necessarily sketchy and does not
do justice to the complexity of his argument. I have only focused here
on the relationship between identity, alterity and ethics in the
Kantian sublime as developed in his third *Critique*: this is the principal
issue I am working through in order to elaborate the discourse of the
feminine sublime, and to justify its ethical underpinnings. It is at this
point that the comparison between Kantian and Levinasian ethics
becomes important for me. While Kant's ethics finds its origin and
justification in the self – with all its accompanying legislative acts,
power struggles and what Lyotard sums up as 'violence' – Levinas
points to the arrival of the other as the source of an ethical sentiment.
Tina Chanter remarks that 'Unlike ... the Kantian dictum according to
which I should treat others with the respect that I would like to
command myself, Levinas' conception of ethics starts not from an
analogy between myself and the other, but precisely from our

differences'.[85] This way of thinking allows for the abandonment of the principle of mastery in an encounter with alterity, as I will explain in more detail in chapter 2. Refusing to assert the self's primacy, Levinas focuses on the vulnerability of the self when facing the other, who is always already 'absolutely other'. The encounter with alterity opens up a chasm between the self, which is never 'present to itself', and the other, whose arrival brings both the sense of incompletion and the promise of bliss. In this way, the allegedly impersonal aesthetics of the sublime creates a possibility of an ethical involvement, an involvement which I want to investigate under the name of the ethics of the feminine sublime. As Simon Critchley explains, ethics, for Levinas,

> is not an obligation toward the other mediated through the formal and procedural universalisation of maxims or some appeal to good conscience; rather – and this is what is truly provocative about Levinas – ethics is *lived* in the sensibility of a corporeal obligation to the other. It is because the self is sensible, that is to say, vulnerable, passive, open to wounding, outrage and pain, but also open to the movement of the erotic, that it is capable and worthy of ethics.[86]

Delineating the possible problems related to Levinas's exposition of sexual difference in his otherwise truly revolutionary ethics, I will propose in chapter 2 that a thinking–loving encounter with the sexuate other be seen as a paradigm of ethical engagement. Tracing the possibility of the 'eruption' of the feminine sublime within the traditional discourse of sublimity, I will draw on the principle of contamination which I have described in this chapter under the name of *décriture féminine*. Open to both thought and desire, to the expelled and the maternal, *décriture féminine* as a discourse of the feminine sublime presents itself as always already polyvocal and plural. It will thus allow me to revisit the concepts of aesthetics, ethics and politics from a feminist perspective and to delineate a new economy of the relationship between the sexes, one which does not depend on the capitalisation of discursive excess.

Notes

1   While this chapter is primarily devoted to the analysis of the principle of *capitalisation* in the traditional discourse of the sublime, its findings will be used in chapter 2, in which I will present a more detailed analysis of the emergence of the modern subject as a side product of the individualist economy of *capitalism*. I will also speculate on the possibility of develop-

ing another economy, one which does not calculate exactly all gains and losses.

2 'By Definition, Art Is a Gesture of Repair: Tomek Kitlinski's Entretien with Hélène Cixous', *Art Magazine*, 4 (1996), 193.

3 Luce Irigaray, *This Sex Which Is Not One*, trans. Catherine Porter (Ithaca, New York: Cornell University Press, 1985), 30.

4 Ernesto Laclau, 'Discourse', in *Contemporary Political Philosophy*, eds Robert E. Goodin and Philip Petit (Oxford: Blackwell, 1994), 433.

5 Ibid., 433.

6 Jacques Derrida, *Positions*, trans. Alan Bass (Chicago: University of Chicago Press, 1981), 59–60. As this passage makes clear, for Derrida 'discourse' is always already marked with the possibility of overflowing.

7 Rosi Braidotti, *Patterns of Dissonance* (Cambridge: Polity Press, 1991).

8 Jacques Derrida, *Spurs: Nietzsche's Styles*, trans. Barbara Harlow (Chicago and London: University of Chicago Press, 1979), 51.

9 Derrida's writings have received a mixed response from feminist theorists. Jane Gallop, for example, sees the need to 'update *Spurs* into the nineties'. She argues that feminists entering the new millennium have become much more aware of the significance of diversity within women's community, to the extent that it is impossible to write about women today without referring to a number of other issues, including race, class, age and sexuality. She invites us to recognise the material reality of women situated outside language, but seems to remain oblivious to the fact that the categories of 'difference' she enumerates are themselves based on the logic of 'sameness' (i.e. a pre-described and identifiable difference, the infinite productivity of which has been limited by selecting what feminists like Gallop consider 'significant differences'). Jane Gallop, '"Women" in *Spurs* and Nineties Feminism', in *Derrida and Feminism*, eds Ellen K. Feder, Mary C. Rawlinson and Emily Zakin (New York and London: Routledge, 1997). (This collection of essays offers a number of thought-provoking interventions into the debates on feminism and deconstruction.) For a more sympathetic account of Derrida's *Spurs* see also Alice A. Jardine, *Gynesis* (Ithaca and London: Cornell University Press, 1985). Even though Jardine recognises the possible violence implied by Derrida's feminist gesture of positioning femininity as 'the non-truth of truth', she also recognises that, especially in his post-1970 writings, Derrida has adopted a number of 'strategies-in-genderisation' which propose 'the feminine' as an alternative logic which can contribute to the 'new vision' of, or within, metaphysics.

10 Jardine, *Gynesis*, 183.

11 Geoffrey Bennington and Jacques Derrida, *Jacques Derrida*, trans. Geoffrey Bennington (Chicago and London: University of Chicago Press, 1993), 143.

12 Ibid., 7.

13 Jacques Derrida, 'Letter to a Japanese Friend', trans. David Wood and Andrew Benjamin, in *A Derrida Reader: Between the Blinds*, ed. Peggy Kamuf (Hemel Hempstead: Harvester Wheatsheaf, 1991).

14 Quoted in Diane Elam, *Feminism and Deconstruction* (London and New York: Routledge: 1994), 23.

15 More detailed analyses of the earlier versions of the sublime can be found in the following books: Thomas Weiskel, *The Romantic Sublime: Studies in the Structure and Psychology of Transcendence* (Baltimore and London: Johns Hopkins University Press, 1976); Peter de Bolla, *The Discourse of the Sublime: Readings in History, Aesthetics and the Subject* (Oxford: Basil Blackwell, 1989); Paul Crowther, *The Kantian Sublime: From Morality to Art* (Oxford: Clarendon Press, 1989); Jean-François Lyotard, *Lessons on the Analytic of the Sublime, Sections 23–29: Kant's Critique of Judgement*, trans. Elizabeth Rottenberg (Stanford: Stanford University Press, 1994); Andrew Ashfield and Peter de Bolla eds, *The Sublime: A Reader in British Eighteenth-Century Aesthetic Theory* (Cambridge: Cambridge University Press, 1996); Barbara Claire Freeman, *The Feminine Sublime: Gender and Excess in Women's Fiction* (Berkeley, Los Angeles and London: University of California Press, 1995).

16 David B. Morris, 'Gothic Sublimity', *New Literary History*, 16:2 (1984–85), 300.

17 'Longinus', *On Sublimity*, trans. D.A. Russell (Oxford: Clarendon Press, 1965), 2. The first treatise on sublimity, *Peri Hypsous*, was for a long time attributed to the third-century Greek philosopher Longinus. It is now believed, however, that the treatise was written as early as the first century AD. Its author is commonly referred to as 'Pseudo-Longinus'.

18 Edmund Burke, *A Philosophical Enquiry into the Origin of our Ideas of the Sublime and the Beautiful* (Oxford: Blackwell, 1967), 57.

19 Crowther, *The Kantian Sublime*, 11, emphasis added.

20 Burke, *A Philosophical Enquiry*, 40, emphasis added.

21 The following passage from Kant's *Critique of Judgement* illustrates how the conflict of the faculties evoked by the sublime is overcome by the supremacy of the mind and its triumph over imagination: '[P]recisely because there is a striving in our imagination towards progress *ad infinitum*, while reason demands absolute totality, as a real idea, that same inability on the part of our faculty for the estimation of the magnitude of things of the world of sense to attain to this idea, is the awakening of a feeling of a supersensible faculty within us; and it is the use to which judgement naturally puts particular objects on behalf of this latter feeling, and not the object of sense, that is absolutely great, and every contrasted employment small. Consequently it is the disposition of soul evoked by a particular representation engaging the attention of the reflective judgement, and not the Object, that is to be called sublime. ... [T]he point of capital importance is that the mere ability even to think it as a whole indicates a faculty of mind transcending every standard of sense'. Immanuel Kant, *The Critique of Judgement*, trans. James Meredith (Oxford: Clarendon Press, 1952), 97–102.

22 Ibid., 97.

23 Crowther, *The Kantian Sublime*, 19.

24 We should distinguish here between the mathematical sublime, in which the object corresponds to the faculty of cognition (i.e. theoretical reason) and the dynamical sublime, in which it is referred to the faculty of desire (i.e. practical reason). In the mathematical sublime we are faced with

what is absolutely great in nature. Even though our imagination feels helpless in the face of this immeasurable greatness, the idea of totality – which is an idea of reason – intervenes to save the self from the momentary arrest of its faculties. In the dynamical sublime it is another idea of reason – the idea of moral agency – that elevates the self beyond the sensory towards its own superiority as a moral being. It is thus only the dynamical sublime that has clear ethical implications. For a detailed discussion of these two modes of sublimity in Kant see Eva Schaper, 'Taste, Sublimity, and Genius: The Aesthetics of Nature and Art', in *The Cambridge Companion to Kant*, ed. Paul Guyer (Cambridge: Cambridge University Press, 1992) and Paul Crowther, *The Kantian Sublime*.

25 Immanuel Kant, *Groundwork of the Metaphysic of Morals*, trans. H. J. Patton (New York: Harper & Row, Publishers, 1964), 88.

26 Crowther, *The Kantian Sublime*, 21.

27 Kant, *Critique of Judgement*, 115–16.

28 Jacques Derrida, *Of Grammatology*, trans. Gayatri Chakravorty Spivak (Baltimore: Johns Hopkins University Press, 1976), 145.

29 Ibid., 145–6.

30 Jean-François Lyotard, *The Inhuman*, trans. Geoffrey Bennington and Rachel Bowlby (Cambridge: Polity Press, 1991), 137.

31 Ibid., 137.

32 Lyotard, *Lessons*, 180.

33 Kant, *Critique of Judgement*, 112–13.

34 Lyotard, *Lessons*, 180.

35 Samuel H. Monk, *The Sublime: A Study of Critical Theories in Eighteenth-Century England* (Ann Arbor: University of Michigan Press, 1960, orig. 1935), 5.

36 Ibid., 3.

37 Derrida, *Spurs*, 67.

38 Freeman, *The Feminine Sublime*, 23.

39 Derrida argues in *Spurs* that 'truth' as the foundation of Western philosophy was represented by the figure of 'woman', which foregrounded the ambiguity of this 'truth'.

40 N. Katherine Hayles, *How We Became Posthuman* (Chicago and London: University of Chicago Press, 1999), 8

41 De Bolla, *The Discourse of the Sublime*, 5–6.

42 Ibid., 9.

43 Ibid., 11.

44 Ibid., 12.

45 This perception of the sublime coincides with Lyotard's claim that the sublime cannot be described in its essence. Instead of putting forward the metaphysical claims regarding the nature of the sublime (i.e. 'This is sublime'), we can only experience the sublime, in all its unpresentability, as a momentary event, leading to a sudden realisation: 'The sublime is like this!'. I will return to Lyotard's discussion of the sublime, expounded, among others, in his 1982 essay, 'Answering the Question: What is Postmodernism?', in Jean-François Lyotard, *The Postmodern Condition: A Report on Knowledge*, trans. Geoff Bennington and Brian Massumi

(Manchester: Manchester University Press, 1986) and *The Inhuman* in a
further part of this chapter.

46 De Bolla, *The Discourse of the Sublime*, 34.
47 Hayles, *How We Became Posthuman*, 8–9.
48 Derrida, *Positions*, 59–60.
49 Freeman, *The Feminine Sublime*, 4.
50 De Bolla, *The Discourse of the Sublime*, 56.
51 Ibid., 65.
52 Ibid., 68.
53 Kant, *Critique of Judgement*, 121.
54 Christine Battersby, 'Stages on Kant's Way: Aesthetics, Morality, and the
    Gendered Sublime', in *Race, Class, Gender and Sexuality: the Big Question*,
    eds Naomi Zack et al. (Oxford: Blackwell, 1998), 227.
55 Luce Irigaray, *I Love To You: Sketch for a Possible Felicity within History*,
    trans. Alison Martin (New York and London: Routledge, 1996), 47.
56 Freeman, *The Feminine Sublime*, 11.
57 Ibid., 11. Freeman is not the only theorist to align the discourse of the
    sublime with femininity recognised as a positive signifier of difference.
    One of the first feminist critics to initiate the re-evaluation of the biased
    gendering of sublimity was Patricia Yaeger. Her articles, 'Toward a Female
    Sublime', in *Gender and Theory*, ed. Linda Kauffman (Oxford: Blackwell,
    1989), and 'Toward a Maternal Sublime', *Genre*, 25:Spring (1992), delin-
    eate the concept of the female/maternal sublime which operates on the
    horizontal rather than vertical, erect or phallic level, and can be encoun-
    tered in the realm of the everyday. However, Yaeger's project is prescribed
    by the notion of 'female generativity' and is merely intended to 'adjust'
    the male sublime to female experience, not to question the founding
    premises of this tradition.
58 Freeman, *The Feminine Sublime*, 7. I am more reluctant than Freeman to
    describe the aesthetics and rhetoric of the sublime as a product of
    'misogyny'. I believe the concept of phallocentrism, which points to the
    Western ideas of language and thought, allows us to overcome the vision
    of 'patriarchy' as constructed by men against 'womankind' and out of
    hatred towards women. The recognition of the 'phallicity' of language,
    and of Western philosophy at large, complicates the network of
    relationships of power: from this perspective, 'misogyny' can be read as
    self-hatred, and men can also be perceived as victims of 'patriarchy'. For
    an interesting account of 'phallocentrism', see Jacques Derrida and
    Christie V. McDonald, 'Choreographies: interview', *Diacritics*, 12 (1982).
59 Yaeger, 'Toward a Female Sublime', 191.
60 Hélène Cixous, Interview with Jonathan Rée for the Channel 4 'Talking
    Liberties' series.
61 Hélène Cixous, 'The Laugh of the Medusa', in *Feminisms*, eds Robyn
    Warhol and Diane Price Herndl (New Brunswick: Rutgers University Press,
    1993), 336.
62 Ibid., 335.
63 Irigaray, *This Sex Which Is Not One*, 213.
64 These metaphors have been inspired by the work of the Polish

philosopher Jolanta Brach-Czaina, whose book *Szczeliny istnienia* (Crevices of Being) is an attempt to trace 'the metaphysics of flesh' in everyday experience. There can be noticed a certain correspondence between her work and that of Cixous and Irigaray, as all three share a fascination, sometimes bordering on perversity, both with the body and with the poeticisation of the philosophical discourse. Chapter 3 explores Brach-Czaina's notion of indwelling the crevices of being, which function as both envelopes (offering protection) and caves (evoking uncertainty and fear).

65 Claire Joubert, 'The "Feminine": A Critical Angle for Poetics', *The European English Messenger*, 8:1 (1999), 27.

66 Ibid., 27–8.

67 Here distinction has to be made between two different meanings contained in the French expression *parler femme*, which was introduced by Luce Irigaray. 'Whereas speaking or writing *like* a woman suggests a linguistic mode available to anyone, if "he" or "she" chooses to use it, speaking or writing *as* a woman depends on deep-seated social, historical, and arguably biological factors that have created gendered subject positions that are far less open to choice', Martin Jay, *Downcast Eyes: the Denigration of Vision in Twentieth-Century Thought* (Berkeley, Los Angeles and London: University of California Press, 1993), 494.

68 Roland Barthes, *Image – Music – Text*, trans. Stephen Heath (London: Fontana Press, 1977), 157.

69 Ibid., 161.

70 'Longinus', *On Sublimity*, 2.

71 Lyotard, *The Inhuman*, 188.

72 Jean-François Lyotard, *The Differend*, trans. Georges Van Den Abbeele (Manchester: Manchester University Press, 1988), 13.

73 Ibid., 13.

74 Ibid., xi.

75 The following passage from *The Differend* foregrounds the relationship between discourse, thought and politics: 'A lot of searching must be done to find new rules for forming and linking phrases that are able to express the differend disclosed by the feeling, unless one wants this differend to be smothered right away in a litigation and for the alarm sounded by the feeling to have been useless. What is at stake in a literature, in a philosophy, in a politics perhaps, is to bear witness to differends by finding idioms for them', 13.

76 Lyotard, *The Inhuman*, 188.

77 Ibid., 84.

78 Lyotard, *The Differend*, xv.

79 Ibid., 115.

80 Emmanuel Levinas, 'Substitution', in *The Levinas Reader*, ed. Sean Hand (Blackwell: Oxford, 1989), 113–14, emphasis added.

81 Quoted in Onora O'Neill, 'Kantian Ethics', in *A Companion to Ethics*, ed. Peter Singer (Oxford: Blackwell, 1993), 178.

82 Crowther, *The Kantian Sublime*, 21.

83 Kant, *Critique of Judgement*, 105.

84 Lyotard, *Lessons*, 52.
85 Tina Chanter, *Ethics of Eros: Irigaray's Rewriting of the Philosophers* (New York and London: Routledge, 1995), 183.
86 Simon Critchley, *Ethics – Politics – Subjectivity* (London: Verso, 1999), 64.

Webwords: what's sublime about spiders?

In his tiny book on the genealogy of spiders' webs, Theodore H. Savory provides us with the following account of this miracle of nature:

> Two quite different mental pictures are normally associated with the words 'a spider's web'. One reader will see a ragged mass of dirt-laden silk in the corner of a room, and will experience a justifiable dislike of the animal which thus adds to her labours as a housewife; while another will see an orb-web hanging in glittering perfection in his garden and will remember his wonder that so beautiful an object should be the work of so small a creature.[1]

Isn't it typical? When it comes to reading, woman is presented as unable to recognise the beauty of the most inconspicuous, reducing its splendour instead to abjection and waste. Equipped with the requisite of both a housewife and a witch, she brushes away the dirt from every nook of the household, aiming to achieve a state of ideal cleanliness and thus pass her daily test of domestic performance. Her pottering around, so mundane and thoughtless, cannot measure up to the conscious appreciation shown by the male connoisseur of art, as the author of *The Spider's Web* implies.

> Man once made himself the point of everything. He organised, she operated. He ruled, she served. He made the great discoveries, she busied herself in the footnotes. He wrote the books, she copied them. She was his helpmate and assistant, working in support of him, according to his plans. She did the jobs he considered mundane, often the fiddling, detailed, repetitive operations with which he couldn't be bothered; the dirty, mindless, semiautomatic tasks to which he thought himself superior. He cut the cloth to fit a salary; she sewed the seams at a piece-rate wage.[2]

The housewife 'naturally' translates the reading experience into physical work, one more chore to be performed within the confines of her domestic space. Interestingly enough, the other kind of reader, for a better contrast a worldly type, is not situated very far from the domesticity of the housewife. Standing in his garden (again, she has 'her labours', he has 'his garden'…), he is prevented from dashing to the affairs of the outer world by the miracle of glittering perfection happening before his eyes. This encounter with the unexpected transports him to the realm of the inverted-divine, i.e. celestial perfection that is taking place here and now, impermanent and feeble, but none the less powerful. But the appreciation of the minimal perspective is nothing new for the housewife, who belongs in the lowlands and does not aspire towards celestial heights. Housewifery can thus signify a wise negotiation of one's ways on earth; it can be read as an attitude of respect towards the little and low. In this light, the act of brushing away 'glittering perfection' presents itself as an image conjured up by the male biologist, who once allowed himself to look down and be carried away by the power of the low horizon, without realising that women had been there before.

Even though it rests upon the traditional binaries such as inside/ outside, nature/culture, and passivity/activity, *The Spider's Web* disrupts this polarisation. It introduces the space of inbetweenness – the garden – where the distinction between work and leisure collapses before the 'natural art product' of the spider's labour. Having left the housewife inside, Theodore H. Savory invites us to step out into the realm where masculinity overcomes its elevation and its phallic fantasy when facing the lowly. The moment the stupefied man reconsiders the earthly and horizontal perspective, the active–passive distinction is blurred. Savory's book on the genealogy of spiders' webs is particularly interesting because of its unfaithfulness to the rigid demands of the 'scientific discourse'. At numerous points when science fails to provide an appropriate image, recourse is taken to metaphor and poeticity takes over. This, in turn, transports the text beyond the framework of the particular: suddenly we seem deprived of the limitations and tightness of the world of the Arachnida and are swept into a conceptual abyss, from the most inconspicuous to the most high.

> The spinning of an orb-web is a spectacle to be watched and watched and watched. Unlike the spinning of many other kinds of web, which grow gradually from a few threads to a thick sheet by a slow accumulation of silk during many days, it is carried through in one continuous operation, occupying from 25 to 50 minutes. From the first it evokes surprise, wonder, bewilderment and admiration, and indeed after the fiftieth watching, when the surprises are fewer because the observer can guess correctly what the spider is going to do next, the wonder and the admiration are scarcely diminished.[3]

The two 'Webwords' chapters I am spinning around the more formal account of the sublime presented in the three main chapters of this book are intended as an illustration – or perhaps even a 'performance' – of the feminine sublime, which is taking place in certain practices produced by women artists. What brings me to the image of the web is the very unpredictability Savory identifies in the act of spinning an orb-web, which disrupts the accumulation of wisdom and undermines the relationship between distance and knowledge. The conflicting feelings evoked by sublime phenomena, including 'surprise, wonder, bewilderment and admiration', immobilise the observer. His or her numerous tactile encounters with the source of both fear and wonder are connected by a thread into a kind of timeless flow, in which linear time gives way to the frozenness of an instant: 'a spectacle to be watched and watched and watched'. But I do not want to claim that women's art is sublime. When talking about Barnett Baruch Newman's paintings, Lyotard indicates the impossibility of looking for the sublime in the actual art object: one should not treat art as the site of the sublime or its incarnation. Rather than declare: 'This is sublime', we must concentrate on the most minute occurrence happening at the exact moment: 'The sublime is like this!'.[4] This does not mean that the sublime occurs independently and outside us, even though it is entirely our task and our responsibility to notice it and engage with it. Unsurprisingly, textual engagement calls for the suspension of conceptual mastery and critical distance. As Roland Barthes contends,

> If I agree to judge a text according to pleasure, I cannot go on to say: this one is good, that bad. No awards, no 'critique', for this always implies a tactical aim, a social usage, and frequently an extenuating image-reservoir. I cannot apportion, imagine that the text is perfectible, ready to enter into a play of normative predicates: it is too much this, not enough that; the text (the same is true of the singing voice) can wring from me only this judgement, in no way adjectival: that's it! And further still: that's it for me![5]

The text as a site of pleasure functions as both a well of good wishes and a bottomless pit, waiting to suck in the lone wanderer and alluring her with the promise of eternal satisfaction. Or, if the metaphor (to which I am consciously taking recourse here, reminding the reader that I do not intend to merely aestheticise the terrible and escape from the physical) of depth sounds problematic, let us turn again to the image of tissue or the spider's web, creatively explored by Nancy K. Miller and other feminist critics. In the theory of the text as arachnology,

> the textual is the textile; and … the text maker, previously known as the author, to the extent that he is still figurable, paradoxically owes his

representation to an undoing: a destabilisation of the terms of identity itself brought about by a breakdown in the boundaries between inside and outside.[6]

The spatiality of the text into which the reader is incorporated not only as an interpreter but first of all as its 'spinner', undergoes a process of restructuring. Reading must contain an element of failure which is produced by the textual network's insoluble knots and tangled threads. Miller emphasises the need for wonder when encountering texts, which is also, significantly, the first condition of the sublime event.[7] She sees textual wanderings – which she describes as 'overreading' – as driven by a desire to open up yet unvisited routes. A tactile journey through the materiality of the text will allow us to bridge the linguistic with the corporeal, and to leave our signature [i.e. 'to put one's finger'] on the body of the text we are visiting:

> The goal of overreading, of reading for the signature, is to put one's finger – figuratively – on the place of production that marks the spinner's attachment to the web. ... This move ... is meant not only to retrieve those texts from the indifference of the aesthetic universal, but to identify the act of this reading as the enabling subjectivity of another poetics, a poetics attached to gendered bodies that may have lived in history.[8]

In my textual encounters with the feminine sublime I want to explore the discourses in which 'woman' is a permanently contested site of meaning. This will enable me to discuss the gendered poetics Miller envisages, but also to examine the instability of gender, which is simultaneously undermined in every act of its affirmation. The novels of the British writer Lisa St Aubin de Terán, the multimedia performances of the American artist Laurie Anderson and the bodily experiments of the French performance artist Orlan are three sets of texts I have chosen for my wanderings. They can all be described as 'gender interventions', revealing 'femininity' to be a mask, or what Derrida calls after Nietzsche 'the untruth of truth', but also projecting new forms of identity and identification. My discussion of the gendered poetics of these texts will draw, to some extent, on the work of Judith Butler. The concept of gender as performative, developed by Butler alongside Austin's theory of performativity in language and Derrida's concept of 'iterability',[9] constitutes a radical critique of rigid gender binaries. Butler has complicated the unproblematic relationship between sex and gender which used to be directly mapped on to the nature–culture matrix. In her theory of gender as performative, performativity must be understood not as a singular or deliberate 'act', but, rather, as the reiterative and citational practice by which discourse produces the effects that it names. … [T]he regulatory norms of 'sex' work in a performative fashion to constitute the materiality of bodies and, more specifically, to materialise the body's sex, to materialise sexual difference in the service of the consolidation of the heterosexual imperative.[10]

One thing Lisa St Aubin de Terán, Orlan and Laurie Anderson have in common is that they all contest the assumed 'representability' of gender, and of the world in general. Putting on the cultural masks of passion, desire, bewilderment and horror, they mimic the 'authenticity' of the sublime discourse of affection and thus expose its constructed and marked character.

For Burke and Kant, the source of the sublime is located in gothic landscapes, such as high cascades of rocks, volcanoes, heavy clouds, or thunderbolts and lightning. All these natural phenomena, perceived from a safe distance (i.e. a position from which one is not threatened by their potential destructive character), 'make our power of resistance of trifling moment in comparison with their might'.[11] The performances of St Aubin de Terán, Anderson and Orlan challenge the previously maintained distance between the subject and object of the sublime encounter. This is the result of these artists' creative engagement with the discourse on and of femininity, and the active/passive dichotomy underlying it. As Mary Ann Doane argues, in the traditional 'ocularcentric' theory of spectatorship, 'woman' is never defined as a perceiving subject. Indeed, she is presented as unable to reflect on her own subjectivity. Defined as a hieroglyphic in Freud's lecture on 'Femininity', she was both an undecipherable enigma and the most universally understandable of signs, collapsing the distance between the signified and the signifier. 'Too close to herself, entangled in her own enigma, [woman] could not step back, could not achieve the necessary distance of a second look.'[12] As a consequence of this 'freezing' of spectatorship, claims Doane, 'woman can never ask her own ontological question'.[13] If sublimity is premised on the distance between the grand object and its spectator, the gazing eye is clearly gendered as male. For a woman to reclaim the gaze in the perception of sublime greatness, she must challenge the boundary between the object of perception and the triumphant, even though threatened, subject. By refusing to identify with the modernist subject of reason constituted in the traditional discourse of the sublime, the three women artists I focus on here foreground the incoherence of identity which underwrites the aesthetics of the sublime.

Here it should become clear that a radical refusal to identify suggests that on some level an identification has already taken place, and identification has been made and disavowed, whose symptomatic appearance is the insistence, the overdetermination of the identification that is, as it were, worn on the body that shows. This raises the political question of the cost of articulating a coherent identity position by producing, excluding, and repudiating a domain of abjected spectres that threaten the arbitrarily closed domain of subject positions. Perhaps only by risking the incoherence of identity is connection possible, a political point that correlates with Leo Bersani's insight that only the decentred subject is available to desire.[14]

In Lisa St Aubin de Terán's *Black Idol* the world is perceived from the moment of passage from life to death, interspersed with shorter or longer trips into the past. *Black Idol* is an attempt to solve the mystery of the death of Harry Crosby, playboy and party-goer, and his young mistress, who were found dead in an apartment of the Hôtel des Artistes in New York in December 1929. The novel starts with a chronology of Harry's life, intermingled with Josephine's biography. Brief entries presented in an encyclopaedic style turn into a bleak monologue which comes, as we learn later, from the lips of the dead Josephine.

How does it feel, Harry? How does it feel to be standing fully dressed now, except for your shoes, your fine polished lizardskin shoes, fitting a cigarette in your amber holder, and striking a match, and listening? How does it feel to be listening to your lonely girl lying back there on a bed a little untidily with her eyes glazed over? Her hands loose at her sides, her lips parted, but not really saying very much, in fact anything at all, or likely to, except for this endless monologue you can't help hearing inside your own head.[15]

Traditional epistemology is defied in the disappearance of the boundary line between life and death. The convention of speaking 'from beyond the grave' is nothing new, but here it is the dead who are given a voice, while the living are silenced and merely reduced to the 'post-mortem' narrative of the former. Josephine's words fill in the brief space between her suicide and Harry's expected death. The monologue is a sinister parody of the death-bed scene, in which the dying character has the final say. Here, it is Harry who is awaiting death, but he has not been granted a voice of his own. In the meantime, Josephine penetrates into his consciousness, pointing out that all his actions, romances, desires and aspirations have been a sublimation of his powerful death wish, and encouraging him to complete their joint 'death project'.

It was on that very day, Harry, that you had your first vision of Death. You felt a chill, crossing the marble hall. You were drawn, hands in your pockets, idle and annoyed, not as you might have expected or planned out through the french windows and into the garden, where the sun on the flowers caught your eye – no. You were drawn into the little sewing room in the other direction, where the light was colder, and a tall figure sat at a table, working with a needle and thread at a piece of old brocade.

You felt a coldness, you told me, and a strange power drawing you in. Death was tall and old. Sewing in her little room, she was dressed in rustling black. A mutch on her head. The face turned away. The fingers out of sight in a pair of black lace gloves. Working. Working along the grey surface of the stiff material.[16]

Death, presented through the imagery of domestic labour, takes on the form of a knitting woman, spinning the threads of destiny. For Harry, Eros is inextricably connected with Thanatos, and the acts of consummation always resemble the scenes of murder and self-annihilation.

For the Greeks, the Fates, the Moirai, were three spinsters – Klotho, Lachesis, and Atropos – who produced, allotted, and broke the delicate contingency of the thread of life. In the folktales of Europe, spindles become magic wands, fates become fairies, and women are abandoned or rescued from impossible spinning and weaving tasks by supernatural entities, godmothers and crones who transform piles of flax into fine linen by means more magical than weaving itself.[17]

Josephine the spinner calls their road to death a 'journey', which signifies progress, development, or passage from the known to the unknown. Harry, a great manipulator, organises his own world, accelerating the time and then delaying it according to his whim. ('Why did you say it was not yet time when I asked you, as I had to ask you, Harry?')[18] The game, however, may last only as long as Josephine does not interfere; as soon as she does, Harry's play with time will be over. But Josephine is not only a master of narrative time but also a mistress (involved in a narcissistic romance with mortality) of life and death. From her self-acclaimed position of the sole speaker she reveals to Harry that she is carrying their 'unborn baby'. Linearity is abandoned here for the sake of a spiral track, where death and life have no sharp boundaries but rather overlap and transmute into each other.

Josephine's scandalous body, 'pregnant death, a death that gives birth',[19] can be read as a version of the Bakhtinian grotesque, which constitutes an opening within the strictly legislated social order. By creating an illusion of the possibility of transgression and excess, this opening in fact assures the stability of the social order which clearly distinguishes between life and death and which constructs a number of taboos protecting against the intrusion of mortality into the everyday. And yet, as Mary Russo notices, such a one-sided semiotic reading of the feminine body as the model of the body politic ignores the social relations of gender, which in Bakhtin's theory remain repressed and undeveloped. Instead, Russo suggests the female grotesque could be analysed through the figure of mimesis, or masquerade. This image foregrounds the parodic aspect of adopting the masculine negative fantasy in order to expose the underlying precariousness of the identity of the male ego, which is threatened by the uncanniness of the feminine and by the enigmas of birth and death.

> This *unheimlich* [uncanny] place, however, is the entrance to the former *Heim* of all human beings, to the place where everyone dwelt once upon a time and in the beginning. There is a humorous saying that 'Love is home-sickness'; and whenever a man dreams of a place or a country and says to himself, while he is still dreaming, 'this place is familiar to me, I have been there before', we may interpret the place as being his mother's genitals or her body. In this case, too, then, the *unheimlich* is what was once *heimisch*, familiar; the prefix '*un*' ['un-'] is the token of repression.[20]

If, according to Freud, love is homesickness, the rendition of the female as both life-giving and dead represses the anxiety that results from the separation from the primary object of desire. A longing for the familiarity of the intrauterine existence is thus replaced by the fear of being suffocated in the lethal folds of woman's flesh. In this way, anxiety is projected onto 'the absolutely other' of the dead female body, which serves as a battleground for the unresolved tension in the male hetero-sexual subject between eroticism and death.

All these anxieties have found reflection in the work of the surrealists, who used to objectify and domesticate the uneasy otherness of the female body. The iconisation of the uncanny, which stands for the fear of castra-tion, but also seduces with the promise of bliss, was supposed to save the male subject from the negative consequences of the encounter with otherness, without depriving him of the desired pleasure. Purely volitional consummation was shifted to the level of the gaze and perpetuated in numerous representations of femininity, fragmentation and death. As Hal Foster indicates,

> [T]his aesthetic has to do less with the beautiful than with the sublime. For convulsive beauty not only stresses the formless and evokes the unrepresentable, as with the sublime, but it also mixes delight and dread, attraction and repulsion: it, too, involves 'a momentary check to the vital forces', 'a negative pleasure'.[21]

Black Idol takes issue with this contorted image of femininity by reversing the schema. The stereotypical fantasies of the male self are brought to extremes in Harry, for whom death bears the features of a mother, a prostitute and a murderer. The fixating gaze, nevertheless, is shifted from the male to the female, as it is 'bewitching Josephine' who directs the whole performance. Her immutable 'evil eye' – which, according to Hal Foster, stands for a castrative threat in our culture – clashes with the provocative fluidity of her narrative. While Harry's eyes have been fixed on the object of his desire, she actually becomes what masculine desire wants to see in her: death incarnate, bordering on perversion and monstrosity, the epitome of the sublime. The negative pleasure of this encounter immobilises not only the bodies of these two characters but also the body of the text, which is reduced to the intermittent flow of the monologue: 'Dreams, then. Dreams. Harry tossed on his bed. Harry with chorus-girl. Harry without. Harry praying. A mystic now, it seems. Betwixt and between. And buying a dog that nobody wants. Harry in pieces. Dreams'.[22] St Aubin de Terán seems to be mimicking masculine anxieties and thus displaying the intrinsic instability of the male ego as produced in traditional psychosexual economy. Josephine is both a version of the surrealists' mannequins and *poupées*, constructed as the site of the uncanny and the representation of the threat of castration and death, and a 'bad copy' of the negative beauty described by Kant and explored by André Breton, Hans Bellmer and other male artists working on the threshold of the modern age.

> [Bellmer's] dolls not only trace a shifting of desire; they also represent a shattering – of the female object, to be sure, but also of the male subject. ... In this regard the *poupées* may go beyond (or is it inside?) sadistic mastery to the point where the masculine subject confronts his greatest fear: his own fragmentation, disintegration and dissolution.[23]

St Aubin de Terán teases the (male?) reader with the fetish of Josephine's silk stockings and lace pretties, equipping her version of Bellmer's doll with a disturbing potential, and thus questioning the passivity of death and the possible resolution of conflict and anxiety. By reversing the 'punishment' exerted by modernist artists on the figure of woman, or, 'more precisely, for her projected representation of this state, of its threat to the patriarchal subject',[24] *Black Idol* mimics the psychoanalytic discourse and the ideas of femininity it produces. Rather than attempt a total repudiation of the objectifying gaze of the threatened male, the novel models Josephine precisely on the premises of the logic of masculine desire; and yet at the same time it undermines this discourse by revealing the very performativity of such a construction.

> To play with mimesis is thus, for a woman, to try to recover the place of her exploitation by discourse, without allowing herself simply to be reduced to it. It means to resubmit herself – inasmuch as she is on the side of 'perceptible', of 'matter' – to 'ideas', in particular to ideas about herself, that are elaborated in/by masculine logic, but so as to make 'visible', by an effect of playful repetition, what was supposed to remain invisible: the cover-up of a possible operation of the feminine in language. It also means to 'unveil' the fact that, if women are such good mimics, it is because they are not simply reabsorbed into this function.[25]

To use Butler's concept of gender as 'citation', we could say that Josephine cites the phallic phantasy of feminine submission by staging the death of the feminine body. The setting for this act, Hôtel des Artistes, highlights the theatrical character of the psychic conflict. Displaced 'twice over' – by the psychoanalytic discourse which constructs femininity as a mask of nonidentity, and by the repetition of this masquerade – Josephine reveals the fragility of sexual identity and the trauma of sexual difference. The modernist artist (here represented in the figure of playboy and party-goer Harry) represses this trauma, only to witness the return of the repressed in the figure of the uncanny. Hal Foster traces the occurrence of this process of repression in many surrealist works, where numerous images acquire the status of fetish, fixating the subject's sexual development on the substitute object which is to save the artist from being exposed to an excessive, and thus lethal, sexuality.

> The fetish in fact results from a real compromise and from a split between denial and affirmation of castration: the fetishist, like the child, at once maintains and abandons the belief that the woman (the mother) has a phallus.[26]

This reconciliation of denial and affirmation is hardly a peaceful compromise, which accounts for the uncertainty the self experiences in its relation to the world. If the mother herself is a site of an irreconcilable contradiction, the world's logical order is ultimately disturbed. Even life and death do not need to be mutually exclusive. The questions Josephine addresses to Harry emphasise the uncanniness of his death and the disturbing familiarity of hers:

> How does it feel to be listening to your lonely girl lying back there on a bed a little untidily with her eyes glazed over? Her hands loose at her sides, her lips parted, but not really saying very much, in fact anything at all, or likely to, except for this endless monologue you can't help hearing inside your own head.[27]

Addressing the other who is to confirm the self's subjectivity, the deceased Josephine disturbs the process of identity-formation: death is precisely the point at which the symbolic network of mirrors producing and reflecting identity is broken. If, as Carole Anne Tyler concludes, 'The subject is the effect of impersonation or mimicry, the assumption of an alienating signifier ('I' or 'you'), and the imitation/repetition of the practices of the apparatus in which it is produced',[28] and if femininity is always already staged as the other of the masculine norm and then represented though the figures of abjection, passivity and death, then positioning a dead woman in the role of the sole speaker and director of this double suicide act exposes the ultimate 'untruth' of feminine identity.

> Never mind, Harry, just be near me and I'll be all right. And be my mirror. After all, it's an age of mirrors, isn't it? You always said we lived in an age of mirrors. Well, they never told me that at Bryn Mawr. They never told me mirrors would break in a jagger of shattering pieces over its granite walls. They never told me in eighteen months I'd be lying on a hard bed in a studio duplex three blocks from the Park, with my clinging skirt on and my shoes off. Lying with my grandmother's best long string of pearls around my neck, and a pair of silk stockings laddered up to the garters from straining my legs around the buttocks of a man wearing a double-breasted jacket from Borks Brothers, and no trousers, and my mouth fixed in a sad Mona Lisa smile, and my hair mussed. No, they never told me that either.[29]

This is not to assert that a masculine identity produced though the recognition of sexual difference is any more stable. It is precisely the disavowal of this instability that has led to the depiction of 'woman' as an 'enigma', her 'mouth fixed in a sad Mona Lisa smile'. Restaging this incoherence of the male ego, Josephine adopts the role of the phallic mother, tender and affectionate, but also destructive and deadly.

> Come over here and feel under my skirt for the twisting blackness of my stocking, and, yes, Harry, you could still do this. You could still lay your

poor head in my lap, and lick. Lick me, Harry. Lick away the tension, the hatred, the fear and the need.[30]

Sarah Kofman argues that in Freud's theory '[w]oman's genital organs arouse an inseparable blend of horror and pleasure; they at once awaken and appease castration anxiety'.[31] Playing with the uncanny feeling evoked by the entrance to what once was man's home, Josephine the spinner exacerbates Harry's anxiety.

> Weaving is an automatic imitation of some bodily function already beyond the weaver's control. She is bound to weave a costume for the masquerade: she is an actress, a mimic, an impersonator, with no authenticity underneath it. She has nothing to reveal, no soul to bare, not even a sex or a self to please. He pulls aside the veils, the webs of lies, the shrouds of mystery, and the layers of deception and duplicity, and finds no comfort, no one there. Only the 'horror of nothing to be seen'.[32]

The deadly threadwork is not finished yet. Josephine the phallic mother does not offer a solution to the riddle posed at the beginning of the novel. As there does not seem to be another world or another story hidden behind the curtain of lace and silk, the veil shrouding its mystery has to stay in place.

> To solve a riddle, is always to bring to light something that has been concealed because of a sexual taboo, it is always to discover (*aufdecken*), to unmask (*entlarven*), to undo the threads that cover over and separate desire from its direct expression. It is to 'unravel', *abspinnen*, the inverse of the task performed by the spider, symbol of the phallic mother, who covers all 'holes' with her phallic cloth.[33]

Black Idol is not disentangled into separate threads but merely rearranges the texture of and displaces some knots in its narration. The tapestry of Josephine and Harry's story, woven out of the monologue spun by Josephine, recoils back on itself, enveloping its own indeterminacy in an act of expansion which excludes progress. The novel invites interpretation, but, having drawn the reader into the knots and loops of its narrative, it tightens its grip.

> [T]there is no crime worse than silence, for it covers women's sex with its 'thick veil', renders it inaccessible, indomitable, implacable: terrifying (*ef-frayante*), in Blanchot's sense. The enigmatic woman neither speaks nor 'betrays herself' through any of her pores. It matters little to her if psychoanalysis withholds its gentleness. She has no need of it, she is sufficient unto herself.[34]

The riddle of Harry and Josephine's death which organises the narrative of *Black Idol* can be read as a parodic displacement of the riddle of 'woman' posed in Freud's famous lecture on 'Femininity'. The novel mocks the desire to know and master sexual difference. Exploring the theatrical imagery Freud uses in his essay, Mary Ann Doane points out that 'the riddle of femininity is initiated from the beginning in Freud's text as a question of masquerade'.[35] Doane writes: 'Masquerade … involves a realignment of femininity, the recovery, or more accurately, simulation, of the missing gap or distance. To masquerade is to manufacture a lack in the form of a certain distance between oneself and one's image'.[36] It is precisely this staging of distance between the image of 'absolute alterity' and the intrinsic lack inherent in the construction of the self that brings me back once again to the problematic of the sublime.

> [T]he feeling of the sublime is a pleasure that only arises indirectly, being brought about by the feeling of a momentary check to the vital forces followed at once by a discharge all the more powerful, and so it is an emotion that seems to be no sport, but dead earnest in the affairs of the imagination.[37]

Now it becomes clearer why both Burke and Kant position distance as the condition of sublimity and the guarantee of the self's intactness. If the sublime is premised on distance, then femininity-as-masquerade reveals that this distance is just a cover-up of the absence, or lack, at work in the construction of selfhood. The self, exposed to the threat of the dangerous object, is able to reassert its own boundaries only by maintaining an appropriate distance between itself and that which it finds threatening. As Christine Battersby explains,

> The appreciation of the sublime is the negation of fear: it requires both an appreciation of the terribleness of the object surveyed and a (simultaneous) transcendence of terror. … For Kant such pleasures are closed off to all except the 'moral man' who has been educated into confidence in the power of his own ego over nature. … According to Kant, this will exclude those who have been taken over by the spirit of trade (*Handelsgeist*), by base self-interest (*Eigennutz*), softness (*Weich-lichkeit*), and cowardice (*Feigheit*). … A 'tender [*weich*] though weak [*schwach*] soul' (that is, an ideal woman) could never have the right attitude of mind; but the non-ideal woman would also be unlikely to qualify.[38]

Springing from the recognition of the irrational fear of sexual difference in the production of the male ego, the feminine sublime collapses the necessary distance between the observer and the grand object. The concept of masquerade, which Luce Irigaray translates into mimicry,[39] allows her to rethink 'feminine identity' from within the masculine discourse of psychoanalysis. While acknowledging the hegemony of psychic processes, Irigaray negotiates a non-utopian space of resistance in which 'woman's' identity can be perceived beyond enigma and lack. By mimicking the master discourse of psychoanalysis, Irigaray calls for an inscription of femininity to be inserted into the masculine discursive construct. Acknowledging the performative production of femininity, she radicalises sexual difference by pointing out that woman's sexuality is always plural and thus 'different from itself'.[40]

> For Luce Irigaray, female anatomy is readable as a constant relation of the self to itself, as an autoeroticism based on the embrace of the two lips which allow the woman to touch herself without mediation. Furthermore, the very notion of property, and hence possession of something which can be constituted as other, is antithetical to the woman: 'Nearness however, is not foreign to woman, a nearness so close that any identification of one or the other, and therefore any form of property, is impossible. Woman enjoys a closeness with the other that is so near she cannot possess it any more than she can possess herself.'[41]

The feminine sublime could thus be perceived as a mimicry of the traditional aesthetics of the sublime which is founded upon 'presuppositions about an innate sexual difference'.[42] By collapsing the distance between the observer and the grand object, however, and thus violating Kant's commandment that 'we must avoid coming too near just as much as remaining too far away',[43] the production of sublimity itself is threatened. Even though sexual difference is an underlying principle of the discourse of the sublime, this difference must be kept at bay. One way of controlling it is by maintaining a radical separation between beauty as associated with feminine gentility and sublimity which represents masculine strength. The interruption of the advocated distance threatens to reveal the inherent gender ambiguity at work in the production of the discourse of the sublime. This is why, as Derrida argues in *Spurs*, distance is the underlying condition of passing off femininity as truth: 'A distance from distance must be maintained. Not only for protection (the most obvious advantage) against the spell of her fascination, but also as a way of succumbing to it, that distance (which is lacking) is necessary'.[44] Investigating the rigid distinction between masculinity and femininity in Burke's *Enquiry*, Barbara Claire Freeman concludes that the feminine body figures the breakdown of the distinction between the sublime and the beautiful. ... Rather than securing boundaries and limits, its very 'smoothness', 'softness', and 'variety' instil 'unsteadiness': this body does not provide a site where distinctions can be fixed but rather represents the point at which they come apart, and the observer, seeking a resting place, 'slides giddily'.[45]

When engaging with the artistic interventions of St Aubin de Terán, Orlan and Laurie Anderson (see the following 'Webwords' chapter), I am drawn to the realm of masquerade in their work. Closing off the gap between the *enigma* of femininity and the *performance* of femininity, they foreground not only the intrinsic instability of gender but also the possibility of constructing new forms of identification. As Doane asserts, 'Female specificity is ... theorised in terms of spatial proximity. In opposition to this "closeness" to the body, a spatial distance in the male's relation to his body rapidly becomes a temporal distance in the service of knowledge'.[46] By replaying the masculine (patriarchal, Freudian) concept of femininity and yet repositioning it a little, these artists reconfigure the available spectrum of women's identities and identifications, shifting it beyond the essentialism of femininity as truth but also beyond the pessimism and passivity of Joan Riviere's masquerade.[47] This search for a new feminine/feminist aesthetics is a complex task, as Joan Key observes in 'The Antidote to the Sublime, or, No Time for Commas':

> The problem is to gain credibility for an aesthetic position that can stand recognisably apart from the validations of the symbolic. In this space there has been a good deal of literature attempting to define an 'other' than the symbolic, which has focused on a dyadic cultural relation based in a positive reading of 'the physical jouissance of the female body'. This does not adapt the simple opposition of 'poor sight' taking up 'no-place' that is left after the completion of 'rich sight', but does require a frank evaluation of everything that is being seen.[48]

I believe that my concept of the feminine sublime might be one such 'antidote' as sought by Key. Understood not as a mere negation of the traditional theory of the sublime, the feminine sublime is both its extension and overcoming, exploring the repressed excessive potential and the imposed distance between the self and the object of its desire. But 'Webwords', which I see as an illustration of this search for the feminine sublime, has a labyrinthine structure. Ariadne's thread does not serve as a pathfinder in my wanderings as it can always be incorporated into the body of this labyrinth. Ariadne, the lady of the maze, can become Arachne, the spider woman, conflated by J. Hillis Miller into Ariachne: the sign of hope and impossibility, closure and expansion. And yet Nancy K. Miller is unwilling to accept the apparent and imposed similarity between the two figures. Her doubts, formulated as a list of questions, are aimed at those readings which grant primacy to similarity for the sake of diminishing irreducible difference:

> [I]f viewed from a position which favours the indeterminacy of meaning and the insecurity of all identity, tearer and torn trade places in a linguistic play of difference, does it follow that no significant difference inhabits the two stories? ... If Arachne and Ariadne change places in the threads of the loom, is nothing lost in this translation?[49]

This is the reservation I take into account in my 'Webwords'. I am aware of the danger inherent in any attempt to discuss women's cultural productions and speculate on the constitutive elements of the feminine sublime. But the recognition of the indeterminacy of the theoretical concept I am working with does not stop me from tracing its 'enactments' or 'performances'. The multiple threads of the discourse of the sublime I weave into my textual wanderings lead us both to Ariadne (who might show us the way) and Arachne. It is this positioning between life, labour, passion and death – mutually non-exclusive and inseparable in either of the myths – that creates a space for the sublime event. The phallicity of the spider woman, recognised as a negative fantasy of the male psychoanalyst, can be read as silencing sexual difference, which is reduced to the countable knots of Arachne's web or, to use another metaphor, to the linearity of Ariadne's thread. By working with the two stories I accept the impossibility of disclosing what has become known as the enigma of sexual difference. But I refuse to leave it only as an enigma. Weaving my 'Webwords', I follow Derrida's reminder: 'Do not forget that to weave (*tramer, trameare*) is first to make holes, to traverse, to work one-side-and-the-other of the warp'.[50]

Notes

1 Theodore S. Savory, *The Spider's Web* (London and New York: Frederick Warne & C. Ltd., 1952), 48.
2 Sadie Plant, *Zeros + Ones: Digital Women + the New Technoculture* (London: Fourth Estate, 1997), 35–6. The influence of Sadie Plant's book on my writing was significant and is reflected in my frequent 'interweavings' of *Zeros + Ones* into my text. Her book is an interesting example of a 'spider-work', one which is spun from multiple threads whose origins cannot always be traced. But I also recognise many problems in Plant's argument. *Zeros + Ones* seems to have been written from the position of a certain impasse, or impossibility, of

presenting a global overview of technology. However, this is also where her argument is most compelling for me, when numerous generalisations, reappropriations and contradictions lead to an infinite entanglement of her discursive threads, which threaten to smother both the spinner and her text.

3 Savory, *The Spider's Web*, 69.

4 See Jean-François Lyotard, *The Inhuman*, trans. Geoffrey Bennington and Rachel Bowlby (Cambridge: Polity Press, 1991), 93.

5 Roland Barthes, *The Pleasure of the Text*, trans. Richard Miller (New York: Hill & Wang, 1975), 13.

6 Nancy K. Miller, 'Arachnologies: The Woman, The Text, and the Critic', in *The Poetics of Gender*, ed. Nancy K. Miller (New York: Columbia University Press, 1986), 271.

7 Chapter 2 discusses the correspondence between wonder/bewilderment and the sublime feeling which can be traced in Plato, Burke and Kant.

8 Miller, 'Arachnologies', 288.

9 Derrida's concept of iterability conveys the sense of repetition which is an unavoidable and necessary condition of linguistic communication. When uttered or written down, words always appear in new contexts and new situations, thus establishing both a continuity and a break with the previous instances in which they were uttered. (For a discussion of the concept of iterability in Derrida see Geoffrey Bennington and Jacques Derrida, *Jacques Derrida*, trans. Geoffrey Bennington (Chicago and London: University of Chicago Press, 1993), 56–70.) Butler applies the logic of iterability to her argument about gender construction: gender does not correspond to some pre-existing essence of identity but is rather produced through a sequence of acts which are, at the same time, old (i.e. recognisable) and new (i.e. contributing to the development of the 'reality' of gender).

10 Judith Butler, *Bodies That Matter: On the Discursive Limits of 'Sex'* (New York and London: Routledge, 1993), 2.

11 Immanuel Kant, *The Critique of Judgement*, trans. James Meredith (Oxford: Clarendon Press, 1952), 110.

12 Mary Ann Doane, 'Film and the Masquerade: Theorising the Female Spectator', in *Writing on the Body*, eds Katie Conboy, Nadia Medina and Sarah Stanbury (New York: Columbia University Press, 1997), 178.

13 Ibid., 192.

14 Judith Butler, *The Psychic Life of Power* (Stanford, California: Stanford University Press, 1997), 149.

15 Lisa St Aubin de Terán, *Black Idol* (London: Pavanne, 1988), 15.

16 Ibid., 28–9.

17 Plant, *Zeros + Ones*, 68.

18 St Aubin de Terán, *Black Idol*, 13.

19 Mikhail Bakhtin, quoted in Mary Russo, 'Female Grotesques: Carnival and Theory', in *Writing on the Body*, 325.

20 Sigmund Freud, 'The Uncanny', in *The Standard Edition of the Complete Psychological Works of Sigmund Freud* (London: The Hogarth Press and the Institute of Psychoanalysis, 1956/197), Vol. 17, 245.

21 Hal Foster, *Compulsive Beauty* (Cambridge, Massachusetts: The MIT Press, 1993), 28.

22 St Aubin de Terán, *Black Idol*, 78.

23 Foster, *Compulsive Beauty*, 107–9.

24 Ibid., 13.

25 Luce Irigaray, *This Sex Which Is Not One*, trans. Catherine Porter (Ithaca, New York: Cornell University Press, 1985), 76.

26 Sarah Kofman, *The Enigma of Woman*, trans. Catherine Porter (Ithaca and London: Cornell University Press, 1985), 86.

27 St Aubin de Terán, *Black Idol*, 15.

28 Carole-Anne Tyler, 'Passing: Narcissism, Identity and Difference', in *Feminism Meets Queer Theory*, eds Elizabeth Weed and Naomi Schor (Indiana: Indiana University Press, 1997), 236.

29 St Aubin de Terán, *Black Idol*, 15.

30 Ibid., 16.

31 Kofman, *The Enigma of Woman*, 85.

32 Plant, *Zeros + Ones*, 24–5. Burke associates the 'horror of nothing to be seen' with the danger inherent in the sublime.

33 Kofman, *The Enigma of Woman*, 95.

34 Ibid., 48.

35 Doane, 'Film and the Masquerade', 177.

36 Ibid., 185.

37 Kant, *Critique of Judgement*, 91.

38 Christine Battersby, 'Stages on Kant's Way: Aesthetics, Morality, and the Gendered Sublime', in *Race, Class, Gender and Sexuality: the Big Question*, eds Naomi Zack et al. (Oxford: Blackwell, 1998), 233.

39 In this way Irigaray moves beyond the fatalism of Joan Riviere's concept of masquerade, which is only seen as an act of resignation and withdrawal. See Joan Riviere, 'Womanliness as a Masquerade', in *Psychoanalysis and Female Sexuality*, ed. Hendrick M. Ruitenbeek (New Haven: College and University Press, 1966).

40 This point seems to escape Judith Butler, who has become increasingly critical of Irigaray's work. Refusing to explore the consequences of this pluralisation of sexuality, Butler accuses Irigaray of essentialising sexual difference and reducing it to the unhelpful binary.

41 Doane, 'Film and the Masquerade', 176.

42 Barbara Claire Freeman, *The Feminine Sublime: Gender and Excess in Women's Fiction* (Berkeley, Los Angeles and London: University of California Press, 1995), 48.

43 Kant, *Critique of Judgement*, 99.

44 Jacques Derrida, *Spurs: Nietzsche's Styles*, trans. Barbara Harlow (Chicago and London: University of Chicago Press, 1979), 43.

45 Freeman, *The Feminine Sublime*, 49–50.

46 Doane, 'Film and the Masquerade', 184.

47 It is worth noticing that parody does not have to be deliberate. The possibility of parody, or masquerade, occurring in a given text already constitutes an appropriate condition for gender re-scription. As Derrida remarks, '[S]omewhere parody always supposes a naivety without withdrawing into an unconscious, a vertiginous non-mastery. Parody supposes a loss of consciousness, for were it to be absolutely calculated, it would become a confession or a law table', *Spurs* , 101.

48 Joan Key, 'The Antidote to the Sublime, or, No Time for Commas', *make: women's art magazine*, 71: August–September (1996), 15.
49 Miller, 'Arachnologies', 283.
50 Jacques Derrida, *Margins of Philosophy*, trans. Alan Bass (Hemel Hempstead: Harvester Wheatsheaf, 1982), xxviii.

2 Between aesthetics and ethics

'Ethics and aesthetics are one'?[1]

I prefer many things not mentioned here to many others
   unmentioned.
I prefer zeroes randomly scattered
to zeroes lined up in rows
I prefer a time of flies to a time of stars.
I prefer to touch wood.
I prefer not to ask how much longer and when.
I prefer consideration of the option
   that there are many ways of being. (Wislawa Szymborska, *Options*)

Sublimity has always been associated with discursive excess. Its first
theorist, Longinus, argues that 'Sublimity is a kind of eminence or
excellence of discourse'.[2] The sublime is thus a useful figure for the
representation of the abundance which characterises our experience
with language. As Paul Crowther observes, the sublime 'is experienced
as profoundly and inseparably connected with – indeed, as *called forth
and projected from* – finite being's struggle to launch itself into and
articulate the world'.[3] Facing the multiplicity of discursive propositions, the self has to cope with the impossibility of making the right
choice or even grasping the full scope of available options. In this
chapter I want to investigate not only how we might come to terms
with this discursive excess of the everyday, but also how we might
follow ethical, rather than contingent, choices in order to make what
I perceive to be the sublime space liveable.

   The exploration of the ethical nature of the sublime should not,
however, be seen as a radical shift from the sublime developed by
eighteenth-century theorists, which is usually described in aesthetic
terms. In fact, as Peter de Bolla asserts:

> [E]ighteenth-century theories on the sublime begin in ethics: the
> ethical systems of Shaftesbury and Hutcheson, for example, are often
> taken as the first examples of an enquiry specifically into the nature
> and causes of the aesthetic, but if either writer can be said to be

interested in aesthetics per se that interest is clearly tempered by their profoundly ethical standpoints.[4]

However, de Bolla observes that ethics functions here as 'a context-ualising and controlling discourse', to which recourse is taken in order to stabilise the discursive boundaries of the sublime. Legislating and normalising the excess produced by sublimity, ethics must be seen as *external* to it. In fact, in all the major works on aesthetics published in the second half of the eighteenth century, which include Burke's *Enquiry*, explicit references to ethics are replaced by psychologism and the newly emergent discourse of subjectivity. But, as I explained in chapter 1, the ethical character of the sublime is clearly foregrounded in Kant's *Critique of Judgement* (1790), in which the dynamical sublime is described as allowing for the attainment of moral consciousness. Faced with overwhelming nature, the self resorts to practical reason, which, for Kant, is always already moral. Grasping the idea of totality, the mind overcomes the temporary weakness experienced by imagin-ation and is thus elevated towards a moral state. As we can see from the above brief overview, it is not possible to trace a strict boundary between aesthetics and ethics in the traditional discourse of the sublime. Indeed, Andrew Ashfield and Peter de Bolla create problems for teleological interpretations of the development of the 'affective' British theory into the Kantian disinterested critique of judgement, interpretations which they sum up as follows:

> The story ends, then, with a proclamation of the aesthetic realm as in some sense autonomous; constructed on rules internal to it, generat-ing affective responses according to its own logic, and generally distinct from all other realms of experience. Consequently, the aesthetic, at least since Kant, has been understood as without political or ethical motivation since its affective registers are, according to the Kantian model, disinterested.[5]

Ashfield and de Bolla perceive British aestheticism, manifested, for example, in Burke's political theories or in Adam Smith's theory of moral sentiments, not as a detached contemplation of art, but as a question of the subject's formation on both an individual and social level. Aesthetics is for them already political, allowing for a fruitful interpenetration between governing and affect.

It is this politico-ethical dimension of sublimity that I want to focus on in this chapter. Influenced by the feminism of sexual differ-ence elaborated by, among others, Luce Irigaray and Hélène Cixous, I am particularly interested in repositioning the self's relationship to the alterity it encounters in the sublime event. This will allow me to provide a different ethical grounding for the discourse of the feminine sublime I develop here. The feminine sublime can thus be seen as a new layer in the palimpsest of the discourses of the sublime, one that retraces, as well as exposes, the radical alterity that has been covered up, to a certain extent, by subsequent discursive thickenings. As Herbert Grabes notices in his article 'Ethics, Aesthetics, Alterity':

> Radical alterity appears in modern aesthetics for the first time with Burke and Kant as the totally strange leading to the experience of the sublime. … [I]n the last two decades, attempts to develop an adequate aesthetic theory of modernist and postmodern art have centred on a revival of the sublime. Largely leaving aside the moral or meta-physical aspect of Kant's concept, the focus in this revival has been on the failure of the imagination when facing extreme alterity, the sense of privation which is even interpreted by Lyotard in an ontological sense as *horror vacui*, the existential threat of nothingness as the absolute other.[6]

Traditionally premised on radical alterity, the sublime depends, at the same time, on the regulation or suppression of this alterity in one way or another. (Chapter 1 lists a number of 'controlling mechanisms' employed by earlier theorists of sublimity, including verbal restraint, maintaining a proper distance from the source of sublime feeling and protecting the self against weakness and effeminacy.) The aesthetic experience of the sublime leads, however, not only to the disintegration of the subject but also to the irruption of *an ethical moment* which foregrounds the irreducible difference of the other and calls the self to respond to this difference. The feminine sublime I propose offers an ethical response to the aesthetic experience of radical alterity, a response which springs from respect for what is absolutely and incalculably different.

Respect for radical alterity

My understanding of ethics arises out of the thought of Emmanuel Levinas, for whom ethics is the first philosophy, situated even before ontology. This 'before' should not be understood in a temporal sense: from a linear perspective, there *is* nothing before being. Rather, it should be read as pointing to the absolute alterity of the other, which collapses the familiar order of Being and calls the self to respond to this alterity. As a result of this calling, 'The Other produces the I by putting it in question'.[7] This possibility, as well as a necessity, of responding to what Levinas defines as an incalculable alterity of the other is the source of an ethical sentiment. Refusing to assert the self's primacy, Levinas focuses on the vulnerability of the self when facing the other, who is always already 'absolutely other', and whose otherness can evoke different reactions in the self. Even though the other can be ignored, scorned or even annihilated, he or she has to be first of all addressed (responded to) in one way or another.

Levinas's ethics is thus based on the recognition of this absolute otherness, which defies mastery and possession: the ethical response consists in responding responsibly to the other and welcoming him or her. Levinas perceives ontology as 'egology', that is a philosophy recognising the primacy of Being and confirming the identity of the self. He argues that 'Western philosophy coincides with the disclosure of the other where the other, in manifesting itself as a being, loses its alterity. From its infancy philosophy has been struck with a horror of the other that remains other – with an insurmountable allergy'.[8] His ethics, coming *before* ontology, takes issue with an egological philosophy which does not question identity, selfhood and sameness, and is therefore based on the logic of totality. Levinas claims that there are no grounds for reducing the strangeness of the other to domestic familiarity, because 'neither possession nor the unity of number nor the unity of concepts link me to the Stranger [*l'Etranger*], the stranger who disturbs the being at home with oneself [*le chez soi*]'.[9]

Interestingly, Levinas's ethics, developed as it is from a religiously inflected, unquenchable metaphysical desire for the absolutely other, abounds in sublime imagery. Levinas's idea of 'responsibility for the other', which has inspired my ethical ruminations, is based on the recognition 'of *the irruption of the face* into the phenomenal order of appearances':[10]

> But, in its expression, in its mortality, the face before me summons me, calls for me, begs for me, as if the invisible death that must be faced by the Other, pure otherness, separated, in some way, from any whole, were my business. It is as if that invisible death, ignored by the Other, whom already it concerns by the nakedness of its face, were already 'regarding' me prior to confronting me, and becoming the death that stares me in the face. ... The Other becomes my neighbour precisely through the way the face summons me, calls for me, begs for me, and in so doing recalls my responsibility, and calls me into question.[11]

When exposed to the alterity of 'the Other and of the Most-High',[12] the self experiences anxiety, elevation and a conflict of the faculties, even though 'this height is no longer the heavens but the Invisible'.[13] For Levinas, the stranger is, paradoxically, both very much like me and at the same time infinitely different. My ethical duty consists in accepting and respecting this alterity without attempting to translate it into familiar terms. The arrival of the other evokes Burkean *horror vacui*, the terror of void and death, a glimpse of both singularity and mortality. Although this arrival may not happen at all, it does not relieve me of the responsibility of awaiting it. If the meeting does finally happen, I can rejoice for having been given this chance of something, rather than nothing, which is the feeling of relief Jean-François Lyotard – for whom Levinas's ethical theory is also extremely important – associates with the contemporary sublime. But the other can never be really grasped in his or her alterity, and this very impossibility disturbs my peace of mind. Faced with what I both fear, due to its strangeness, and desire, I am called into question in all my self-sufficiency and pride. And even though an ethical encounter with the other is always a relation of reciprocity, it does not amount to equal measurement. Levinas asserts that 'A calling into question of the same ... is brought about by the other. We name this calling into question of my spontaneity by the presence of the Other ethics. The strangeness of the Other, his irreducibility to the I, to my thoughts and my possessions, is precisely accomplished as a calling into question of my spontaneity as ethics'.[14] His ethics is extremely important in its reconceptualisation of the ideas of identity and sameness in Western philosophy. By positioning 'the feminine' as a mark of radical alterity ('the feminine is not added to an object and a Thou antecedently given or encountered in the neuter'[15]), Levinas creates a 'radical break in the hegemony of Eleatic being as oneness, sameness, unity, allowing the other to remain other without being reduced to the logic of the same'.[16] This is why his ethical thinking can offer a groundbreaking intervention into the ideas of identity and alterity produced by and producing the traditional discourse of the sublime. Levinas positions alterity as always already preceding the I and thus as irreducible to this I. Ethics is for him born out of the necessity of responding to this radical and incalculable alterity, an alterity which defies suppression and annihilation.

Levinas's theory, interesting in its recognition of ethics beyond justification, and positioning 'the feminine' as a sign or radical alterity, seems nevertheless to foreclose on the sexual aspect of the encounter with the other. In *Totality and Infinity* this encounter is organised around the concept of 'fecundity', leading, as a consequence, to the transformation of unchannelled sexuality into the visible fruits of 'love'. Identified, in a somewhat contradictory way, with virginity, voluptuousness, eroticism and pretence, femininity is also associated with the passivity of the 'Beloved'. Levinas's ethics is constructed in opposition to Eros, which stands for profanation, immodesty, obscurity and ambiguity. The face, which is the site of the ethical, represents, in turn, divinity, morality, height and eminence:

> The principle 'you shall not commit murder', the very signifyingness of the face, seems contrary to the mystery which Eros profanes, and which is announced in the femininity of the tender. In the face the Other expresses his eminence, the dimension of height and divinity from which he descends. In his gentleness dawns his strength and his right. The frailty of femininity invites pity for what, in a sense, is not yet, disrespect for what exhibits itself in immodesty and is not discovered despite the exhibition, that is, is profaned.[17]

The virginity of the feminine, which yearns to be violated, serves for Levinas as a figure of the autarchy of the other. Due to its links with eroticism and profanation, and because of its uncertain situation between purity and lust, it is ultimately confined to the darkness of the non-ethical night. But femininity, which in the earlier part of *Totality and Infinity* is also described as a dwelling and a welcome, can, according to Derrida, be read beyond its stereotypical characteristics (i.e. private interiority, apolitical domesticity, etc.). Instead, in *Adieu to Emmanuel Levinas* Derrida proposes we read *Totality and Infinity* – without forgetting about the 'androcentric attribution' it so clearly makes – as a 'sort of feminist manifesto'. This is how Derrida justifies his argument: 'This text defines the welcome par excellence, the welcome of welcoming the absolute, absolutely originary, or even pre-originary hospitality, nothing less than the pre-ethical origin of ethics, on the basis of femininity. That gesture reaches a depth of essential or meta-empirical radicality that takes sexual difference into account in an ethics emancipated from ontology'.[18]

It is precisely Levinas's perception of femininity as organising the ethical universe and thus undermining the unity of being that is taken up by Luce Irigaray, whose ethics of sexual difference constitutes a radical feminist proposal for encountering and respecting incalculable alterity.

The 'feminine' of sexual difference

Taking further Heidegger's claim that 'each age has one issue to think through, and only one',[19] Irigaray claims that it is precisely the issue of sexual difference which in our age 'could be our "salvation" if we thought it through',[20] but this 'only one' issue of sexual difference she promotes is fragmented and multiple. For Irigaray, sexual difference does not reinstate the binary difference between the two genders, nor does it refer to the essential universality of Being. Instead, it proposes a new way of thinking which takes corporeality and sexuality into account. The acknowledgement of the sexual aspect of living beings is an acceptance of lack (where the recognition that 'I am sexed' stands for 'I am *not everything*'); it is a sign of both our limitation and communality. Sexual difference thus reveals that we are neither universal (i.e. sex-less) nor singular.[21] In this way, Irigaray's ethics of sexual difference denounces 'the spirit of capitalisation': it accepts that in the relationship between two selves 'something cannot be capitalised'.[22]

Irigaray argues that the question of sameness and difference remains unanswered in Levinas's *Totality and Infinity*. Pointing to the decisive role of sexuality and corporeality in the formation of identity, she problematises Levinas's concept of alterity by asking:

> Who is the other, if the other of sexual difference is not recognised or known? Does it not mean in that case a sort of mask or lure? Or an effect of the consumption of an other [*Autre*]? But how is transcendence defined? Furthermore, this non-definition of the other, when the other is not considered to have anything to do with sexual difference, gives rise to an infinite series of substitutions, an operation which seems to me non-ethical. No one can be radically substituted for the other, without depriving the other of identity.[23]

Thanks to her concept of sexual difference, Levinas's other – both a stranger and 'in all essential aspects like me' – becomes both embodied and embedded in the materiality of the everyday.

For Irigaray, an ethical relation involves not only a face-to-face encounter but also a body-to-body proximity. The sexuate other, to use Irigaray's term, is summoned before the self and is to be approached, touched and caressed, but not subjugated or appropriated. She describes the suddenness and immediacy of this encounter with the other in the following terms:

> To arrive at the constitution of an ethics of sexual difference, we must at least return to what is for Descartes the first passion: wonder. This passion has no opposite or contradiction and exists always as though for the first time. Thus man and woman, woman and man are always meeting as though for the first time because they cannot be substituted one for the other. ... This feeling of surprise, astonishment, and wonder in the face of the unknowable ought to be returned to its locus: that of sexual difference. ... It does not try to seize, possess, or reduce this object, but leaves it subjective, still free.[24]

Irigaray here emphasises that the other's positioning body-to-body with me evokes a wonder which results from the ultimate difference, and thus unknowability, of this other. It needs to be emphasised that her ethics of sexual difference should not be reduced to what Judith Butler calls 'the heterosexual matrix'. On the contrary, her theory is aimed at disentangling the paternal hom(m)oeroticism of Levinas's philosophy, which she terms the 'culture of men-amongst-themselves'.[25] There is more than the penis that differentiates man from woman for Irigaray. Playing with the notion of *jouissance*, that is infinite sexual and corporeal pleasure which allows for temporary proximity and demands involvement without annulling self-identity, she depicts a whole new ground for their sexuate meeting. She is also interested in exploring the fecundity of the 'between-women' community, in which irreducible sexual and corporeal difference is played out in numerous acts of sexual experience which cannot be translated into masculine economy. The wonder evoked by the appearance of the other results from the strangeness of that other mixed with erotic sensation, previous memory of the joint experience of the motherly flesh and the promise of mutual recognition and closeness. An aesthetic experience of the contemplation of the other's face thus opens up an ethical space. Sexualisation is released here from the confinement of eros and introduced to the realm of the ethical. Moving beyond Levinasian logic of fecundity, which is '[s]terile, if it were not for the child',[26] Irigaray turns the passive Beloved into an active loving woman, giving birth to life *before* the birth of the child. The lovers bestow life on each other: that, according to Irigaray, 'cannot be perceived as profanation'.[27] But she also recognises that such an immersive encounter with the sexuate other can pose a threat to the male lover: 'Always alien to the intimacy of the mucous, not crossing the threshold, still remaining outside, the lover continues to caress *until he founders in some abyss*'.[28]

The ethics of the feminine sublime

A correspondence can be noticed between the fear and astonishment of the self when faced with the infinitely other, as described by Irigaray, and when coming across the infinitely great. Burke depicts that latter passion, which he describes as sublime, in the following way: 'astonishment is that state of the soul, in which all its motions are suspended, with some degree of horror. In this case the mind is so entirely filled with its object, that it cannot entertain any other'.[29] However, Burke's is a clearly polarised relationship between an impersonal, though threatening object, and a self fighting for self-preservation. The necessary distance between them is a guarantee of the self's ultimate victory, which also allows the self to expel and suppress any threatening or excessive element, as Barbara Claire Freeman indicates in *The Feminine Sublime*. The feminine sublime, in turn, in its exploration of the irreducible alterity of the other, not only redefines space and time in the manner akin to the traditional sublime,[30] but it also delineates the provisional boundaries of the meeting parties. The mutual wonder of both sides excludes the position of mastery the self might adopt toward the threatening object. Thus in the feminine sublime we have two selves not only exposed to each other, but also needing each other for the assertion of their subjectivity. Moral responsibility, understood as a readiness to be 'for' rather than 'with' the other, is therefore, to quote Zygmunt Bauman, 'precisely the act of self-constitution'.[31]

Such an encounter with the irreducible alterity of the other can generate both fear and desire. The self strives to get closer to the object of its longing, but is at the same time pulled back by the potential danger related to the unknown. Hence the other of the amorous encounter can also be seen as a powerful opponent, whose difference and imagined greatness evoke the self's respect. In his *Enquiry* Burke declares that 'it is impossible to look on any thing as trifling, or contemptible, that may be dangerous'.[32] He notices that several languages 'bear a strong testimony to the affinity of these ideas. They frequently use the same word, to signify indifferently the modes of astonishment or admiration and those of terror. θαμβος is in Greek, either fear or wonder'.[33] The fear of the unknown, overwhelming the self, is combined here with the appreciation of the unfamiliarity of the other. However, in the feminine sublime fear is eroticised by desire. This is why the self may prefer a dangerous meeting with the object of its wonder to the distanced but safe appreciation of this object. A direct encounter of this kind is certainly risky. The anxiety evoked by this encounter does not just reflect the fantasised fear of castration or death in the folds of the *vagina dentata*: it rather refers to each side's uncertainty about the other's response to his or her arrival.

Perceived as a sign of innocence and lasciviousness, of closure and excess, the signifier 'femininity' destabilises the binary logic of the phallogocentric discourse. Following Levinas's claim that ethics occurs discursively, I want to turn my attention to the exploration of the discursive framework of the ethics of the feminine sublime. Regulated by the logic of *décriture féminine*, i.e. 'writing of the impossible description' winding its way along bodily folds,[34] the ethical is not limited to the luminosity of the day here. It can also be found in the dark nooks and crevices of the linguistic and the corporeal. This allows me to look for ethics in the discursive spaces of the aesthetic and the poetic, and perhaps arrive at what Mireille-Calle Gruber calls 'poethics': 'the conjunction of poetry and philosophy. Where writing frees itself of a form of "realism", that is to say simplistic conventions, to give itself full latitude to think. To become a "thinking-writing"'.[35] This kind of discourse remains open to interweaving and contamination; it takes delight in the instances when communication breaks down and gives way to the corporeal enactment of poetry, to a desirous gasp, to a deadly embrace. The ethics of the feminine sublime recognises the absolute alterity from which the earlier theorists of sublimity tried to escape: it envelops ethical encounters in the ambivalence of corporeal textuality, which does not easily distinguish between affect and thought, or pleasure and pain.

It is this uncertainty, or undecidability, of the ethics of the feminine sublime that distinguishes it from the 'positive', normative programme of feminist ethics as exposed by Seyla Benhabib in her 1992 book, *Situating the Self*. Even though I take issue with Benhabib's ethical theory, I do recognise the radical novelty of her project, which is intended to move beyond the 'totality' of a masculine ethics towards a recognition of 'the concrete other'. But, at the same time, I cannot accept the indisputable knowability of the other upon which Benhabib's ethics relies:

> The standpoint of the concrete other ... requires us to view each and every rational being as an individual with a concrete history, identity and affective-emotional constitution. In assuming this standpoint we abstract from what constitutes out commonality, and focus on

individuality. We seek to comprehend the needs of the other, his or her motivations, what she searches for, and what s/he desires. Our relation to the other is governed by the norms of equality and complementary reciprocity: each is entitled to expect and to assume from the other forms of behaviour through which the other feels recognised and confirmed as a concrete, individual being with specific needs, talents and capacities.[36]

It seems to me that Benhabib does not really depart from what Levinas perceives as a totality. Her relationship with the other, whose alterity is recognised and respected, involves a mastery the self exerts over this otherness. Knowledge here amounts to possession and leads to the reduction of the incalculable difference to the categories elaborated and controlled by the self. It is thus based on the appropriating logic of the intellect, which Levinas has described as follows:

> [I]n knowledge there also appears the notion of an intellectual activity of a reasoning will – a way of doing something which consists precisely of thinking through knowing, of seizing something and making it one's own, of reducing to presence and representing the difference of being, an activity which *appropriates* and *grasps* the otherness of the known.[37]

Benhabib's emphasis on particularities which are to be situated alongside universals stems from her belief in the possibility of the prior conceptualisation of the ethical. This is precisely the kind of ethics that does *not* precede ontology, but rather reasserts the rationality – or sensitivity – of moral selves, whose identity remains unquestioned. The recognition of the need for particularity seems problematic, especially if this particularity is presented as coherent and stable. If attention is paid to the most minute detail, the identity of the self which is faced with alterity, as well as the identity of the other, which undergoes destabilisation in every instance of the recognition of detail, will be suspended. In turn, this most serious and radical recognition of alterity and concreteness annuls the possibility of the ethical perceived as a pre-defined set of moral rules. This allows me to see ethics as *a possibility of,* or *need for, ethics*: constantly deferred but never releasing the self from the obligation to respond respectfully to the irreducible particularity of the other. But how can we conceptualise ethics without relying on the clearly defined notion of the other?

In *Feminism and Deconstruction*, Diane Elam asserts that a departure from the pre-defined notion of subjectivity is not only possible, but also necessary, if the consequences of feminist and deconstructive interventions are to be taken seriously. As a result, a new form of ethics will emerge, which will be different from ethics perceived as a traditional branch of philosophy:

> [A] turn away from subjective autonomy produces an ethics which is not a question of individual choice or individual care for the other. ... [B]y taking a distance from pragmatism, this ethics gives rise to an account of groundless solidarity. [Here] ethical decisions are not made on the basis of pre-established norms. ... Rather than judging on the basis of a system of rules, political activism becomes the search for the rule that may do justice to the case. This search is necessarily endless.[38]

And indeed, deconstruction seems to me to provide a useful means of explaining the ethical dimension of the sublime. In particular, deconstruction can offer us an 'ethical' way of thinking about difference, since its constant exploration of meaningful entities prevents them from fossilising into the totalities Levinas fears. By revisiting the notions of otherness, selfhood and ethics itself, deconstruction creates a radical investigative territory on which the principle of undecidability serves as a guarantee that ethics will *always* and *continually take place*. As Elam notices, 'This search [for the rule] is necessarily endless'. In his interview with Jean-Luc Nancy entitled 'Eating Well', Derrida confirms the ethical character of deconstruction in the following terms:

> In order to recast, if not rigorously re-found a discourse on the 'Subject', on that which will hold the place (or replace the place) of the subject (of law, of morality, of politics – so many categories caught up in the same turbulence), one has to go through the experience of a deconstruction. This deconstruction (we should once again remind them who do not want to read) is neither negative nor nihilistic; it is not even a pious nihilism, as I have said. ... [T]here is a duty in deconstruction.[39]

In the feminine sublime, this duty springs from the call of the other, whose otherness can never be ultimately grasped, and whose arrival is not guaranteed. And yet the mechanism of deconstruction is activated whenever an event occurs; whenever the other speaks to me and initiates an encounter. As Simon Critchley puts it in *The Ethics of Deconstruction*, 'Derrida writes, paying careful attention to the reflexivity of the statement, *Ça se déconstruit* ("It deconstructs itself", the *Ça* being a translation of both Freud's *Es* – the Id, the unconscious – and

a homophone for *Sa* – *savoir absolu*, absolute knowledge ...). It deconstructs itself whenever something takes place'.[40] This is not to say that
deconstruction is a passive enterprise, but rather to foreground a
certain unavoidability of a deconstructive event, which can either be
acknowledged (just as the other can be welcomed in his or her
otherness) or can be overlooked and ignored.

The ethics of the feminine sublime is based on a recognition of
this uncertain character of the encounter with the alterity of the
other, which is devoid of the guarantee of its occurrence. The
feminine sublime embraces the indeterminacy of sublime experience,
in which the exact balance between pain and pleasure cannot be
reached, and in which the self's security and solipsism are threatened
by the intrusion of the other. As this other is a corporeal being, the
ethical encounter occurring under the aegis of sublimity will not
escape sexualisation. Occurring in the shadow of Burkean *horror vacui*,
the feminine sublime affirms femininity as a non-negatively marked
sign of difference. Represented for me through the metaphor of
décriture féminine, i.e. 'writing of an impossible description', it is
written in multiple voices, thus foregrounding the irreducible alterity
of the other, 'without appeal to the truth of a presocial identity'.[41] The
ethics of the feminine sublime, which refuses the passage to the
universal and which does not 'consume' alterity in the name of liberal
politics, is thus less restrictive than the feminist ethics of the kind
proposed by Benhabib. But it is also more difficult, because its search
for ethical justification, for the source of the voice of the other and his
or her exact positioning, can never be terminated. This indeterminacy
generates the need to constantly explore ethical questions and revisit
discursive interlacings. As Grabes explains:

> What is important in this indeterminacy can, even after close
> scrutiny, be only slightly reduced, yet by no means resolved. Thus,
> even upon closer acquaintance through repeated reading, the
> essential alterity not only remains intact, but actually increases in the
> interminable process of sense making. It may become so intense,
> indeed, that the imagination fails totally and, in the face of a
> seemingly boundless indeterminacy, only the idea of infinity seems
> adequate. Yet instead of the feeling of an increase of power – as is
> postulated in the Kantian sublime – through a sudden awareness of
> the superiority of reason over nature, the glimpse of the abyss of
> unresolvable indeterminacy creates instead a feeling of the absolute
> powerlessness of reason in the postmodern art.[42]

Grabes focuses here specifically on what he terms 'postmodern art', which for him provides a new context for the experience of sublimity, one in which the superiority of Kant's reason is suspended when facing what he terms 'the abyss of unresolvable indeterminacy'. The feminine sublime draws pleasure from this irreducible indeterminacy which reason cannot think. Recognising the problematic status of the distinction between 'real life' and 'art' as the representation of this life, I would like to look at the image – or perhaps enactment – of the 'loving encounter' as a possible 'testing ground' for this indeterminacy of the feminine sublime. In the loving encounter, the self is exposed to the infinite alterity of the other, its physicality, eroticism and desire. As Freud explains in 'The Uncanny', love is often described as the feeling of homesickness, driving the self to re-enact the primary unity with the other in the substitute relationships of adult life. But love should not be perceived here as a cultural universal. Instead, it can be experienced through indeterminate singular events, which foreground its specificity and locality, and which evoke the Burkean passions of pain and pleasure.

Every event of the sublime can only be a temporary flicker. Suspended between an act of awaiting the other (fraught with Burkean *horror vacui*) and the moment of his or her appearance (resulting in the recognition which Lyotard describes as 'the sublime is like that!'), it lacks permanence. As Derrida explains, 'In the feeling of the sublime, pleasure only "gushes indirectly". ... The schema here is that of a dam. ... The maximum pressure lasts only an instant (*augenblicklich*), the time it takes to blink an eye, during which the passage is strictly closed and the stricture absolute. Then the dam bursts and there's a flood.'[43] Deciding to give way to its desire which overcomes fear, the self considers itself capable of seeing the other again and faithfully awaits one more instant of the other's embrace. The ethics of the feminine sublime I put forward is thus necessarily a-rational, because it needs the suspension of the disinterested judgement of reason, which might dissuade the self from opening itself to the flood of desire and pursuing its amorous engagement. It is not my intention, however, to construct a binary opposition which would privilege madness over clear thinking. Contrarily, I believe the feminine sublime necessitates reason as a decision-maker, but I am referring here to the reason which is aware of its limitations and open to affect. I would like to return here to Ashfield and de Bolla's discussion of eighteenth-century aesthetics in which they state that: 'the British tradition insists that the affective is based in human experience and human nature, and that by necessity the aesthetic cannot, therefore, be understood as a separate realm. ... This is why the British tradition insists upon the social, ideological and finally cultural basis of the aesthetic realm'.[44] The apparent separation between aesthetics as the sphere of sensual perception combined with feeling, and ethics as the territory of moral conduct directed by reason, is not sustainable, as the self, elevated by sublime experience, is found to be more conducive to ethical action.

I am consciously avoiding to provide a fully fledged definition of the feminine sublime, instead allowing metaphors to protect the fragility of this notion. Suspended between aesthetics and ethics, between reason and affect, and between grandeur and abjection, the feminine sublime can be attacked for its non-essentiality, or conceptual vagueness. To justify my 'retreat to metaphor', I would like to quote Drucilla Cornell, for whom the metaphor 'show[s] what cannot be stated':

> [T]he use of metaphor, or allegory, is not utilised as part of academic chic. Such devices are used to be faithful to the truth of paradox, to show what cannot be stated. ... But there is an ethical moment in the endless demonstration of this paradox. It is the significance of this ethical moment that is particularly crucial for feminism. The demonstration of the limit of meaning loosens the binds of convention. The knots are loosened rather than re-enforced by philosophy. This challenge to any attempt to philosophically secure the bounds of meaning implicitly defends the possibility that we operate within an ever wider field of meaning. As the boundary recedes, we have more space to dream and reimagine our forms of life.[45]

Exploring the limits of meaning and its links with excess, abjection and waste, the feminine sublime can be seen as an ethical proposition for the necessarily disparate encounters of the heterogeneous world. It is not an easy ethics: it requires that the self expose its vulnerability and come to terms with the undecidability which characterises the moment of awaiting the other. According to William Blake, 'The most sublime act is to set another before you'.[46] Risking both annihilation and eternal dissatisfaction, the self is motivated by the promise of redemption from sluggishness and stasis, even though its salvation were a mere instant. The traditional wisdom of the capitalist exchange has to be abandoned here for the sake of a different economy, which is not focused on keeping the balance of gains and losses, but rather on infinite expenditure towards the other's needs. Such a decision will always seem mad in the eyes of the calculating capitalist; and yet proportionate economy fails when faced with the spending of affect. The encounter with the other has to be a gift, with love functioning both as its driving force and justification.

After the subject

> The thought of life is capable of thinking the loss, capable of knowing that life does not advance by means of a system in the Hegelian way of reinjecting, reincorporating what it could leave. On the contrary, the thought of life is capable of accepting that something cannot be capitalised. That is the thought of Derrida, a deconstruction, a critique; a denunciation of the spirit of capitalisation which is purely artificial and produces nothing but death. (Hélène Cixous, 'Interview')

In his monumental study of sublimity, *The Discourse of the Sublime*, Peter de Bolla explores the link between the discourse on the sublime and the discourse on national debt, both of which emerged in the Seven Years War period of 1756–63. He is particularly interested in establishing how one can manage the excess produced by these two discourses. The emergence of the autonomous subject is presented here as one of the outcomes of what could be termed the capitalist economy of the sublime. 'The discourse on the debt effects the capitalist description of the subject – still very much with us and under which we are represented – in which the discursive excess is identified as the mark of individuality; it brings about the field of representation in which difference determines and ratifies person; difference in and to excess becomes the defining feature of the indivi-dual and sanctions the subject.'[47] This kind of transaction reflects the overall way of thinking about identity in Western culture: the capital-ist logic, which is based on the exact calculation of gains and losses, always attempts to reduce excessive, incalculable alterity to sameness.

Taking into account the excessive potential of the sublime – a potential which, as I demonstrated in chapter 1, seems to have been silenced in the masculine aesthetic tradition – I want to argue that it is possible to conceptualise the subject beyond the discourse of capital-ism. The notion of the feminine sublime allows me to revisit the sublime's discursive excess in search for the forms of subjectivity that do not try to reduce difference to sameness or capitalise on loss. One such attempt has been undertaken by Eduardo Cadava, Peter Connor and Jean-Luc Nancy, who in 1991 edited a collection of essays entitled *Who Comes After the Subject?*. Indicating the need to rethink the Cartesian–Kantian–Hegelian model of subjectivity, which has dominated Western philosophy, the title of this collection has a sublime character: it points to the unexpected arrival of the unknown ('Who comes?'), which may or may not happen. But rather than either simply abandon the notion of subjectivity or proclaim 'a return to the subject' as if the critique of subjectivity had not happened at all, perhaps we should accept that the question of the subject can be approached only *as a question*, demonstrating the need for the permanent investigation of subjectivity. As Derrida observes in his interview with Jean-Luc Nancy entitled 'Eating Well', which has been included in this collection:

> If we still wish to speak of the subject – the juridical, ethical, political, psychological subject, etc. ... , it is first of all necessary to submit to the test of questioning the essential predicates of which all subjects are the subject. ... It is necessary to question this authority of the being-present, but the question itself neither offers the first nor the last word. ... This vigil or beyond of the question is anything but precritical. Beyond even the force of critique, it situates a respon-sibility as irreducible to and rebellious toward the traditional category of 'subject'. Such a vigil leads us to recognise the processes of *différance*, trace, iterability, ex-appropriation, and so on. These are at work everywhere, which is to say, well beyond humanity. A discourse thus restructured can try to situate in another way the question of what a human subject, a morality, a politics, the rights of the human subject are, can be, and should be. Still to come, this task is indeed far ahead of us.[48]

We should not be misled here by Derrida's prophetic 'to come', indicating the future of subject politics and ethics. Rather, this 'to come', which reappears in his discussion of 'arriving democracy' in *Politics of Friendship*, is permanently deferred. Even if one is prompted to respond to the question of the subject and his or her rights and duties, the moment of arrival at the correct answer gives way to an act of 'arriving', i.e. being on-the-way to the subject, ethics and demo-cracy. Therefore these new forms of subjectivity should be seen as constantly contested, setting off the machinery of differentiation which breaks through fixed definitions. Derrida argues that

> Something of this call of the other must remain nonreappropriable, nonsubjectivable, and in a certain way nonidentifiable, a sheer

supposition, so as to remain other, a singular call to response or to responsibility. This is why the determination of the singular 'Who?' – or at least its determination as subject – still remains problematic. And it should remain so. This obligation to protect the other's otherness is not merely a theoretical imperative.[49]

In this context, ethics can be understood, in a Levinasian way, as a response to the voice of the other. This voice can only be heard from far away or perhaps merely imagined as a promise of an encounter that may or may not take place. This form of ethics – which I describe as the ethics of the feminine sublime – is not reduced to the code of moral behaviour, as it produces an ethical situation not only in every singular act of waiting for the other, but also when his or her voice addresses me and I accept (or reject) this call. Here, the sublime springs from uncertainty. The ethics of the feminine sublime can therefore be described as 'wandering ethics', being permanently 'on-its-way'. Denying capitalisation, the ethical encounter with the other, which has not been underwritten by the promise of success or gain, is marked by both excess and lack. Consequently, it evokes sublime feeling, which for Burke results from the 'terrible uncertainty of the thing described':[50]

> We are first prepared with the utmost solemnity for the vision; we are first terrified, before we are let even into the obscure cause of our emotion; but when this grand cause of terror makes its appearance, what is it? is it not, wrapt up in the shades of its own incomprehensible darkness, more aweful, more striking, more terrible, than the liveliest description, than the clearest painting could possibly represent it?[51]

In Burke, sublimity results from the terror of the vision 'to come', but this terror is soothed – even if not 'balanced' – by the promise of the vision's arrival. What Cixous calls 'the denunciation of the spirit of capitalisation' in deconstruction differentiates the ethics of the feminine sublime, (mis)guided by deconstructive signposts, from the ethics which de Bolla associates with the early discourse of the sublime:

> [T]he repositioning of moral economy takes into account both the fact that bankruptcies occur in the individualistic pursuit of profit, and that society becomes corrupt through the degeneration of morals brought about by selfish profiteering. ... It follows from this that great pressure must be placed on the conjunction between the individual and the state, between public interest and private gain, in order to create the discourse within which its revalued ethics of collective

individualism can be read as an ethics, not as the more brutal vicissitudes of economic pragmatism. ... This production of the body of the state should be seen in terms of the legislation and control of a discursive excess.[52]

The discursive excess of eighteenth-century sublimity, which I discuss in chapter 1, is here converted into ethics. Excess is controlled by representing public debt within the bounds of control. It is seen as a regulated quantity within the economy, rather than as a superfluous one. Ethics thus comes *in place of* excess, ruling out the instability of the subject that has emerged as a side-product of the discourse of the sublime. In this context, however, ethics signifies nothing more than a codified collection of morals, warding off disturbance or 'over-spilling' on the level of both the individual and the state.

And yet Derrida indicates that 'the sublime, if there is any sublime, exists only by overspilling: it exceeds cise and good measure, it is no longer proportioned according to man and his determinations'.[53] Debt and loss should not thus be seen as unnatural and unwanted products of a miscalculated business transaction. If, as Derrida claims in *The Post-Card*, 'To borrow is the law'[54] of the economic order which depends on speculation, moral economy – imposed in order to cover up individual and social corruption – in fact reveals what it intends to hide: that debt is an intrinsic feature of an economic exchange. Derrida argues that 'Without borrowing, nothing begins, there is no proper fund/foundation [*fonds*]. Everything begins with the transference of funds, and *there is interest in borrowing*, this is even its initial interest. To borrow yields, *brings back*, produces surplus value, is the prime mover of every investment'.[55]

The ethics of the feminine sublime is therefore not the exact opposite of the moral economy de Bolla describes. Instead, it should be seen as a recognition of the principle of debt and the experience of loss, which are at work in any transaction with the other. Rather than guard against corruption, the ethics of the feminine sublime is rooted precisely in corruption, alterity and foreignness perceived as an intrinsic part of the experience of the self. In this ethics, the acceptance of corporeality and desire, born out of the respectful recognition of the other's difference, will result in the annulment of the subject's secure distanced position. The preservation of this distance is for Burke a guarantee of maintaining the subject's integrity and of controlling the excess that the sublime event could unleash. But in this 'new' model of subjectivity, the subject is not formed a priori: it is a product of the event in which it participates. The subject only emerges as a response to the coming of the other, who is assured about his or her being in this very encounter and not before. The word 'response' refers us to the concept of dialogism, preparing the grounds for the emergence of the self *before* the other, whose coming-into-being is a recognition of, and a response to, the alterity against which the self's own difference can be formulated. The subject can thus be described in Derrida's words as the 'finite experience of nonidentity to self, as the underivable interpellation inasmuch as it comes from the other'.[56] It is produced only *in* the meeting, and this very meeting is an indication and a confirmation of the subject's precarious status. The chance of nothing happening at all and of an instant termination of the event – the fears that Burke associates with the uncertain arrival of the sublime – erase the possibility of returning to the Enlightenment model of subjectivity.

Donald Wesling and Tadeusz Słamek's book, *Literary Voice: The Calling of Jonah*, is another example of late-twentieth-century attempts to rethink the traditional Western concept of the subject. The authors of *Literary Voice* propose instead a dialogic subjectivity which inhabits the borderline between at least two consciousnesses and which recognises the equal-to-self role of others in its constitution. Developing the parable of the call of Jonah, Wesling and Sławek notice that 'Every human word implies the existence of the other. It also implies that the speaker has a kind of otherness within; voice enters humans easily and literally obliges humans to enter into others, a situation that holds special terrors for some'.[57] Terror is here linked with bliss, since the event of being called by one's name and forced to step out and assume responsibility, although risky, can transform the mundane into the extraordinary. Interestingly, for Wesling and Sławek dialogism is situated beyond communicative success: like the sublime, to which the authors of *Literary Voice* resort to explain their concept of minimal articulation, it is devoid of the guarantee of a communicative event taking place to the satisfaction of both parties involved. Wesling and Sławek emphasise the singular and irreducible character of every encounter, which always occurs in the local, 'horizontal' perspective. Such an encounter remains inscribed in the paradigm of minimal articulation, haunted by

> the ghost of revelation which must speak from under the subsoil of tone in order to break into petrified formulae of language. ... The minimally articulate, then, leaves the domain of socially accepted

utterances; or, if it uses these, it is only after a terrifying experience of hearing the voice from behind a chair. It is only outside social discourses that the abyss could be thought and expressed. If articulation is insertion of an utterance into a network of contexts, then the articulation of the inarticulate is such an insertion into a context which cannot be specified, an insertion into the territory which defies easy contextualisation and begs for the association with the sublime or supernatural.[58]

The minimally articulate is explained through the workings of the sublime, which erupts in the articulate discourse and manifests itself in 'corporeal speech' (in its verbal forms such as sexual *jouissance*, hysteria and glossolalia, but also in non-verbal forms, including touch, gesticulation, and dance). Due to its links with the spasmodic and the inarticulate, minimal articulation poses a threat to the autonomy of a subject who is a master of his own reason and who remains fully capable of his own self-critique. The femininity of the minimally articulate comes as a mark of alterity and excess, disrupting the rigidity of a logical discourse, clearly articulated philosophy and strictly confined knowledge. The discourse of the feminine sublime embraces the discursive overspilling which has not been restrained by bodily closure. The untameable flow of minimal articulation guarantees the ethical singularity of the discursive event, as if always occurring for the first time.

The economy of the gift

> The madness ... is a certain excess of the gift. (Jacques Derrida, *Given Time*)

A sexuate encounter is initiated by the other's call and established by the self's response to it. As a consequence, both the other and the self can emerge as separate and different, though never ultimately fixed, entities. By opposing the dialectical logic of capitalist exchange, the 'economy of desire' regulating this encounter remains open to the untamed and insubordinate circulation that can always be interrupted by some form of either lack or excess.

This economy, defying the principles of capitalist exchange, is frequently represented through the concept of the gift. In his essays *Given Time* and *The Gift of Death*, Derrida challenges our everyday understanding of the gift as something we possess on reception, or something we pass on to another person, usually in association with some kind of celebration. Traditionally, gifts are exchanged both in private – on birthdays, Christmases, St Valentine's days, etc. – and in public – on state visits of different ranks. It is precisely this exchange-ability of the gift that Derrida exposes as contradictory to the very essence of the idea of 'giving' when he says: '[The gift] must not circulate, it must not be exchanged, it must not in any case be exhausted, as a gift, by the process of exchange, by the movement of circulation of the circle in the form of return to the point of depar-ture.'[59] Working against the logic of debt and gratitude supporting the circle of symbolic exchange, the gift disrupts traditional economy. To retain its status of a gift (rather than a token for some kind of grace or favour, be it the lover's affection, international co-operation or the feel-good factor), it has to remain unspeakable, or even inconceivable, which saves it from being reduced to the familiar economy based on the exact calculation of gains and losses.

The feminine sublime, deprived of the promise of the other's arrival, is inscribed in the unexpected, even violent, logic of donation and generosity that the gift calls for. As Derrida argues in *Given Time*, the gift, sublime in its sudden arrival, 'must be irruptive'. Violence is the condition of the gift, as a donee is often taken by surprise, against his or her will, and transported beyond him- or herself. In *The Gift of Death*, Derrida writes that in Judeo-Christian cultures being presented with the gift of one's identity (i.e. being called in and recognised as the subject by the other), remains inscribed in a wider framework of the parabolical Christian offering, the shared *mysterium tremendum*: 'the terrifying mystery, the dread, fear and trembling of the Christian in the experience of the sacrificial gift. This trembling seizes me at the moment of becoming a person, and the person can become what it is only in being paralysed [*transie*], in its very singularity, by the gaze of God'.[60] We should remember from our earlier discussion of the dimension of height in sublimity that, for Emmanuel Levinas, the height and indescribability of God represent the absolute alterity of the other. This other deserves to be answered *as if he were God*. The ethical character of this act results from the fact that the call of the other can be rejected. An act of taking responsibility for the other, encouraged by the promise of bliss and fulfilment, must result in an overcoming of the paralysing fear of nothingness. And yet, this ethical moment is premised upon unavoidable danger and risk. As Derrida explains, '[Responsibility] must always run the risk of conversion and apostasy: there is no responsibility without a dissident and inventive rupture, with respect to tradition, authority, orthodoxy, rule, or doctrine.'[61] The initial decision that is handed to the other as a gift carries with it a lethal threat of eruption and destruction: communication can always turn into chaotic babble; meaning can perish under the thrust of the minimally articulate and the discursive overspill can turn out to be too demanding for the other to accept it. The possibility of rejection constitutes the very essence of the gift.

Abolishing the logic of practical reason and economic exchange, the gift of an ethical response to the other demands a different logic. This particular logic goes against *logos*, 'which means at once reason, discourse, relation, and account'.[62] Lyotard points out that there is 'something of the sublime in capitalist economy',[63] which means that the logic of calculation always produces its own bastard child, the unspent, and thus undermines the circularity of its own principle of perfect exchange. The feminine sublime should not therefore be seen as another 'version' of the sublime, but rather as a re-exploration of 'the unspent' in the discourse it produces and reflects. It thus demands an ultimate offering to the other, to whom I owe absolute responsibility, but it also denies the sacrificial aspect of this offering: the gift, as Derrida has explained, to retain its status of a gift, has to be immediately and absolutely forgotten. The gift that the feminine sublime calls for consists of the ultimate spending of the self. As Derrida puts it, 'What is given – and this would also represent a kind of death – is not some thing, but goodness itself, a giving goodness, the act of giving or the donation of the gift. A goodness that must not only forget itself but whose source remains inaccessible to the donee.'[64] Burke's fear of death inherent in the sublime experience will not be annulled by consolation resulting from the performance of a merciful act: though the goodness which is required here is to amount to infinity (i.e. total expenditure, without capitalising anything), it has to remain unmentioned, secretive and silent. This is the meaning of the self-sacrifice that foregrounds the irreplaceable singularity of both the donor and the donee. Answering the question: 'On what condition does goodness exist beyond all calculation?', Derrida justifies the madness of the ethics of the gift as follows:

> On the condition that goodness forget itself, that the movement be the movement of the gift that renounces itself, hence the movement of infinite love. *Only infinite love can renounce itself and, in order to become finite, become incarnated in order to love the other, to love the other as a finite other.* This gift of infinite love comes from someone and is

addressed to someone; responsibility demands irreplaceable singularity. Yet only death or rather the apprehension of death can give this irreplaceability, and it is only on the basis of it that one can speak of a responsible subject, of the soul as conscience of self, of myself, etc.[65]

It is this link between love and mortality – understood as singular events and not 'cultural universals' – that I am particularly interested in exploring in the feminine sublime. The deadly aspect of the sublime event, which testifies to its singularity, is also a guarantee of its ethical character. Levinas claims that it is only in the face of death that the other and the self are confirmed in their singularity and irreplaceability. The scandal of the gift of death can be redeemed by and through affect, generating a different logic from the capitalist economy of exchange. Sacrifice is not motivated here by prospective gain or reward; on the contrary, the possibility of the repayment of this sacrifice has to be ruled out. Following Derrida's speculations on goodness, we can conclude that the 'mad' economy of the feminine sublime can be justified through love, which cannot rest on the promise of the other's arrival. Amorous spending threatens to disrupt the progress and development of a sexuate encounter – i.e. towards matrimony, child-bearing and family genealogy – with its demand for absolute consummation.

This economy of infinite spending calls for a rethinking of the gender laws which underwrite it. Derrida notices that the biblical parable of Abraham sacrificing his son Isaac in accordance with God's orders, and thus trying to reconcile affect with responsibility, functions on an exclusive father–son level. Woman features here only as non-presence. She is deprived of the possibility of challenging the extremity of the laws imposed by God and followed by his patriarchs. This prompts Derrida to ask, 'Would the logic of sacrificial responsibility within the implacable universality of the law, of its law, be altered, inflected, attenuated, or displaced, if a woman were to intervene in some consequential manner? Does the system of this sacrificial responsibility and of the double "gift of death" imply at its very basis an exclusion or sacrifice of woman?'[66] Derrida leaves the question is suspense, to which he frequently takes recourse when faced with 'the woman question'. Trying to imagine Sarah's horror and awe resulting from the impossibility of understanding the logic of the male hierarchy, but also from being excluded from this logic which was both kept secret and exposed on the altar on Mount Moriah, I want to open this ethics of sacrifice and the gift of death to femininity. This amounts to revealing sexual difference where it surreptitiously manifests itself. Hence the *feminine* sublime can be read as a counter-logic of infinite expenditure, motivated by the infinity of love which suspends the restraint of certain social practices based on mutuality, avoidance of risk, distance and non-involvement. It also involves the acceptance of what Sylviane Agacinski calls 'the experience of weakness' associated with falling in love, i.e. with the recognition of the self's need for the other. This is not to confirm the misogynist association between women and affect, as opposed to men's rationality and self-guard. The sacrifice does not amount to one person sacrificing herself for the sake of the other and thus perpetuating the social power structure. On the contrary, sacrifice is situated here beyond the dichotomy of gender, although femininity as a mark of difference, excess and 'the non-truth of truth' helps to open the rigidity of the unfair model of relations between the sexes. Infinite spending does not therefore conform with the old cultural model of domesticised womanhood, which has to be controlled in order to maintain patriarchal dominance: it signifies rather a different economy that regulates the relations between the sexes without capitalising on them (e.g. in the form of socially prescribed aims of the relationship, strict birth control policies, anti-abortion legislation, the policing of gay lovers or gay parents, etc.).

This economy which is not one

Irigaray identifies the source of this economy of excess, which over-comes the opposition between the linguistic and the material, in women's plural sexuality. Against man's dominant phallic economy, she opposes women's autoeroticism, represented by the two lips constantly touching and caressing each other. Here, woman is no more seen as lacking a sex organ; on the contrary, 'She has at least two of them, but they are not identifiable as ones. Her sexuality, always at least double, goes even further: it is *plural*'.[67] In the past, women functioned as objects in man's symbolic exchange. Passed from fathers to husbands, they were not granted a subjectivity of their own. Instead, they were reduced to a symbol, while at the same time themselves remaining outside symbolisation, as the language which regulated their social position did not belong to them. And yet women were also able to forge insurgent unions within and among themselves, taking recourse to madness, mysticism and other forms of implosion or explosion, which Michel de Certeau has described as 'the right to exercise language *otherwise*'. Discussing mystical texts which offer a new treatment of language, de Certeau points to the ability of these texts to go beyond normative discursive traditions: 'They are beaches offered to the swelling sea; their goal is to disappear into what they disclose, like a Turner landscape dissolved in air and light. An ab-solute (un-bound), in the mode of pain, pleasure, and a "letting-be" attitude (Meister Eckhart's *gelazenheit*), inhabits the torture, ecstasy, or sacri-fice of a language that can *say* that ab-solute, endlessly, only by erasing itself'.[68]

The feminine sublime is one such discourse which utilises the 'right to exercise the language otherwise'. In the experience of the feminine sublime, the exact balance between pain and pleasure can-not be reached, while the self's security and solipsism are threatened by the intrusion of the other. The feminine sublime thus challenges the reductive logic of phallogocentric discourses, which reduce woman's sexual pleasure to the reproduction of the species. As Cixous argues in 'The Laugh of the Medusa', woman refuses to be constrained by the traditional perception of herself as mother and 'a source of goods': 'The woman arriving over and over again does not stand still; she's everywhere, she exchanges, she's the desire-that-gives'.[69] Accord-ing to Cixous, woman 'doesn't "know" what she's giving, she doesn't measure it; she gives, though, neither a counterfeit impression nor something she hasn't got. She gives more, with no assurance that she'll get back even some unexpected profit from what she puts out. She gives that there may be life, thought, transformation. This is an "economy" that can no longer be put in economic terms.'[70] She is a giver, 'the locus for the other', and thus she participates in this discourse of unrequited exchange. This does not mean that she does not receive pleasure, but rather that this flow of pleasure exceeds the linear logic of the masculine economic exchange. Cixous points out that Man can distribute his 'gifts' only in meeting the other. He needs to enter another space to leave his gift there but what he takes in return is pleasure. This questions the nature of his gift, which becomes only an item of exchange, or a form of *payment* for his pleasure. But woman's pleasure defies the economy of capitalisation. For both Cixous and Irigaray, woman's sexual pleasure is irreducibly plural and cannot thus be restrained by any regulatory discursive practices. The ethical encounter occurring under the aegis of the feminine sublime cannot thus escape sexualisation. It also opens up residues of uncon-

strained excessive pleasure, in which the economy of desire undermines the logic of exact calculation.

The physicality of language developed in the discourse of the
feminine sublime, with its emphasis on pain and pleasure, or torture
and ecstasy, disturbs the order of Man's world. This loosening of
regulations suspends the authority of the legislators of the discursive.
The economy of the unspent has its source in the relationship of non-
identity and alterity between women, in which there is always room
for the trace of the corporeal other. According to Irigaray, this insurgent
economic order 'upsets the linearity of a project, undermines the goal-
object of a desire, diffuses the polarisation toward a single pleasure,
disconcerts fidelity to a single discourse.'[71] The discourse of the feminine sublime, in its opening towards the minimally articulate, breaks
with the logic of sacrifice promoted by patriarchy. In phallogocentric,
patriarchal economy the gift element of the relationship between the
sexes is reduced to 'natural duty', which could be read as a version of
the Kantian moral law.

The Kantian sublime is based on the sacrifice of imagination.
Nature, which Lyotard terms 'a first gift' (or, to quote Kant, 'the
given', the present "wealth"', and 'the *Stoff* of free natural form'),
must be 'sacrificed on the altar of the law'.[72] Even though, as Kant puts
it, imagination deprives *itself* of its freedom, its self-sacrifice can be
seen as an inevitable response to a higher law. According to Lyotard,
'The law of practical reason, the law of the law, weighs with all its
weight on the law of productive imagination. It uses it'.[73] This sacrifice
is based on a 'calculation of interest', supplementing the loss of
imaginative productivity with the feeling of respect, but this is a kind
of transaction that cannot *not* take place. As a result, the gift of
imagination is recuperated by the law which ensures that there is no
permanent overspill in the sublime. The sacrificial violence of imagination remains inscribed in what Derrida terms 'a calculation': 'The
imagination gains by what it loses. It gains by losing'.[74] However, in
Derrida's reading of the Kantian sublime delineated in *The Truth in
Painting* we will not find the kind of accusatory tone Lyotard uses for
his reading of the 'Analytic of the Sublime'. Instead, Derrida goes to
great lengths to demonstrate that the sacrificial economy of the
Kantian sublime, an economy which is based on the exact calculation
of gains and losses, exists only when threatened by overspilling (i.e.
that its alleged violence is already open to a certain vulnerability and
wounding). Represented by the concept of the colossal, which is used

to present the unpresentable, a concept 'almost too big for presentation', the sublime is framed by a number of textual devices. The 'almost too' phrase used by Kant is one of them, signalling 'a certain categorical fixity' of the concept used. This 'almost too' refers, according to Derrida, to our power of apprehension: deprived of the sluice of the 'almost too', our facultary powers would collapse when faced with absolute unpresentability. But the erection of the colossal – and thus the wider framework of sublime experience – can only be upheld, as Kant very well realises, thanks to the maintenance of proper measurement and distance. The colossal – whose 'cise' refers to both its size and cut – is thus constantly threatened with the possibility of castration and detumescence. Derrida confirms that the Kantian sublime takes man's body as its primary object and 'the measuring and measured unit of measure'. If, for Kant, 'that is sublime in comparison with which all else is small',[75] the presentation of its unpresentability by means of the colossal (which, as Derrida says playfully, 'if we were in a hurry, we'd translate this as: of the phallus which doubles the corpse', only to warn us that 'you must never be in a hurry when it's a matter of erection'), points to its dependence on nature. '[N]ever be in a hurry when it's a matter of erection, let the thing happen'.[76] Sacrificed to the superelevation of the moral law, nature retains ultimate power over its erection. This is probably why 'In Kant's examples, this relationship of body to body is one of body to stone. Even before the colossal rises up, and you already sense that it will be of stone, stony, petrified or petrifying'.[77]

But why does the principle of morals need such an impenetrable protection? What if the negative pleasure of the sublime were not to be ultimately superseded by the seriousness of the law? What if we were to replace the solidity of the stone colossus with the bodily folds which permanently touch each other? What if, finally, the calculation of the facultary economy was to allow for the inflow of the economy of desire? Would this create a means of bringing about what Irigaray has called a 'fecund exchange between the sexes'?

In praise of moderation

I would like to postulate here that such a fecund exchange, ruled by the unruly logic of the ultimate spending of goodness, can be accomplished through what Derrida calls 'infinite love'.[78] As Derrida puts it, 'Only infinite love can renounce itself and, in order to become finite, become incarnated in order to love the other as a finite other. This gift of infinite love comes from someone and is addressed to someone; responsibility demands irreplaceable singularity.'[79] Derrida draws here on the Levinasian concept of an ethical relationship, whose singular character can be guaranteed by the irreducible transcendence of the absolutely Other. This 'ethics without foundations' proposed by Levinas is developed as an affective (i.e. pre-rational) response to the sudden arrival of the Other, whose alterity evokes wonder and respect. Love here signifies the special character of the encounter with otherness, suspended between grandeur and frailty, or pleasure and pain. Levinas acknowledges that 'Love aims at the Other; it aims at his frailty [*faiblesse*]',[80] but he also recognises the elevated, epiphanic character of the Other. This uncertain position of the Other, combined with the necessity of infinite spending that the encounter requires, determines the sublime character of the loving relationship.

Burke does not demonstrate similar courage in his sublime adventures, nor does he share Levinas's desire for proximity to the source of his tumultuous passions. He is aware that the bewilderment the self experiences when facing the infinitely great threatens its stable positioning. However, fear can be diminished by the self's conscious action. Placing themselves 'at certain distances'[81] or introducing 'certain modifications' – whose character Burke does not quite specify – humans are able to exert special power over both their emotions and the outside world. The development of wonder and astonishment is thus prevented, as such uncontrollable passions could bring us to the verge of danger and death. Instead, Burke concentrates on the overcoming of danger and the ultimate triumph of the self. '[W]hen we *recover our health*, when we *escape an imminent danger*, is it with joy that we are affected? The sense on these occasions is far from that smooth and voluptuous satisfaction which the assured prospect of pleasure bestows. The delight which arises from *the modifications of pain*, confesses the stock from whence it sprung, in its solid, strong, and severe nature.'[82]

In *The Theory of Moral Sentiments*, published two years after Burke's *Inquiry* (1759), Adam Smith advises similar moderation in the way emotions ought to be experienced and manifested. 'It gives us spleen ... to see another too happy, or too much elevated, as we call it, with any little piece of good fortune. We are disobliged even with his joy; and, because we cannot go along with it, call it levity and folly. We are even put out of humour if our companion laughs louder or longer at a joke than we think it deserves; that is, than we feel that we ourselves could laugh at it.'[83] Smith's faith in the objectivity and stability of the self's position, which allows the self to judge unerringly, is typical of the Enlightenment theories of both the individual and society. Smith and Burke were active politicians, so their interest in man's flamboyant feelings was closely linked with their understanding of his role in the social organism, an organism which was significantly perturbed and unstable during the revolutionary period. Just as the tumult of political transformations was to result in the stability of the state, the upheavals the individual experienced eventually led to the emergence of a coherent, better self: morally and emotionally sane and politically conscious. That is why Burke and Smith allowed no room for excess on either the individual or the social level. Though wonder combined with surprise and admiration was for Smith one of the most important passions, the rule of propriety was to prevent it from spinning out of control.

This logic works along the lines of Aristotle's rule of the mean: passions that are too strong need moderation, presented as a return from the position of uncertainty to what is familiar, solid and safe. As Alasdair MacIntyre concludes in *A Short History of Ethics*, 'For the love of the person, as against the goodness, pleasantness, or usefulness of the person, Aristotle can have no place'.[84]

Love as a hyperbole of friendship

Aristotle's ethical theory, which has to a large extent shaped Western concepts of goodness and duty, is based on the expulsion of affect. And even though the friendship (*philia*) he recommends as the most perfect relationship between humans is contrasted with the selfishness and uselessness of love (*eros*), I intend to demonstrate that the two remain inseparable in Aristotelian ethical tradition. Exploring the tension between friendship and love in this tradition, I will postulate that the irresolvable character of this tension can be analysed through the concept of the sublime. This will lead me to define a singular loving encounter – situated at the crossroads between *philia* and *eros* – as a paradigm for the ethics of the feminine sublime. But it is not my intention to merely enact a shift from the Aristotelian concept of friendship to a vague, ahistorical notion of love. The loving encounter I discuss in the context of the feminine sublime will be developed precisely from a tradition of friendship, which – for the reasons I will expound below – has expelled this love and turned it to its opposite.

Analysing the ethical character of an encounter with infinite otherness, I will yet again part ways with Levinas, whose ethical theory has inspired my ethics of the feminine sublime. It strikes me that Levinas seems baffled by the excess of love he encounters, and thus has to reduce it to the manageable figures of control: frail femininity; the passivity of the female Beloved; eroticism perceived as the negation of ethics; and parenthood seen as the culmination of fecundity. In my discussion of love and friendship, I want to draw special attention to the logic of calculation and moderation which accompany these two notions in the Western tradition. My reading of the feminine sublime as an amorous relation thus responds to the idea of love as described by Plato and Aristotle, and later developed by a number of other philosophers. This is a very specific tradition, which accompanies the development of the discourse of friendship, or *philia*, in Western philosophy.

My investigation can be seen as a speculation on Derrida's project carried out in his *Politics of Friendship*. Following Derrida's argument, I want to focus on the encounter between the discourses of friendship and love in Aristotle's ethical theory, and their relation to the figures of proportion and excess. I intend to demonstrate that love has served as the silenced 'other' of this discourse of friendship, produced alongside the more elevated *philia* in order to visualise the discrepancy between the desirable and the unwanted. The reason this retracing of the Aristotelian tradition of friendship is important from a feminist point of view is that, as Derrida notices, 'the figure of the friend, so regularly coming back on stage with the features of the *brother* ... seems spontaneously to belong to a *familial, fraternalist* and thus *androcentric* configuration of politics'.[85] And if, as I argued earlier, the aesthetics of the sublime always already has ethical and political implications, the ethics of the feminine sublime needs to address the fraternalist tradition that has shaped our understanding of the concepts of ethics and politics. This investigation of the brotherly-masculinist aspect of this tradition will, in turn, allow me to rethink the rigidity of the gender-exclusive concepts of politics and ethics.

The notion of *eros* I am using here can be linked to the idea of *philia*, which was developed in Plato and Aristotle, and since then has been presented as both friendship's excess and overcoming. It is worth noticing that the fraternal tradition of friendship relies for its coherence and continuation on what Derrida calls 'the double exclusion of femininity' from its premises. And yet it is not the aim of my project to open friendship to women, since friendship itself, to retain its status of friendship, needs this very exclusion and the resulting protection of the male lineage. Instead, I propose to look under the protective veil of friendship – or perhaps just peer through the uneven threadwork of its texture – which has been imposed by certain philosophers, in order to explore the source of their anxiety.

Before I go any further with my investigations, I should acknowledge that I am aware of Derrida's attempt to address 'the woman question', or rather the absence of this question, from the tradition of *philia*. Developing the technique he applied in *The Gift of Death*, when discussing the masculinisation of the logic of the sacrifice as enacted by Abraham, Derrida spins a network of questions concerning the absence of 'woman' or 'sister' from the paradigm of friendship. However, he leaves all these questions in suspense, as if unable or unwilling to proceed any further. And yet, by withholding the answer, Derrida may be performing a political act of posing femininity *as a question*, both present in its challenge to the previous certainties and non-present in its withdrawal of ultimate answers. I would not like to discredit this gift made towards 'woman' and women, since I am conscious of the uncomfortable position of the speaker 'for' and 'in the name' of women that Derrida certainly wants to avoid. But I would like to take over the multiple threads he has left untangled in various places and weave my own reading of the tradition of *philia*, which will allow me to question the restrictive gendering of friendship.

Traditionally, fraternal friendship had to remain exclusive. The expulsion of alterity and the silencing of sexual difference constituted its very premises. The democratic tradition of 'freedom, equality, fraternity' did not recognise femininity as difference, but rather translated it into sameness, which allowed for the establishment of a 'fraternity'. In political declarations based on the democratic ideal there was room for a sister as long as she was exactly like a brother, and nothing else than a brother. Aware of the exclusivity of this version of politics and democracy, in *Politics of Friendship* Derrida remained faithful to the brotherly tradition. Clearly, Derrida chose to write a book on friendship, representing a particular tradition of thought and posing certain unavoidable questions concerning that tradition. It is as much as he could, or perhaps wanted to do, maybe for the sake of friendship itself which needed this very weakening if it was still to be perceived as an ethico-political option.

It is significant that a certain anxiety about the precarious nature of friendship is visible in the discourse of its constructors, from Aristotle, through Bacon, Montaigne and Nietzsche, among others, to Derrida. Aristotle's ethics is based on the rule of the mean: happiness as the highest good is assured by virtue, which is situated between the extremes of excess and deficiency. Pathos, defined as the intensity of emotion, is considered a vice, and cannot provide happiness. Instead, Aristotle considers friendship (*philia*), described as 'some sort of excellence or virtue ... indispensable for life',[86] to be an ideal relationship between people.

In the *Nicomachean Ethics* Aristotle postulates the need for proportion, emphasising the importance of reciprocity and equal exchange between friends. '[E]ach partner receives in all matters what he gives the other, in the same or in a similar form.'[87] 'Thus, each partner both loves his own good and makes an equal return in the good he wishes for his partner and in the pleasure he gives him.'[88] 'In sum, the friendships we have so far discussed are based on equality; both partners receive and wish the same thing from and for one another, for instance, pleasure for material advantage.'[89] Such a relationship is based on the logic of symbolic exchange, where loss is turned into profit and excess is annulled. Both partners bring exactly the same amount into this transaction, which, according to Derrida's reading of the gift, cannot be called *presenting* each other with friendship, but rather can only be described as a trade. The self knows what the other will offer, but the other's expenditure will always be balanced with the self's gift. Embarking upon this exchange of virtue, both sides make sure that no risk is involved. The *Nicomachean Ethics* implies the presence of an external rule, embodied in the form of the highest good, which regulates such encounters and guarantees justice. Purified from the threat of risk, friendship is characterised here by stability. Aristotle contrasts it with affection, which 'resembles an emotion, while friendship is rather a characteristic or lasting attitude'.[90]

Aristotle goes to great lengths to draw attention to the element of proportion in friendship, which saves it from turning into something unpredictable and dangerous. Its potential excess is perceived as disturbing: it therefore needs to be excluded by imposing rules and regulations on the etiquette of *philia*. But Aristotle's dialogue on friendship starts, interestingly, 'at the crossing of who knows how many *passages, routes or aporias* with love'.[91] Indeed, for Aristotle, 'being in love means to have something like *an excess of friendship*'.[92] As Derrida observes,

> The *Eudemian Ethics*, for example, inscribes friendship, knowledge and death, but also survival, from the start, in a single, *selfsame* configuration. The same here is none other than the other. It has at least the figure of the other. The necessary *consequence* of this strange configuration is an opportunity for thought. Beyond all ulterior frontiers between love and friendship, but also between the passive and active voices, between the loving and the being-loved, what is at stake is 'lovence' [*aimance*].[93]

Friendship is thus not differentiated from love by some *natural law* that would ascribe harmony and proportion to the former and disruption to the latter. On the contrary, in order to be retained as friendship, and not to be confused with its dangerous neighbour *eros, philia* needs the invention of *social rules* which will shelter it from its voluptuous other. It needs to be enveloped in a protective veil of silence, which amounts to acknowledging its fragility. Recognising the mechanism applied by more or less faithful practitioners of the Aristotelian tradition of *philia*, Nietzsche – one of the 'brothers' Derrida engages with in his *Politics of Friendship* – admits that the truth of friendship is its illusion, 'for such human relationships almost always depend upon the fact that two or three things are never said or even so much as touched upon: if these little boulders do start to roll, however, friendship follows after them and shatters'.[94] This is perhaps why both Nietzsche and Derrida are so protective about friendship. Recognising the importance of this silence practised through centuries, both philosophers understand the precarious, but also precious, nature of friendship. As a consequence of this realisation, they resort to repression and silence, allegedly for friendship's own good. We are thus left with two questions: What do these philosophers really know about friendship to feel so strong a need to protect it at all cost? And what is it exactly that friendship needs protection from? As Derrida concludes:

> Friendship does not keep silence, it is preserved by silence. From its first word to itself, friendship inverts itself. Hence it says, saying this to itself, that there are no more friends; it avows itself in avowing that. Friendship tells the truth – and *this is always better left unknown*. The protection of this custody guarantees the truth of friendship, its ambiguous truth, that by which friends protect themselves from the

error or the illusion on which friendship is founded – more precisely, the bottomless bottom founding a friendship, which enables it to resist its own abyss. *To resist the vertigo or the revolution that would have it turning around itself.* Friendship is founded, in truth, *so as to protect itself from the bottom, or the abyssal bottomless depths.*[95]

Friendship is here positioned on a liminal territory, quivering from repressed excitement and unfulfilled desire. Suspended between the economy of the gift which does not calculate gains and losses and the practicality of instrumental reason, friendship suffers from the contortions of the unspoken. The silence advocated by its practitioners is never an absolute silence, but, as Derrida suggests, an implied silence: 'This is nothing other than a certain way of speaking: secret, discontinuous, aphoristic, elliptic, just in disjointed time to avow the truth that must be concealed; hiding it – because it is deadly – to save life'.[96] The aporias of non-speech can be a germinating ground for the seeds of passion, which cause an eruption in the discursive surface the Aristotelian tradition has constructed. And yet, as Wesling and Sławek notice, not only is the minimally articulate (which borders on silence) 'marked by a certain lack of loyalty to itself, but also by excess: it has to overflow, exceed, its own sphere to become known, signalled, indicated'.[97] This linguistic earthquake can be easily extended to the territory of the other's body, which will not be able to house and suppress the Great Mystery of friendship's illusion. We enter here the forbidden, or rather forgotten, territory of the interlacing between the friendly and the corporeal. Invented and supported by the fraternal guild, friendship has relied on the expulsion of the body, and constructed itself in opposition to *eros*. By addressing this anxiety which underlies friendship's stability, we expose friendship to the 'abysmal bottomless depths' it has tried to avoid. Faced with the realm of the bodily, friendship is confronted with sexual difference, which can be a source of fearsome vertigo.

This vertiginous experience results from the elevated position friendship has been awarded by its legislators. Placed amidst starry skies and mountain peaks, it has refused to look down on what it ousted below. 'In antiquity the feeling of friendship was considered the highest feeling, even higher than the most celebrated pride of the self-sufficient sage.'[98] Ushered to unattainable heights, spiritual friendship was constructed in opposition to the lowlands and badlands of the everyday. To retain its spiritual character, friendship has tended to rely on the closure and 'sealing' of the body. This has led to the elaboration of the concept of 'friendship without proximity', a concept which, nevertheless, does not exclude closeness. The need for distance which has been advocated in friendship[99] may have resulted from a fear of being annihilated by possessive desire, something Nietzsche has associated with what he demeaningly called the 'things people call love'.[100] Shunning the excess of affection and denying the insatiable hunger for physical and emotional consummation, the legislators of the filial tradition have resorted to distance. But, surprisingly, this distance is constantly interrupted by insurgent acts of reaching for the otherness of the other, which may eventually lead to immersion and loss. As Aristotle claims, an ideal friendship amounts to an achievement of 'one soul in two bodies' – a bizarre communion of the physical and the spiritual. Sentenced to this constant fluctuation between the closeness of the other's home and the need to remain a stranger to it, *philia* reveals its uncanny side. '"Good friendship"', explains Derrida in his reading of Nietzsche, 'certainly supposes a certain air, a certain tinge (*Anstrich*) of intimacy, but one "without actual and genuine intimacy". It commands that we abstain "wisely", "prudently" (*weislich*), from all confusion, all permutation between the singularities of you and me.'[101]

Freud's concept of the uncanny, embracing the contradictory meanings of 'being at home' and 'being a stranger to the home', is a useful figure for the investigation of friendship. Rejoicing in the homeliness of the other's dwelling – which is evocative of the primal unity with the envelope of the mother's body – one also has to maintain a distance, and difference, between one's abode and that of one's friend. Friendship thus presents itself as an impossible task of longing for the home of the other, a task relating to the memory of that home, but also to its intrinsic otherness which can never be domesticated. Derrida is aware of this paradox when he explains that

> the friend is the friend of what he desires, but if he can desire only that which he lacks, and if what is lacking can only be that of which he has been deprived (that which has been taken away), then one must indeed imagine that before this feeling of privation, and precisely in order to experience it, friendship (*philia*), *qua eros* and *epithumia*, must indeed be found to be linked to what is proper, suitable, appropriate and familiar (*oikeios*) to it.[102]

Friendship always looks both towards the past and the future, trying to recuperate what it has lost. The forgotten familiarity of the past turns the present moment into a spectre, haunting those who try to reenact the lost closeness in the aporia of the current moment.

The gift of friendship, offered without an expectation of reciprocity, attacks this circular economy of returning home. This marks a departure from Aristotle's proportionate version of *philia*, though it is worth mentioning here that Derrida notices some contradictions in Aristotle's logic of proportion.[103] Derrida's reading of Aristotle opens the uncanny ambiguity of friendship to two important issues: *epithumia* (desire) and *eros*. The lack experienced by a friend presupposes his prior possession of the knowledge about what he is now missing. But this story of past closeness is characterised by a certain sterility, resulting from the exclusion of the corporeal from the concept of *philia*. In this way, the home/hearth of the other is rendered a purely social and political concept. Rather than correspond to the envelope of the other's body, both protecting and connecting him to the surrounding world, this a-physical notion of home prevents bodily encounters from taking place under the aegis of *philia*. The total dis-eroticisation of the uncanny, corresponding to the 'forgetting' of sexual difference, produces the very (im)possibility of fraternal friendship.

'Love, if there is such a thing, if there were such a thing'

Irigaray's ethics of respect for sexual difference poses a challenge to the impasse created by the fraternal practice of exclusion. By defending the identity of a woman lover, who should not be treated as a mere receptacle for the seed of male affection, Irigaray dreams of a different economy, one that could regulate the spending of affect. 'The beloved woman's face illuminates the secret that the male lover touches on. Shining with a new light, bathed in a horizon that goes beyond intention, her face expresses what is hidden without disposing of it in a meaning. It is full of what cannot be said but is not nothing – thanks to the already and the not yet.'[104] The encounter between the one and the other is governed by the unpresentable, because both parties bring to the encounter an irreducible alterity which cannot be ultimately grasped. The other's arrival can therefore evoke wonder, which Lyotard perceives as the self's rejoicing at the fact that unpresentability does not amount to vacuum. Rather, it can be acknowledged and ascertained in presentation itself: 'Here and now there is this painting [which, in this context, I allow myself to interpret as the representation, reflection or icon of the other's face, given that Lyotard's concept of the sublime extends from the aesthetics of high art to the politics of everyday life – J.Z.], rather than nothing, and that's what is sublime.'[105] The appearance of the other is a presentation, 'but it presents nothing; it is, that is, presence.'[106] In the feminine sublime, the self is constantly surprised by the arrival of the other, who in certain aspects resembles the self, but who is also irreducibly different. There can be no absolute certainty regarding this arrival. The event of meeting the other can only be a temporary flicker, a touch or a caress, which will leave some imprints on the memory, but which will not fossilise into the monument of love.

The feminine sublime can thus redefine power relations by affirming the inscrutable alterity of *both* parties involved. It inscribes their encounter in the affective framework, which excludes pre-calculated equality and mastery. Born at the interstices of love and friendship, it responds to the call of what Derrida terms 'lovence', i.e. a dissymmetrical act of loving the friend before finding out about his or her reciprocity. In this way, the feminine sublime opens itself to the affect expelled from the proportionate exchange of the patriarchal order. Drawing on the principle of hospitality which underlies the economy of the gift, the ethics of the feminine sublime is justified by amorous acts of infinite spending. However, it has to be emphasised once again that love should not be seen here as a cultural universal, but rather as an intrusion of the principle of hospitality into the fraternal discourse of friendship. As Derrida concludes, 'The suspensive modality of the possible, which seems to cause the "epoche" of a declaration of love, signifies maybe that love can belong only to the order of faith or testimony, not at all to that of proof or certainty. Neither knowledge nor assurance, only a "love, if there is such a thing, if there were such a thing – I would love you, because I love you"'.[107]

The sexuate ethics of respect for the alterity of the other demands the suspension of a desire to rule over otherness, which is to save 'lovence' from closure. The amorous encounter does not take place only once, but is in the constant process of occurring. As Irigaray states, 'The act of love is neither an explosion nor an implosion but an indwelling. Dwelling with the self, and with the other – while letting the other go. ... Which will always remain on the threshold, even after entering into the house'.[108] This permanent undecidability distinguishes 'lovence' from the humanist project of love. This allows me to conceptualise 'love' beyond patriarchal reciprocity, which needs to control and legislate affection and fecundity. 'Lovence' does not rule out the possibility of marriage or childbirth, but neither does it perceive them as its necessary conditions or its markers of validity. Kant's objectifying idea of marriage as mutual possession has to be seen as defying the ethical responsibility towards the alterity of the other. This is why Sylviane Agacinski is baffled by Kant's perception of 'amorous engagements'. She confesses:

> I admit that I am not able to understand very well exactly how the reciprocity of possession, the fact that the two spouses are things in each other's eyes according to a rigorous reciprocity guaranteed by a contract, can restore their personality. This would rather resemble a sort of mutual disrespect and a possible unleashing of a reciprocal and legal hold over one another. The experience of the commitment of those who are in love [*l'engagement amoreux*] could suggest something else: rather than a double mastery or hold over each other, it could be a shared weakness.[109]

The experience of shared weakness excludes mastery and ensures the recognition of lack and alterity in every 'amorous engagement'. Teleology thus gives way to instantaneousness, as 'amorous engagements', built from disparate singular events, cannot be neatly arranged into a coherent 'love story'. Love as longing for the original envelope is re-enacted in numerous visits to the homes of one's lovers. For these visits to remain ethical and not to result in frustration or disappointment, one should not forget that the other is not the mother, and that the closure and security of the primary home cannot be recuperated. The *unheimlich*/uncanny is then the most personal experience, which should teach one respect for the ungraspable difference of the other. Fascinated with the idea of the infinite differentiation of identity, Cixous stresses the temporariness of both the self and its relationship with the other:

> I will never say often enough that the difference is not one, that there is never one without the other, and that the charm of difference (beginning with sexual difference) is that it passes. It crosses through us, like a goddess. We cannot capture it. It makes us teeter with emotion. It is in this living agitation that there is always room for you in me, your presence and your place. I is never an individual. I is haunted. I is always, before knowing anything, an I-love-you.[110]

There is always a danger that indwelling in the other could turn into a desire to occupy and subjugate the foreign land. And yet one has to remember that an invitation to the house of the other is a gift. An act of violence would be a threat to 'lovence', which does not mean that it is better to leave the house safely locked. The haunted I must risk numerous encounters: if the door of the house is not left open in the gesture of both esteem for the alterity of the other and trust, the amorous ethics of respect will be replaced by the pragmatism of a self-contained ego.

Eros Pteros: blinded by love

[I]t is impossible to love and to be wise. (Francis Bacon, 'On Love')

Doubly encoded as madness and wisdom, love fluctuates in Plato's *Phaedrus* between these opposite poles. After Socrates's re-evaluation of madness as originating from the divine source, Lysias's arguments against the excess of affection are put in question. But the contest between the two rhetors is more than just an exercise in presenting contradictory opinions: when the debate develops,[111] it turns out that the terms used in the debate have been defined differently by its participants. Rather than aim at proving how wrong Lysias has been in his negative evaluation of love, Socrates undermines his understanding of what love *is*. Lysias presents love in economic terms as a sum of gains and losses. '[L]overs bring into account not only the kindnesses they have shown but also the losses they have incurred in their own affairs on account of their passion, and when they add to this the trouble they have undergone they consider that the debt they owe to their favourites has been discharged long ago.'[112] He is aware of the danger such an exchange inheres, as the invested capital may never be reciprocated. We should remember that this insistence on mutuality and proportion will be later maintained by Aristotle. Lysias's declaration, '[T]he truth may be that it is not the most insistent that you should favour, but those best able to make a return',[113] could have been used by Aristotle in his defence of friendship as compared with the excess of affection. Accepting the provisionality of an amorous relationship and the risk of losing more than one has invested for Plato does not agree with a virtuous man's desire for mastery, which he would like to retain over himself and his friends. The loss of control must then be evil and should be avoided. As Lysias asserts,

> The conviction which impels us towards excellence is rational, and the power by which it masters us we call self-control; the desire which drags us towards pleasure is irrational, and when it gets the upper

hand in us its dominion is called excess. Excess has many categories and takes many forms and goes by a variety of names. Whichever of these forms is most in evidence confers upon its possessor its own peculiar name, an acquisition which is far from being honourable or valuable.[114]

In response to Lysias's doubts, Socrates conjures up Eros Pteros, a feathery god of love. He defines love as a regrowth of the wings of the soul, which signifies a movement from proportion to excess. The imagery of swelling and overgrowth prevails in his depiction of the changes love causes: 'As the nourishing moisture falls upon it the stump of each feather under the whole surface of the soul swells and strives to grow for its root. ... So now it is all in a state of ferment and throbbing'.[115] Along with love comes chaos, which erases the soul's self-complacency and exposes it to the danger of collapse. The spatiality of the world in which love reigns is incessantly transformed, and this transformation happens in the atmosphere of fervour, disorder and threat. The struggle against the tightness of the soul is arduous, and cannot be alleviated by the promise of the soul's closure and healing. Love for Socrates, then, is inextricably intertwined with physical pain, but this pain can be soothed by the pleasure resulting from the remembrance of the beloved's beauty. Striving for beauty does not present itself as an easy task. It requires immersion in one's physicality and leads, as a result, to bodily suffering:

> In this state of *mingled pleasure and pain* the sufferer is *perplexed by the strangeness of his experience* and struggles helplessly; *in his frenzy* he cannot sleep at night or remain still by day, but his longing drives him wherever he thinks that he may see the possessor of beauty. When he sees him and his soul is refreshed by *the flood of emanations* the closed passages are unstopped; he obtains a respite from his pains and pangs, and there is nothing to equal the sweetness of the pleasure which he *enjoys for the moment*.[116]

The attainment of love – depicted here as a search for beauty – is always temporary and cannot be taken for granted. As Plato indicates, the lover is driven wherever he 'thinks he may see the possessor of beauty', which indicates the uncertainty and impermanence of the amorous quest. The feelings beauty evokes in the lover are always contradictory. Suspended between pleasure and pain, but still ready to risk immersion in the floods of affection, *ego affectus est* is also *ego furioso*, preferring the madness of love to the moderation of detachment. Plato's beauty does not guarantee satisfaction; on the contrary, it produces turmoil and confusion, transporting imagination to the level where the idea of the lover exceeds all that can be thought about him or her. This incommensurability of affect and thought is both disconcerting and pleasing.

Though Plato opposes the pursuit of wisdom with the pursuit of love, the latter is also motivated by the desire for knowledge. Not only does it lead one towards the cognition of his or her beloved, which is to provide intellectual satisfaction, but it also promises corporeal pleasure. The quest for love can thus be seen as a sexuate form of the search for wisdom, which Plato wants to purify from the desire 'to see, to touch, to kiss [the lover], and to share his bed'.[117] This is what in Tadeusz Rachwał and Tadeusz Sławek's book, *Representations of the Erotic*, is described as 'the wisdom of desire', which lacks the permanence of the traditional body of knowledge. The wisdom of desire is a mere flicker, situated between darkness and light. As Rachwał and Sławek argue, 'When we speak about the blindness of love, we remember this necessary lack of vision which constitutes the wisdom of desire, a radical dim-sightedness which does not deprive one of vision and knowledge but, on the contrary, makes them possible. Love tactics is out of necessity what Derrida describes as *tactique aveugle*, "a strategy without finality"'.[118]

To be able to see, one needs to go blind. However, visual perception does not signify here preconditioned seeing, which is focused on selected objects, but rather one's self-exposure to unlimited light that will delineate one's perceptive horizon. Love thus requires the suspension of the position of the seer/sire. Only then can one gain access to the unlimited residues of Eros, deposited in the space between poverty and expenditure.[119] Such a dubious positioning does not ascertain profit, as the logic of the gift of love requires the abandonment of one's hope for enrichment. In 'Plato's Pharmacy' Derrida exposes the ambiguous character of Plato's concept of the gift (*pharmakon*), which signifies both a cure and a poison. The gift of love therefore presents itself as simultaneously curative and wounding. Janus-faced Eros, the dispenser of amorous gifts, is both a healer and a killer, poisoning one's senses with the illness of love, but also soothing the pain evoked.

Love as a problem of sight

As we can see, love is thus not only a problem of knowledge but also of sight. Though, on the one hand, Plato insists on a radical separation between the two ('For sight is the keenest of our physical senses, though it does not bring us knowledge'),[120] he also emphasises the role of sight in the cognition of ideal forms:

> [T]he newly initiated, who has had a full sight of the celestial vision [who is in the possession of knowledge about divinity? – J.Z.], when he beholds a god-like face or a physical form which truly reflects ideal beauty, first of all shivers and experiences something of the dread which the vision itself inspired; next he gazes upon it and worships it as if it were a god, and, if he were not afraid of being thought an utter madman, he would sacrifice to his beloved as to the image of a divinity. Then, as you would expect after a cold fit, his condition changes and he falls into an unaccustomed sweat; he receives through his eyes the emanation of beauty, by which the soul's plumage is fostered, and grows hot.[121]

Plato's distinction is based on his opposition between ideal forms and their copies, the former belonging to the realm of truth, the latter merely depicting its distortion. As perception is always already stained with delusion, Plato does not accept the momentary cognition of the lover's beauty as the core of divine wisdom, which is for him immutable and perfect. Blindness, in turn, seems to be a natural human condition. This is why people need Eros the philosopher, who will turn their gaze towards heaven, rather than Eros the poet, who will only perpetuate false images and mere reflections of perfection. 'Beauty, as we were saying, shone bright in the world above, and here too it still gleams clearest',[122] concludes Plato. Too strong a light may lead to temporary blindness, resulting here from the *excess* of light rather than its lack. Turning their gaze towards divinities, mortals put themselves at the risk of seeing too much. This is the price they must pay to experience the transformation and transport of love. Motivated by the promise of the 'emanation of beauty' and 'the sweetness of pleasure', they overcome the shivering and 'the dread which the vision itself inspires' for the sake of partaking of the immense residues of satisfaction. And yet the excess of a good thing, emitting too strong a light to be endured by the human eyes, turns the marriage between divinity and mortality into an unattainable fantasy. In Plato, the sexuate encounter with the alterity of the other can only be a flicker, a counter-rational and unlawful glance smuggled to the outer world, always threatened with the possibility of losing sight, or getting lost in the abyss.

Feminism beyond the gaze

Woman takes pleasure more from touching than from looking, and her entry into a dominant scopic economy signifies, again, her consignment to passivity: she is to be the beautiful object of contemplation. While her body finds itself thus eroticised, and called to a double movement of exhibition and of chaste retreat in order to stimulate the drives of the 'subject', her sexual organ represents *the horror of nothing to see*. A defect in this systematics of representation and desire. A 'hole' in its scoptophilic lens. It is already evident in Greek statuary that this nothing-to-see has to be excluded, rejected, from such a scene of representation. Woman's genitals are simply absent, masked, sewn back up inside their 'crack'. (Luce Irigaray, *This Sex Which Is Not One*)

The problem of sight has always been implicated in the discussions of the sublime. While Burke warns against 'look[ing] at anything as trifling, or contemptible, that may be dangerous',[123] in his *Critique of Judgement* Kant speaks about the 'astonishment amounting almost to terror, the awe and thrill of devout feeling, that takes hold of one when gazing upon the prospect of mountains ascending to heaven, deep ravines and torrents raging there, deep-shadowed solitudes that invite to brooding melancholy, and the like'.[124] The objects and phenomena described as sublime disrupt the peace of mind by defying sensual perception (though in Kant especially this categorisation is not clear, as he tends to situate the source of sublimity both in the inner feelings of the observer and in the external objects themselves).

Burke and Kant's privileging of sight in cognition is characteristic of Enlightenment ocularcentrism, which establishes vision as what Martin Jay calls 'the dominant scopic regime of the modern era'. Having embraced the ocularcentric perspective, the modern self relies for perception on 'the unblinking eye of the fixed gaze rather than the fleeting glance'.[125] The failure of the eye is 'naturally' excluded from the prescribed continuous observation, which is conducted by the immobile organ of sight. This infallible human eye is modelled upon the eye of providence. It is therefore not surprising that perception must involve success, defined as a complete and undistorted registration of external reality on the retina. If sight is inextricably linked with success, that is with the possibility – as well as necessity – of seeing something, rather than nothing, the sublime can stand for the underlying inadequacy that affects the bearer of the Enlightenment legacy. It is the site of the failure of the ocularcentric project.

One can find multiple solutions to this potential failure which threatens vision. Burke, for example, draws satisfaction from a belief that 'When we know the full extent of any danger, when we can accustom our eyes to it, a great deal of the apprehension vanishes'.[126] 'The terrible uncertainty' is clarified when the eyes accommodate themselves to obscurity and are able to distinguish some details in what seemed impenetrable and thus frightening. Though Burke feels safer in lightness, which can under certain circumstances *become* sublime, he privileges darkness as a true source of sublimity. The opposition between the two does not, however, seem tenable, as Burke understands them as only functions of the eye. Exposed to darkness, the eye eventually manages to overcome the terror of the dark and adjust to – or discover – lightness. Significantly, light, 'which by its very excess is converted into a species of darkness',[127] can threaten with blindness as much as darkness can. If perception and sublimity depend on the behaviour of the eye, the contrasting terms turn out to be overlapping. Burke is particularly interested in the actual moment of transgression, when the two extremes meet, producing a dazzling spectacle: 'A quick transition from light to darkness, or from darkness to light, has yet a greater effect.'[128] Even though the eye has no time to get used to the changing scene, the pain of its strained muscles can be soothed by the pleasure of watching the volatile spectacle.

The sublime thus challenges the mastering fixed gaze by imposing upon the viewer the uncertainty of the fleeting glance. By revealing the porous nature of the gaze itself – stained with the possibility of the blind spot, with the exertion of the eye quickly strained in its motionless stare, and with the danger of non-exact representation – the mobile glance does not fear error. Contrarily, blindness and distortion are its very premises, allowing for the mysterious performance of instability happening between subsequent blinks.

The ethics of the feminine sublime I develop here challenges the gaze, with its rigid active/passive dichotomy, as a principle of its relation to alterity. In her celebrated essay, 'Visual Pleasure and Narrative Cinema', Laura Mulvey reveals a patriarchal bias embedded in the concept of the gaze. 'In a world ordered by sexual imbalance, pleasure in looking has been split between active/male and passive/female. The determining male gaze projects its fantasy onto the female figure, which is styled accordingly.'[129] Woman is seen here as a frozen image of the castrated other, which positions her as inferior to Man, but her implied castration also poses a threat to his completeness. Reducing her to the category of an object fixated as the erotic basis of the voyeur's pleasure wards off men's implied insecurity. As Irigaray notices, woman 'is to be the beautiful object of contemplation'.[130] Significantly, Burke uses the female body as the foundation for his description of beauty, which he contrasts against sublimity:

> Observe that part of a beautiful woman where she is perhaps the most beautiful, about the neck and breasts; the smoothness; the softness; the easy and insensible swell; the variety of the surface, which is never for the smallest space the same; the deceitful maze, through which the unsteady eye slides giddily, without knowing where to fix, or whither it is carried.[131]

And yet uncertainty creeps into Burke's discourse on beauty, as the female body fails to provide a secure grounding for the masculine aesthetics of dominance. Analysing the dizziness that is produced in Burke by the sight of the feminine body, Freeman accounts for his scopophilia and the difficulty of its gratification in the following way: 'The absence of a fixed point of view or visual focus produces disorientation; unlike the male, the beautiful female body defeats our expectation of a centre and instead becomes the occasion of a giddiness, or vertigo'.[132] The gaze promoted by Burke is a sign of both repression and oppression. It introduces sexual subjugation as a way of exerting power over the threatening, a mechanism to be observed in the traditional aesthetics of the sublime. This is why the *feminine* sublime I am working with, which is to be seen as an ethics of respect towards the other, must transcend the immobility of the gaze and the distance it implies. It needs to divert the one-sidedness of the look which, traditionally, always returns to the gazer. 'But how realisable is such a renegotiation in everyday life?', asks Kaja Silverman in *The Threshold of the Visible World*. Although Silverman does not assure us about the inherent success of such an ethical project, she insists that we should not feel exempt from the responsibility of trying to renegotiate the relation between the ego and the object:

> No look can extricate itself in any absolute way from the snares of the self. It can only work ceaselessly, with that all-too-limited knowledge to which consciousness has access, to undo the projections through which it rids itself of lack, and the incorporations through which it arrogates to itself what does not belong to it. Over and over, this struggle will end in failure, or, at most, partial and transitory success. However, the impossibility of ever finally achieving these goals does

not liberate us from the ethical necessity of renewing the project of which they are a part every time it fails.[133]

The feminine sublime as I understand it could opt for such a less fixating interaction, allowing for a form of a 'visual caress' which involves more than the eyes. Looking the other deep in the eyes does not result in getting to know her by sight since, by focusing on the abyss of the other's eyes, the observer remains blind to the other's corporeal aspect. As Derrida indicates in his *Memoirs of the Blind*, 'The staring eye always resembles an eye of the blind, sometimes the eye of the dead, at that precise moment when mourning begins: it is still open, a pious hand should soon come to close it; it would recall a portrait of the dying. ... [S]eeing the seeing and not the visible, it sees nothing. This seeing eye sees itself blind'.[134] Exposure to 'too much sight' is always threatened with the possibility of blindness: of seeing the abyss of seeing – which is reminiscent of Burkean *horror vacui* – rather than the presence of the other. If in its encounter with the other the self pursues the self-identity between seeing and knowing – to be detected, for example in the Latin etymology of *ver* (to know) and *vider* (to see) – it will have to deal with frustration resulting from the project's distortion and incompleteness. If, on the other hand, the amorous encounter is guided by the instantaneousness of the flicker, then nonpresence has to be accepted as a necessary component of the blink, which is different, nevertheless, form a phenomenological 'perfect' *Augenblick*. Derrida reminds us that 'There is a duration to the blink, and it closes the eye'.[135]

As the feminine sublime works along the principle which Derrida describes as 'catching a glimpse – or not',[136] the certainty of the encounter with the other is suspended. It is worth noticing that Burke associates similar uncertainty with the occurrence of the sublime event. There is always a possibility of nothing happening at all, but the lack of the ultimate guarantee does not release the self from the responsibility – or even possibility – of awaiting it. As both Plato and Burke observe, too much light can be as pernicious as total darkness and may result in the pain of the blinded eyes and the disappointment of the self. If some kind of failure is a necessary prerequisite of an encounter with the other, and if one can never be properly sheltered from blindness in the course of his or her amorous quest, the understanding of blindness itself invites transformation.

Choosing blindness

Rather than as a curse or punishment happening *a posteriori*, blindness may be perceived as a choice. This attitude may appeal to the subject who is aware of its limitations and does not desire mastery over the other. The ethics of blindness does not denigrate sight as opposed to the other senses, but rather creatively explores the crevices and gaps resulting from the imperfection of representation. This recognition of the blind spot of sight calls for its supplementation by other senses. Touch, for example, can focus the self's attention on the texture of the other's body and guide the hand in the direction of the intraceable curves of the silhouette which defies freezing by the self's gaze. Renouncing the triumphalism of ocularcentric philosophy, imperfect sight recoils back upon itself when dazzled by the greatness of the other. The origin of this greatness lies in alterity, towards which the ethical self is predisposed to adopt an attitude of positive bewilderment. As the mastering gaze can be easily punished by too radiant a lustre, the self that does not cherish a fantasy of its extraordinary positioning will suspend any desire to appropriate the difference.

Arriving before the other as a blind man/woman, one does not need to give up the willingness to know. But the wisdom of an amorous encounter is different from the enLIGHTened knowledge of the scopic regime, reducing the other to an object of perception. Instead, for a respectful encounter with the alterity of the other to take place, the wisdom of a seer is needed. It will be pointed inwards and suspended between lack (i.e. not seeing anything) and excess (i.e. having access to another dimension). Derrida writes in *Memoirs of the Blind*: 'The blind do not want to know, or rather, would like not to know: that is to say, not to see. *Idein, eidos, idea*: the whole history, the whole semantics of the European *idea*, in its Greek genealogy, as we know – as we see – relates seeing to knowing'.[137] However, Derrida does not reinstate the opposition between sight and idea on the one hand, and blindness combined with the rejection of a clear concept on the other. If sight is imperfect per se and always stained with error, blindness emerges as the only option that assures dignity in the face of the unpresentable. But blindness amounts to the renouncement of a desire for knowledge only in the sense of not relying on preconceived ideas of the other, which are the product of the mastering gaze. A blind person represents a desire for the alterity of the other, which is manifested in the gesture of his or her outstretched hands. This is an attitude of expectation, which obtains reassurance from an illogical belief that the awaited gift, or encounter, will happen. The open eyes would guarantee the purity of transaction: the exchange of goods could be properly evaluated, which would rule out potential cheating. Blindness, in turn, excludes the possibility of knowing the value of the other's gift. It does not even allow one to check whether the gift is going to happen at all and then prepare oneself for it.

The desiring self reveals its vulnerability. Derrida notices that the gesture of outstretched hands not only prevents one from falling but is also a reminder of the possibility of the fall. He states that 'the blind are beings of the fall, the manifestation always of that which threatens erection or the upright position'.[138] A blind person finds him- or herself on the verge of falling, and has to seek the other in order to ensure that the fall does not happen. The other's arrival is, nevertheless, a matter of individual responsibility rather than necessity. There is always a chance of *nothing* happening, which for Burke constitutes the greatest threat in the experience of the sublime. Suspended between falling to the ground and into the other's arms, the blind challenge the phallic logic of erection and oneness. The ethics of blindness inheres the possibility of detumescence, which poses a threat to elevation and vertical representation. 'The almost too large' of the colossal, which in Kant qualifies the presentation of a concept which is 'almost too large for any presentation' (and which, as Derrida playfully observes, 'if we were in a hurry', we would translate as 'the phallus which doubles the corpse')[139] is exposed to the possibility of failure: its wilting, collapse and annulment. The feminine sublime, encouraging us to peer through the veil which protects the self-defeating greatness of the colossal, proposes a faltering ethics, founded upon the uncertainty it poses before its potential followers. The horizontal gesture of the outstretched hands interrupts the phallicity of the symbolic exchange. Blindness, perceived here as a choice and not punishment or disaster, is more interested in the lowlands. Instead of concentrating on uprightness and centrality, it explores the commonplace, down-to-earth and everyday.

The celebration of blindness in the feminine sublime releases the abundant residues of sensuality in the sublime encounter. Sight gets dethroned from its privileged position: from now on it will have to accept its fallibility, which results from its 'flickering nature'. Its blind spots create the possibility of a different kind of seeing. Drawing the contours of the other's body with one's hand does not guarantee perfect cognition, but it may promise infinite pleasure for *both* sides, and not only the gratification of the greedy voyeur. Blindness is then sexuated, as it recognises the sexual difference of the meeting parties. Discussing the painter's attempt to capture his identity in the self-portrait, Derrida points to the difficulty, bordering on horror and madness, inherent in the perception of non-sexuated sameness:

> The one, the other, knows at least one thing: that he would never know how to be accessible as such, and especially not to knowledge, neither beforehand nor after. All symmetry is interrupted between him and himself, between him, the spectacle, and the spectator who he also is. There are now only spectres. In order to get out of this, it is necessary, at the very least, to share out the roles in the hetero-portrait, indeed in sexual difference.[140]

Freud has taught us that to love means to get to know somebody: it is thus not surprising that self-love should crumble if not supported by the reliable body of knowledge. For a solipsistic self, self-identity can neither be confirmed, as there is nothing against which the self could be mirrored, nor can it be absolutely denied. It is the arrival of the other that can save one from this horror of non-identity. Derrida confirms that it is through an encounter with sexual difference that the self finds solace. But the feminine sublime is not a permanent remedy for fragmented selves, as the encounters happening under its aegis are contingent and have a temporary character. However, a promise of seeing oneself in the mirror of the other's eyes and touching the difference through the veil of blindness can save the self from the sense of loneliness and loss. This loss will not be ultimately overcome, but an amorous encounter will at least lead to the sharing of this weakness with the other. Falling into the other's arms requires the amorous predisposition of what Derrida calls 'lovence', i.e. of opening towards the other, his or her corporeality and caress. Exploring the positionality of the English and French expression 'falling in love', Agacinski concludes that they both 'say the same thing: a fall is involved, or rather, the experience of weakness, through which existence would discover, or rediscover itself, in the mode of absence, the fact of its non-presence to itself'.[141]

Since the feminine sublime represents for me an ethics of respectful attitude towards difference and excess, I do not intend to restrict this excess by delineating strict conceptual boundaries within which this ethics can function. Every encounter adds a new story to the repertoire of the feminine sublime. An encounter with the other, guided by the ethics of the fleeting glance which necessarily incorporates blindness, rather than by the law of the fixating gaze, can be compared to an act of tracing, sketching, drawing or even writing. As the story of the feminine sublime can never be completed, I have to take recourse to illustrations, images and metaphors, which help me to find paths for the curvilinear meanings that refuse to be pinned down. This is why I want to refer again to Derrida's discussion of drawing/writing presented in his *Memoirs of the Blind*. Even though Derrida puts more emphasis on drawing, and sometimes clearly differentiates it from writing, in some other places the clear distinction between the two seems to collapse. In the Afterword to Cixous' *Rootprints* entitled 'Fourmis', *Lectures de la Différence Sexuelle*, Derrida argues that sexual difference can only be 'read, interpreted, deciphered and decoded', but not seen. I would therefore like to read his story of writing and otherness alongside Cixous' fable of writing and alterity, and to trace the possible contours of the space of the feminine sublime at the interstices of their texts.

Derrida writes:

> What happens when one writes without seeing? A hand of the blind ventures forth alone or disconnected, in a poorly delimited space; it feels its way, it gropes, it caresses as much as it inscribes, trusting in the memory of signs and supplementing sight. It is as if a lidless eye had opened at the tip of the fingers, as if one eye too many had just grown right next to the nail, a single eye, the eye of a cyclops or one-eyed man. This eye guides the tracing or outline [trace]; it is a miner's lamp at the point of writing, a curious and vigilant substitute, the prosthesis of a seer who is himself invisible. The image of the movement of these letters, of what this finger-eye inscribes, is thus sketched out within me. From the absolute withdrawal of an invisible centre or command post, a secret power insures from a distance a kind of synergy. It coordinates the possibilities of seeing, touching, and moving. And of hearing and understanding, for these are already words of the blind that I draw in this way.[142]

Cixous writes:

> Writing is working; being worked; questioning (in) the between (letting oneself be questioned) of same *and of* other without which nothing lives; undoing death's work by willing the togetherness of one-another, infinitely charged with a ceaseless exchange of one with another – not knowing one another and beginning again only from what is most distant, from self, from other, from the other within. A course that multiplies transformations by the thousands.

> And that is not done without danger, without pain, without loss –
> of moments of self, of consciousness, of persons one has been, goes
> beyond, leaves. It doesn't happen without expense – of sense, time,
> direction.[143]

Writing the story of the other can be understood as an attempt to trace one's own territory and acknowledge its separateness from the realm of the other's dwelling. Drawing the boundaries between itself and the other it wants to know/love, the self ventures into the darkness of the unknown. Maintaining this distance, it hopes for proximity, knowing that it will have to learn how to live with uncertainty and lack. The awareness of this paradox does not stop one from trying, that is from tracing the contours of the other's body with one's caressing hand: 'a hand of the blind ventures forth' to prevent one from the fall. Writing the story of the other does not rely on pre-calculated profit. Pain and loss are part of this enterprise, which to a capitalist investor may appear mad. But in the shadow of the feminine sublime the horror of the dark can be overcome. This horror is in fact emphasised by patriarchal thinking to propagate 'the infamous logic of antilove' and antinarcissism, which is founded upon the economy of proportion.

In *drawing the other* I *draw an ethical contract*, promising to tell the other my (horror) story and listen to theirs, and giving the surface of my body to the amorous inscription of the other's caress. The feminine sublime, recognising blindness as a sign of abandoning one's position of mastery, necessitates the prospect of the fall, and the spectre of death, as a guarantee of the singularity of the event and the promise of respect. The feminine sublime happens at the interstices of death, but it is not a funereal ethics: when provisionality and finality are accepted, the picture of a more meaningful and wiser event can be drawn.

Notes

1 The title for this section comes from Wittgenstein's *Tractatus Logico-Philosophicus* and has been used by Diané Collinson as a title for her article published in *The British Journal of Aesthetics*, 25:3, (1985). The ideas included in this part of the chapter have been developed from my article, 'The Feminine Sublime: Between Aesthetics and Ethics', which appeared in *Women: A Cultural Review*, 9:1 (1998).
2 'Longinus', *On Sublimity*, trans. D.A. Russell (Oxford: Clarendon Press, 1965), 1.

3 Paul Crowther, *The Kantian Sublime: From Morality to Art* (Oxford: Clarendon Press, 1989), 167.
4 Peter de Bolla, *The Discourse of the Sublime: Readings in History, Aesthetics
   and the Subject* (Oxford: Blackwell, 1989), 32.
5 Andrew Ashfield and Peter de Bolla eds, *The Sublime: A Reader in British
   Eighteenth-century Aesthetic Theory* (Cambridge: Cambridge University Press,
   1996), 2.
6 Herbert Grabes, 'Ethics, Aesthetics, Alterity', in *Ethics and Aesthetics: The
   Moral Turn of Postmodernism*, eds Gerhard Hoffmann and Alfred Hornung
   (Heidelberg: Universitätsverlag C. Winter, 1996), 23.
7 Tina Chanter, *Ethics of Eros: Irigaray's Rewriting of the Philosophers* (New
   York and London: Routledge, 1995), 90.
8 Emmanuel Levinas, 'The Trace of the Other', in *Deconstruction in Context*,
   ed. Mark C. Taylor (Chicago: University of Chicago Press, 1986), 346.
9 Emmanuel Levinas, *Totality and Infinity*, trans. Alphonso Lingis (Dordrecht,
   Boston, London: Kluwers Academic Publishers, 1969), 39. Levinas's account
   of the alterity of the self arriving before the other resembles Freud's
   description of the uncanny, in which the unknown side of the allegedly
   familiar is revealed.
10 Emmanuel Levinas, 'Ethics as First Philosophy', in *The Levinas Reader*, ed.
   Sean Hand (Blackwell: Oxford, 1989), 82.
11 Ibid., 83.
12 Levinas, *Totality and Infinity*, 34.
13 Ibid., 35.
14 Ibid., 43.
15 Ibid., 256.
16 Chanter, *Ethics of Eros*, 202–3.
17 Levinas, *Totality and Infinity*, 262.
18 Jacques Derrida, *Adieu to Emmanuel Levinas*, trans. Pascale-Anne Brault
   and Michael Naas (Stanford: Stanford University Press, 1997), 44.
19 Luce Irigaray, 'Questions to Emmanuel Levinas', in *The Irigaray Reader*, ed.
   Margaret Whitford (Oxford: Blackwell, 1991), 5.
20 Ibid., 5.
21 This point was made by Diane Perpich in her paper 'Rethinking the Subject
   of Ethics: From Incarnation to Sexual Difference' presented at the 'Gendering Ethics/The Ethics of Gender' conference held at the University of
   Leeds on 23–25 June 2000.
22 'By Definition, Art Is a Gesture of Repair: Tomek Kitlinski's Entretien with
   Hélène Cixous', *Magazyn Sztuki/Art Magazine*, 4/96, 193.
23 Irigaray, 'Questions to Emmanuel Levinas', 181–2.
24 Luce Irigaray, *An Ethics of Sexual Difference*, trans. Carolyn Burke and
   Gillian C. Gill (London: The Athlone Press, 1993), 12–13.
25 Irigaray, 'Questions to Emmanuel Levinas', 178.
26 Irigaray, *An Ethics of Sexual Difference*, 187.
27 Ibid., 201.
28 Ibid., 189, emphasis added.
29 Edmund Burke, *A Philosophical Enquiry into the Origin of our Ideas of the
   Sublime and the Beautiful* (Oxford: Blackwell, 1967), 57.

30 The sublime of Burke and Kant causes the freezing of the distance separat-
    ing the self from sublime phenomena. This immobilised spatial relation-
    ship can be linked to the instantaneous character of the sublime event. Its
    momentariness captures and envelops the self in its entirety, depriving it
    of the sense of the passage of time. Thus the self becomes a mirror for the
    overwhelming sublime object, which can explain why Kant is so hesitant
    about the actual situation of sublimity, characterising both external
    objects and the ideas of our mind. For a further discussion of the problem
    of space in Kant see Liliana Barakońska and Małgorzata Nitka, 'A Reading
    of Distance in the Kantian Sublime', in *The Most Sublime Act*, eds David
    Jarrett, Tadeusz Rachwał and Tadeusz Sławek (London: University of
    North London Press), 1996.
31 Zygmunt Bauman, *Postmodern Ethics* (Oxford: Blackwell, 1993), 14.
32 Burke, *A Philosophical Enquiry*, 57.
33 Ibid., 8.
34 My concept of *décriture féminine* arises, on the one hand, out of Lyotard's
    notion of *décriture*, i.e. 'writing of an impossible description', and, on the
    other, out of Cixous' idea of *écriture féminine,* i.e. feminine writing. For a
    detailed discussion of the feminine sublime and its relation to the above
    concepts see chapter 1.
35 Hélène Cixous and Mireille Calle-Gruber, *Rootprints*, trans. Eric Prenowitz
    (London and New York: Routledge, 1997), 79.
36 Seyla Benhabib, *Situating the Self: Gender, Community and Postmodernism in
    Contemporary Ethics* (Cambridge: Polity Press, 1992), 159.
37 Emmanuel Levinas, 'Ethics as First Philosophy', 76.
38 Diane Elam, *Feminism and Deconstruction* (London and New York: Rout-
    ledge, 1994), 106–8.
39 Jacques Derrida, '"Eating Well", or the Calculation of the Subject: An
    Interview with Jacques Derrida', in *Who Comes After the Subject?*, eds
    Eduardo Cadava, Peter Connor and Jean-Luc Nancy (New York and London:
    Routledge, 1991), 107–8.
40 Simon Critchley, *The Ethics of Deconstruction* (Oxford: Blackwell, 1992), 22.
41 Elam, *Feminism and Deconstruction*, 69.
42 Grabes, 'Ethics, Aesthetics, Alterity', 25. Even though the sublime has
    recently been associated with 'postmodern' aesthetics, I try not to overuse
    this term, whose conceptual boundaries have been infinitely stretched.
    When I speak about 'the postmodern' – as I will in further parts of this
    book – I remain faithful to Lyotard's use of this term, introduced in *The
    Postmodern Condition* and especially his essay 'Answering the Question:
    What Is Postmodernism?', included in that volume. Lyotard does not treat
    the postmodern as a linear overcoming of the modern, but rather as a
    certain mode of thinking which erupts *within* the modern. I am also
    interested in John D. Caputo's concept of 'another postmodernism',
    which he links to the philosophy of Derrida, Levinas and Lyotard: 'I
    would say that Derrida's dream of justice, his dream of the innumerable –
    along with Levinas' dream of the justice due "*l'infini*" and with Lyotard's
    dream of a "sublime" justice – are all just such new, more salutary,
    empowering myths, postmodern myths, if that is not too paradoxical,

myths of justice that inspire *another* postmodernism'. 'Dreaming of the Innumerable: Derrida, Drucilla Cornell, and the Dance of Gender', in *Derrida and Feminism*, eds Ellen K. Feder, Mary C. Rawlinson and Emily Zakin (New York and London: Routledge, 1997), 154.

43 Jacques Derrida, *The Truth in Painting*, trans. Geoff Bennington and Ian McLeod (Chicago: University of Chicago Press, 1987), 128.

44 Ashfield and de Bolla, *The Sublime*, 4.

45 Drucilla Cornell, 'What Is Ethical Feminism?', in *Feminist Contentions: A Philosophical Exchange*, eds Seyla Benhabib et al. (New York and London: Routledge, 1994), 94–5.

46 William Blake, *Complete Writings*, ed. Geoffrey Keynes (Oxford: Oxford University Press, 1969), 151.

47 De Bolla, *The Discourse of the Sublime*, 14–15.

48 Derrida, 'Eating Well', 109.

49 Ibid., 110–11.

50 Burke, *A Philosophical Enquiry*, 63.

51 Ibid., 63.

52 De Bolla, *The Discourse of the Sublime*, 134–5.

53 Derrida, *The Truth in Painting*, 122.

54 Jacques Derrida, *The Post-Card*, trans. Alan Bass (Chicago: University of Chicago Press, 1987), 384. For a discussion of the relationship between capitalist exchange and the logic of the gift, see also Jim Vinh, 'The Economics of Hospitality', *Foreign Body*, vol. 6, http://www.hydra.umn.edu/fobo

55 Derrida, *The Post-Card*, 384.

56 Derrida, 'Eating Well', 103.

57 Donald Wesling and Tadeusz Sławek, *Literary Voice: The Calling of Jonah* (New York: State University of New York Press, 1995), 25.

58 Ibid., 63.

59 Jacques Derrida, *Given Time: I. Counterfeit Money*, trans. Peggy Kamuf (Chicago and London: University of Chicago Press, 1992), 7.

60 Jacques Derrida, *The Gift of Death*, trans. David Wills (Chicago and London: University of Chicago Press, 1995), 6.

61 Ibid., 27.

62 Derrida, *Given Time*, 35.

63 Quoted in Barbara Claire Freeman, *The Feminine Sublime: Gender and Excess in Women's Fiction* (Berkeley, Los Angeles and London: University of California Press, 1995), 59.

64 Derrida, *The Gift of Death*, 41.

65 Ibid., 50–1, emphasis added.

66 Ibid., 76.

67 Luce Irigaray, *This Sex Which Is Not One*, trans. Catherine Porter (Ithaca, New York: Cornell University Press, 1985), 28.

68 Michel de Certeau, *Heterologies: Discourse on the Other*, trans. Brian Massumi (Manchester: Manchester University Press, 1986), 81.

69 Hélène Cixous, 'The Laugh of the Medusa', in *Feminisms*, eds Robyn Warhol and Diane Price Herndl (New Brunswick: Rutgers University Press, 1993), 348.

70 Ibid., 348. The concept of woman as the repository of gifts should not be

understood in essentialist terms. In the Afterword to *The Hélène Cixous Reader*, Mireille-Calle Gruber writes: 'The human which Hélène Cixous explores has nothing to do with "humanism" nor with any anthropocentrism. What she places on the scene are the perspectives of a 'human better' (recent interview) by which all frontiers are crossed. The being human enters in floods and expands from its others, vegetal, mineral, animal: knows itself to be dust, convolvulus (*Dedans*), butter (ibid.), air (*L'Ange*), body-fruit (*Vivre l'orange*); recognises its arch-vegetal kinship (*La*), its wounds of terrible meat (*Déluge*), and that it is necessary to have brushes to clean shoes. The souls too (*Beethoven a jamais*). So it is, doubtless, that the reader has the feeling of emerging strengthened by the crossing of these texts: we are strengthened by our weaknesses, by our dichotomies, by our censures. By our lacerations. Hélène Cixous gives us these. Let us make no mistake: she does not reconcile us. She gives us the gift of the irreconcilable', in *The Hélène Cixous Reader*, ed. Susan Sellers (London and New York: Routledge, 1994), 210.

71 Irigaray, *This Sex Which Is Not One*, 30.

72 Jean-François Lyotard, *Lessons on the Analytic of the Sublime, Sections 23–29: Kant's Critique of Judgement*, trans. Elizabeth Rottenberg (Stanford: Stanford University Press, 1994), 188–9.

73 Ibid., 189.

74 Derrida, *The Truth in Painting*, 131.

75 Immanuel Kant, *The Critique of Judgement*, trans. James Meredith (Oxford: Clarendon Press, 1952), 97.

76 Derrida, *The Truth in Painting*, 126.

77 Ibid., 141.

78 This notion of love challenges the logic of proportion and impermeability organising the philosophical rationalist discourse. Sylviane Agacinski points to the fear of eruption and unruly corporeality associated with the so-called 'philosophical subject', of whom Kant is for her the primary representative. There seems to be something comical, even pathetic, in the efforts Kant makes in his everyday existence not to let himself be bothered or surprised by his body. Following an account given in the memoirs of Kant's last secretary, Wasianski, Agacinski explains: 'a permanent vigilance, very strict rules for living – not to sweat, not to cough, not to sneeze, so to 'breathe exclusively through the nose' – to digest well, to be comfortable in his clothes. ... So many examples of techniques capable of making this celibate philosophical machine function neatly. ... One should ask, as a very serious question, why Kant tolerated neither coughing nor sneezing (and no doubt, in all likelihood any sort of spasm). Indeed, it seems clear that the autonomy of a subject that coughs is, if not gravely, at least distinctively weakened. A free subject must know how to prevent itself from coughing'. Sylviane Agacinski, 'Another Experience of the Question, or Experiencing the Question Other-Wise', in *Who Comes After the Subject?*, 17.

79 Derrida, *The Gift of Death*, 50.

80 Levinas, *Totality and Infinity*, 256.

81 There can be noticed a correspondence between 'certain distances'

advocated by Burke and Kant's reservation: 'provided our own position is secure, [the sublime phenomenon's] aspect is all the more attractive for its fearfulness'. Kant, *Critique of Judgement*, 110–11.

82 Burke, *A Philosophical Enquiry*, 38, emphasis added.
83 Adam Smith, *The Theory of Moral Sentiments* (Indianapolis: Liberty Classics, 1976), 57.
84 Alasdair MacIntyre, *A Short History of Ethics* (London: Routledge and Kegan Paul, 1967), 180.
85 Jacques Derrida, *Politics of Friendship*, trans. George Collins (London and New York: Verso, 1997), viii.
86 Aristotle, *Nicomachean Ethics*, trans. Martin Oswald (Indianapolis: Bobbs-Merrill Co., 1962), 214.
87 Ibid., 221.
88 Ibid., 224.
89 Ibid., 226.
90 Ibid., 224.
91 Derrida, *Politics of Friendship*, 7.
92 Aristotle, *Nichomachean Ethics*, 268. The word 'hyperbole', translated into English as 'excess', remains, nevertheless, linked to scarcity and privation. It was used by Aristotle twice, as Derrida indicates in his reading of a double context in which it appeared in the *Eudemian* and *Nicomachean Ethics*. '*Second hyperbole*. The example of love, of sensuous love, as it is translated. Eros is a "hyperbole" of *philia*. A hyperbolic scarcity. Eros addresses only one at a time (*pros ena*). But this is also the case with great friends, those friends the poets praise. These hymns to friendship always concern couples. Never more than two friends.' Derrida, *Politics of Friendship*, 212.
93 Ibid., 7.
94 Quoted in Derrida, ibid., 53.
95 Ibid., 53, emphasis added.
96 Ibid., 54.
97 Wesling and Sławek, *Literary Voice*, 64.
98 Friedrich Nietzsche, *The Gay Science*, trans. Walter Kaufmann (New York: Vintage Books, 1974), 124.
99 Such a distance is advised, for example, by R.W. Emerson. On the one hand, Emerson glorifies passion in man's encounter with nature, but he also emphasises the need for detachment and separation in relationships with others. He distances himself from affect by taking recourse to theatrical imagery. In this way, he justifies his recommendation for distance as springing from respect. In his essay *Friendship*, Emerson instructs us as follows: 'Treat your friend as a spectacle. ... Stand aside. Give those merits room. Let them mount and expand. Be not so much his friend that you can never know his peculiar energies, like fond mammas who shut up their boy in the house until he is almost a grown girl. Are you the friend of your friend's buttons, or of his thought?' (Ralph Waldo Emerson, *Essays* (New York: Thomas Y. Crowell Company, 1926), 151). The American philosopher gets entrapped in the opposition between bodily contact (one may wonder what could be hidden behind these buttons, and how these precious intellectual residues can be wasted by

being stained with some kind of 'improper' or 'impure' fascination) and immersion in the friend's thought. Emerson certainly tries to recuperate friendship from profanation, which is why he warns us: 'You shall not come near a man by getting into his house.' (153) He believes that the distinction between distance and proximity, or indwelling, as Irigaray will term it, saves the relationship with the other from abjection and helps maintain its highest value. Hence closeness has to be denied, as the truly precious encounter happens on the level of thought: it does not involve touch, caress, or even sojourning in the proximity of the other's home. I would like to give credit here to another version of friendship, which was depicted by the American writer Henry David Thoreau in *A Week on the Concord and Merrimack Rivers* (New York: Signet Classics, 1961). Thoreau's friend recognises the uncertain (or 'flickering') status of friendship and does not eschew affection. Though the love of a friend may be perceived as a sublime experience, since it should transfigure, refine and elevate (230), Thoreau stresses the corporeal character of this relationship. Thus, the distance advocated by Emerson is suspended. Thoreau declares: 'My friend is ... flesh of my flesh, bone of my bone. ... We do not live far apart.' (245) It is also worth noticing that Thoreau does not depict friendship as an exclusively male relationship, but rather emphasises the attraction between the sexes. He also recognises the special quality of their friendship. ('Friendship is, at any rate, a relation of perfect equality', 234.) Sexual difference is acknowledged without being annulled here, which saves his concept of 'perfect equality' from dissolving into colonising sameness.

100 As Nietzsche writes in *The Gay Science*, 'Here and there on earth we may encounter a kind of continuation of love in which this possessive craving of two people for each other gives way to a new desire and lust for possession, as shared higher thirst for an ideal above them. But who knows such love? Who has experienced it? Its right name is friendship' (89). For Nietzsche, friendship is both a prolongation and an elevation of love, or rather of 'the things people call love', which he does not respect. Nietzsche's love stands for lust and the possession of the lover's body and soul. Due to its ultimate egoism, it is seen as lower and meaner than the advocated friendship. As Derrida remarks, Nietzsche's friendship loses the permanence of Aristotle's *philia* and moves into the realm of uncertainty and instantaneousness, but it is still perceived as a highly desirable goal.

101 Derrida, *Politics of Friendship*, 62.

102 Ibid., 154.

103 Discussing Aristotle's recommendation that in the relationship between two friends it is advisable to love rather than to be loved, Derrida concludes: 'This incommensurability between the lover and the beloved will now unceasingly exceed all measurement and all moderation – that is, it will exceed the very principle of a calculation. It will *perhaps* introduce a disorder in the organisation of the Aristotelian discourse', ibid., 10.

104 Irigaray, *An Ethics of Sexual Difference*, 211.

105 Jean-François Lyotard, *The Inhuman*, trans. Geoffrey Bennington and Rachel Bowlby (Cambridge: Polity Press, 1991), 93.

106 Ibid., 81.

107 Derrida, Foreword to *The Hélène Cixous Reader*, x.
108 Irigaray, *An Ethics of Sexual Difference*, 44–5.
109 Agacinski, 'Another Experience of the Question', 16.
110 Cixous, Preface to *The Hélène Cixous Reader*, xviii.
111 The 'debate' between the two rhetors presented in *Phaedrus* is actually Socrates's response to Lysias's speech, as Lysias himself does not appear directly but is merely quoted by his friend Phaedrus.
112 Plato, *Phaedrus*, trans. Walter Hamilton (Harmondsworth: Penguin Books, 1995), 6–7.
113 Ibid., 10.
114 Ibid., 16.
115 Ibid., 37.
116 Ibid., 37–8, emphasis added.
117 Ibid., 44.
118 Tadeusz Rachwał and Tadeusz Sławek, *Representations of the Erotic* (Katowice: Wydawnictwo Uniwersytetu Śląskiego, 1996), 10.
119 In Plato's *Phaedrus* Eros is presented as the son of Penia (Poverty) and Poros (Plenty).
120 Plato, *Phaedrus*, 36.
121 Ibid., 36–7.
122 Ibid., 36.
123 Burke, *A Philosophical Enquiry*, 57.
124 Kant, *Critique of Judgement*, 120–1.
125 Martin Jay, *Downcast Eyes: the Denigration of Vision in Twentieth-Century Thought* (Berkeley, Los Angeles and London: University of California Press, 1993), 81.
126 Burke, *A Philosophical Enquiry*, 58–9.
127 Ibid., 80.
128 Ibid., 80.
129 Laura Mulvey, 'Visual Pleasure and Narrative Cinema', in *Contemporary Film Theory*, ed. Anthony Easthope (London: Longman, 1993), 116.
130 Irigaray, *This Sex Which Is Not One*, 26.
131 Burke, *A Philosophical Enquiry*, 115.
132 Freeman, *The Feminine Sublime*, 56.
133 Kaja Silverman, *The Threshold of the Visible World* (New York and London: Routledge, 1996), 173.
134 Jacques Derrida, *Memoirs of the Blind*, trans. Pascale-Anne Brault and Michael Naas (Chicago: University of Chicago Press, 1993), 57.
135 Quoted in Jay, *Downcast Eyes*, 500.
136 Derrida, *Memoirs of the Blind*, 1.
137 Ibid., 12.
138 Ibid., 21.
139 Derrida, *The Truth in Painting*, 126.
140 Derrida, *Memoirs of the Blind*, 68.
141 Agacinski, 'Another Experience of the Question', 15.
142 Derrida, *Memoirs of the Blind*, 3–4.
143 Hélène Cixous and Catherine Clément, *The Newly Born Woman*, trans. Betsy Wing (Manchester: Manchester University Press, 1986), 86.

Webwords: from the spider's web to cyberspace

Just as individuated texts have become filaments of infinitely tangled webs, so the digital machines of the late twentieth century weave new networks from what were once isolated words, numbers, music, shapes, smells, tactile textures, architectures, and countless channels as yet unnamed. Media become interactive and hyperactive, the multiplicitous components of an immersive zone which 'does not begin with writing; it is directly related rather to the weaving of elaborate figured silks'. The yarn is neither metaphorical nor literal, but quite simply material, a gathering of threads which twist and turn through the history of computing, technology, the sciences and arts. In and out of the punched holes of automated looms, up and down through the ages of spinning and weaving, back and forth through the fabrication of fabrics, shuttles and looms, cotton and silk, canvas and paper, brushes and pens, typewriters, carriages, telephone wires, synthetic fibers, electrical filaments, silicon strands, fiber-optic cables, pixeled screens, telecom lines, the World Wide Web, the Net, and matrices to come.[1]

The spider's web has been incorporated by the late-twentieth-century world as a material connection between the disparate spheres of labour, communication and storage. As Sadie Plant notices in *Zeros + Ones*, its status is not explicitly metaphorical, nor should it be perceived just as a development of the earlier version of the product of nature. In the network of contemporary technologies and communication devices, images from the allegedly separate domains of nature and culture are positioned side by side to produce an uncanny coupling: a cyborg.

By the late twentieth century, our time, a mythic time, we are all chimeras, theorised and fabricated hybrids of machine and organism; in short, we are cyborgs. The cyborg is our ontology; it gives us our politics. The cyborg is a condensed image of both imagination and material reality, the two joined centres structuring any possibility of historical transformation.[2]

The image of the cyborg – by now an institutionalised presence in the matrix of both academic and mainstream technocultures – has been acclaimed for its reworking of the conceptual division between organism and machine and its 'subversion' of traditionally mapped knowledge. And yet this concept poses numerous ontological problems which often remain unaddressed by its theorists: Is the cyborg merely a metaphor or a material presence? Is it a product of post-industrial capitalism or have 'we' always been cyborgs? Does it signify a shift towards the 'post-human' or is it an exponent of the intrinsic impurity of the human? Does cybertechnology transcend the body or does it offer new possibilities of sexualisation and embodiment? A thorough discussion of these points exceeds the scope of this chapter, but I will approach some of these questions in my encounter with the cyborg, perceived here as an insubordinate feminist icon.[3]

To begin with, describing the cyborg as a hybrid of human and machine can appear problematic, as this definition relies on the absolute separateness of the two concepts and thus constructs a fantasy of identity without difference. Instead, the cyborg can rather be seen as signifying an intrinsic instability of the boundary between what is traditionally perceived as human and machine. This instability, or impurity, has come to the fore through the exposure of unprecedented couplings offered by the late-twentieth-century technologies. But if the cyborg is to be a useful concept for a feminist agenda which takes into account the constructedness of both 'nature' and 'culture' as we know them, we have to move beyond somewhat limiting descriptions of cyborgs as 'people with electronic pacemakers, artificial joints, drug implant systems, implanted corneal lenses, and artificial skin'.[4] In all these examples, the cyborg names a 'human being' whose body has been prosthetically extended by means of technology. The coupling of separate but recognisable entities only confirms the division between the natural and the artificial. To offer a conceptual promise to feminism and gender studies, perhaps cyborgs could rather be seen as figuring the uncertain and performative character of identity and the way it is channelled into sexualised bodies and genders. In what follows, I will thus use the term 'cyborg' to refer to a *process* of what I describe as queering/querying identity and identification, and not to some essence of being.[5] In fact, Haraway's 'original' definition of the cyborg focuses on the moment of encounter and transgression, and not on the cyborg's essence:

> The cyborg appears in myth precisely where the boundary between human and animal is transgressed. Far from signalling a walling off of people from other living beings, *cyborgs signal disturbingly and pleasurably tight coupling*. Bestiality has a new status in this cycle of marriage exchange.[6]

Interestingly, in order to convey the incommensurability of the feelings of fear and delight evoked by the cyborg, Haraway takes recourse to the rhetoric of the sublime. Similarly, Claudia Springer argues in 'The Pleasure of the Interface' that 'The contradictory discourse on cyborgs reveals a new manifestation of the simultaneous revulsion and fascination with the human body that has existed throughout the western cultural tradition'.[7] It is clear from the above statements that there is no point in celebrating the absolute novelty of the cyborg: disguised by the techno-metaphors of virtual reality, 'postmodern' cyborgs evoke modernist automata, creatures born out of the psycho-social conflict at the heart of the society which both feared and desired technology. Cyborgs can thus be seen as beings of uncertain ontology, signifying the instability of identity and the problematic boundedness of the human.

What I find particularly interesting in representations of the cyborg is the way in which the machinic is frequently gendered as feminine. This seems to constitute a shift from representing women solely through images of pre-cultural nature. Andreas Huyssen points out that the association between women and machines was first made in the eighteenth century. This mechanism of representation was employed to displace male anxieties over increasing industrialisation on to women, who were then defined as harbingers of threat and destruction. As Huyssen explains:

> There are grounds to suspect that we are facing here a complex process of projection and displacement. The fears and perceptual anxieties emanating from ever more powerful machines are recast and reconstructed in terms of the male fear of female sexuality, reflecting, in the Freudian account, the male's castration anxiety. This projection was relatively easy to make; although woman had traditionally been seen as standing in a closer relationship to nature than man, nature itself, since the 18th century, had come to be interpreted as a gigantic machine. Woman, nature, machine had become a mesh of significations which all had one thing in common: otherness; by their very existence they raised fears and threatened male authority and control.[8]

The construction of machines and automata fulfilled the male dream of self-mothering and self-sufficiency: it was 'the promise of creation outside woman, of identity free of difference, of self-conception without death'.[9] If the automaton can be seen as displaying the repression of sexual difference and the simultaneous projection of this difference on to the femininised, subordinate clockwork figurine, then the cyborg can be read as a mimicry of the modernist automaton. Although this mimicry can take a number of different forms, I would like to focus here on mimetic performances by women artists and theorists searching for new modes of self-identification. To return to the argument I developed in the first part of 'Webwords', mimicry can provide a non-utopian viable political option for these theorists of gender who neither want to resort to a prediscursive essentialist identity nor believe in the possibility of creating 'entirely new' identities, which would not be marked by the Law of the Father governing representation and language. Indeed, as Luce Irigaray concludes, 'There is, in an initial phase, perhaps only one "path", the one historically assigned to the feminine: that of mimicry. One must assume the feminine role deliberately. Which means already to convert a form of subordination into an affirmation, and thus to begin to thwart it'.[10]

Weaving their threads through the webs of contemporary communication devices and computer networks, women challenge the teleological rationale of the IT discourse with a circular logic of the repetitive spin. Following what Irigaray describes as the 'only one path assigned to the feminine', they adopt various cyborgian masks through their participation in networked performances. In this way, a new 'cyber-politics' of representation is being developed, allowing for bold provocations of self-authorising and self-fragmentation.[11] But this search for new forms of identification is not easy: it depends to a large extent on the material produced in and by the tradition of representation which is now being questioned 'from within'. This is why for me cyborgs do not represent a triumphal overcoming of the gendered body and self, but rather an intrinsic queerness – even uncanniness – of identity and the problematic boundedness of embodiment. The feminist use of the cyborg can thus be seen as a performance of imposed subordination through the discourse of technology, with a possibility of thwarting it. And yet it should not baffle us that cyberspace abounds in the images of seductively submissive vamps, with virtuality translated into voluptuousness. Feminists do not 'own' the cyborg, whose representations appear in numerous examples of popular culture, simultaneously projecting and disrupting 'the truth of femininity'. These representations do not refer to any original Cyberform, but rather simulate the idea of its origin. As Sadie Plant explains in a somewhat rebellious manner:

> Cybernetic feminism does not, like many of its predecessors, including that proposed in Irigaray's recent work, seek out for woman a subjectivity, an identity or even a sexuality of her own: there is no subject position and no identity on the other side of the screens. And female sexuality is always in excess of anything that could be called 'her own'. Woman cannot exist 'like man'; neither can the machine. As soon [as] her

mimicry earns her equality, she is already something, and somewhere, other than him.[12]

For Plant here cyberfeminist mimicry foregrounds an encounter between the material and the virtual, which leads to the suspension of any fantasy we might cherish of grasping 'the wholeness' of identity and capturing the 'truth of woman'. At the same time, it allows us to move beyond the pessimism of earlier descriptions of 'woman as masquerade' as presented by Sigmund Freud and Joan Riviere. For both Freud and Riviere, women were sentenced to the melancholic repetition of ascribed feminine roles which had been written for them in the patriarchal gender script.[13]

But embracing a cyberfeminist stand does not mean that a total reversal of the script is possible: the search for new forms of self-fashioning always involves the risk of incompleteness and failure. This is why the concept of the sublime, presenting the idea of the unpresentable rather that providing us with the solace of a good form, is useful in my project. Lyotard argues that the sublime 'allows the unpresentable to be put forward only as the missing contents'.[14] Consequently, I do not expect new technologies to provide me with positive images of womanhood, but rather to facilitate a performance of the lack which is inherent in the very idea of identity. Nevertheless, this 'negative' performance will not amount to the silencing and withdrawal of women from the stage of identity, even though we have to acknowledge that the sublime event – as Burke has recognised – always involves the danger of *horror vacui* (i.e. nothing happening at all). The identities we are looking for are therefore always tentative and provisional, signifying the intrinsic instability of the self and revealing a lack, or gap, at the core of 'being'. As Jennifer González states, 'the cyborg is like a symptom – it represents that which cannot otherwise be represented'.[15]

> There is no authentic or essential woman up ahead, no self to be reclaimed from some long long past, nor even a potential subjectivity to be constructed in the present day. Nor is there only an absence or lack. Instead there is a virtual reality, an emergent process for which identity is not the goal but the enemy, precisely what has kept at bay the matrix of potentialities from which women have always downloaded their roles.[16]

I want to explore this emergent process of liquidising (not liquidating!) identity by looking at the work of two artists: Orlan and Laurie Anderson. The French performance artist Orlan and the American multimedia artist Laurie Anderson contest the assumed 'representability' of gender, and of the world in general. Putting on the cultural masks of passion, desire, bewilderment and horror, they mimic the 'authenticity' of the sublime discourse of affection and thus expose its constructed and marked character. Both artists challenge the alleged primacy of nature by staging bold, even shocking, encounters between the human and the nonhuman. Breaching the distance between the subject who is exposed to the disturbingly pleasing experience of the sublime and the terrifying object, they incarnate sublimity by giving their body to 'art'. Their projects go beyond the disinterestedness of Western aesthetics to address a number of political and ethical issues.

> After decades of ambivalence towards technology, many feminists are now finding a wealth of new opportunities, spaces and lines of thought amidst the new complexities of the 'telecoms revolution'. … virtuality brings a fluidity to identities which once had to be fixed; and multi-media provides a new tactile environment in which women artists can find their space.[17]

Indeed, cyborgian hybridisation, in its openness to an encounter with irreducible alterity, has ethical consequences. Haraway explicitly declares in her manifesto: 'This essay is an argument for pleasure in the confusion of boundaries and for *responsibility* in their construction'.[18] Interestingly, for both Haraway and Chris Hables Gray – author of the celebrated 'Cyborg Bill of Rights' – the ethics and politics of the cyborg are founded upon the American legal discourse. The individual is for them simply 'extended' in the process of cyborgisation, but his or her intrinsic singular rights remain unquestioned.[19] Jill Marsden accuses Haraway of being unable to tolerate the full cyborg coupling of science and politics, and thus 'appeal[ing] to a security system of humanist values to protect her cyborg from illicit, anarchic and random liaisons. Perhaps in the desire to hold sway over a future that is potentially "monstrous" for the economically vulnerable, she reinscribes the dialectical illusion of transcendent control in the guise of an ethical sensibility'.[20] But if we follow Derrida's contention that 'the future is necessarily monstrous: the figure of the future, that is, that which can only be surprising, that for which we are not prepared',[21] this vulnerability, resulting from the lack of mastery over the future, does not merely affect the economically impoverished. And even if resorting to the bill of rights wards off the monstrosity of the cyborgian future, it does not explain why democracy with its manifestos and rights of the individual would not itself be affected by the monstrous cyborg, perhaps to such a degree that relying on the democratic framework of society would become impossible.

> A monster is always alive, let us not forget. Monsters are living beings. The monster is also that which appears for the first time and, consequently, is not yet recognised. A monster is a species for which we do not yet have a name, which does not mean that the species is abnormal, namely, the composition or hybridisation of already known species. Simply, it *shows* itself [*elle se* montre] – that is what the word monster means – it shows itself in something that is not yet shown and that therefore looks like a hallucination, it strikes the eye, it frightens precisely because no anticipation had prepared one to identify this figure.[22]

Derrida's insistence on the withdrawal of our expectations regarding the arrival of the monster, his abandonment of the desire to 'possess' the monster, whose very monstrosity is only preserved in the deferral of its arrival, draw our attention to the element of unexpectedness characterising the future. What we are presented with is the promise itself, which deprives us of the possibility of devising an ethics based on identity and presence: 'it shows itself as something that is not yet known'. There can be noticed a similarity between Derrida's depiction of awaiting the monster and Lyotard's discussion of awaiting the sublime: both withhold the ultimate guarantee as to what will actually arrive. This suspension of a desire to master the future does not lead, nevertheless, to the abandonment of the vigil (which can be equally kept or abandoned, because the future – the monster – will be arriving anyway). This attitude constitutes the anti-foundational basis for what I call the ethics of the feminine sublime. Responsibility for the future, and for the monster that it is/brings, does not stem from any transcendental order. The ethical moment springs from a response to the lack of knowledge about what will arrive (i.e. the fear of what Burke terms '*horror vacui*'), combined with a decision to await it and the recognition that 'no anticipation had prepared one to identify this figure'. This kind of decision cannot therefore be taken once and for all: it has to be constantly retaken.

Thus from a feminist–deconstructive point of view the figure of the cyborg can signify the suspension of knowledge and judgement about the future, with the recognition of the possibility of what Marsden calls 'illicit, anarchic and random liaisons'. Derrida helps us recognise that 'Among the paths through which Nature erupts in our experience a mistake always remains possible – a *Vergreifen* or bastardy'.[23] The feminine sublime, which remains open to the experience of unexpected arrival and eruption, inheres the possibility of bastardy, disaster and death. And yet the ethics of the feminine sublime does not take recourse to pre-defined rights or duties. The responsibility it puts forward brings about the constant need for decision-making (even if that decision amounts to disinterestedness).

The work of Orlan and Laurie Anderson, among others, can be perceived as having been produced from the perspective of 'awaiting the monstrous'. Cyborg technology creates opportunities for rewriting the identity matrix and pushing the boundaries of the self. Their projects are not underwritten by any guarantee: in cyborgian couplings 'a mistake always remains possible'. If modernist automata were the representations of sterility, offering the promise of creation outside woman, feminist cyborgs can be seen as figures of bastardy, questioning the compartmentalisation of nature and technology as pre-defined entities that were only brought together in the late-twentieth-century post-industrial age.

> A visual representation of this new being through an imaginary body provides a map of the layers and contradictions that make up a hyperhistorical 'positive-unconscious'. In other words, the cyborg body marks the boundaries of that which is the underlying but unrecognised structure of a given historical consciousness. It turns the inside out.[24]

The French artist Orlan, whose performances have caused sensation in the art world since 1960s, has undergone a series of operations as part of a project entitled *The Reincarnation of St Orlan*. Exposing her body on the technological altar of plastic surgery, with its cultural taboos and rituals of beauty, Orlan challenges the traditional ideal of perfection and the possibility of ever achieving a 'perfect fit'. Without renouncing the pain involved in the operation, Orlan defies the ultimate objective of plastic surgery: thus her selection of the chin of Boticelli's Venus, the nose of Diana and the forehead of Mona Lisa only exposes the roughness of the stitching that holds European aesthetics together. Choosing from among the traditional Western representations of femininity, she exposes the cruelty of the gendered beauty myth which also bears an unambiguously 'white' inscription. Thus Orlan's (anti?)aesthetic project, which results in what Haraway describes as 'disturbingly and pleasurably tight coupling' between the human and the nonhuman, is intrinsically political. As Michelle Hirschorn argues,

> [Orlan's] work raises serious questions concerning identity, societal taboos against opening the body, the mind/body dualism, the often acrimonious relationship between women and technology, the limits of art and language, physical pain, representations of the female grotesque, myths of femininity, private and public domains, the long legacy of colonisation that western medicine has exerted over female bodies, as well as the historic relationship between art and life that is inherent within the tradition of avant-garde performance throughout the twentieth century.[25]

Exposed not only to the mastering touch of the surgeons' scalpels but also to the anxious but persistent gaze of the audience who are invited to witness her gory performances, Orlan 'is making a spectacle out of herself'. There is something scandalous in her 'continuing fascination with woman as fetish and her own absorption within that fetishistic desire',[26] which manifests itself as a willingness to cater for the voyeuristic interests of those witnessing her transformation. Mary Russo claims that, for a woman, making a spectacle out of herself has to do 'with a kind of inadvertency and loss of boundaries':[27] and it is precisely the transgression of the boundary lines between pleasure and pain, and beauty and horror, that situates Orlan's work in the aesthetic of the sublime. For Burke and Kant, woman could only be seen as beautiful, while the sublime was associated with strength, virility and masculinity. But Orlan does not want to pursue the beauty ideal through her art. By insisting on the fragmentation and detachment of a woman's body, something which used to be seen as a passive object immobilised by the male gaze, Orlan challenges nature with technology in order to achieve what can be described as the 'unnatural face' – the mask.

But in what sense can her 'cyborgisation' of the body be seen as feminist? If indeed Orlan manages to transgress the 'bad fit' of femininity with its sexist, racist and homophobic assumptions, what kind of costume does she don in the end? And in what sense can such a gender- and sex-redressing offer a conceptual challenge for women in search of new modes of self-fashioning? Even though some critics dismiss Orlan's work as a naïve attempt to change the costume of her identity 'at the drop of a hat', perhaps her project foregrounds the intrinsic difficulty and uncertainty of gender identity and identification? Finally, is what the artist herself describes as 'woman-to-woman transsexualism' only a tasteless parody of the painful process of 'real transsexualism' which in public perception is only skin-deep?[28] Or would Orlan's work rather fit in with Sadie Plant's radical, anti-essentialist view of transsexualism as presented in *Zeros + Ones*?

> [T]here is no such thing as being human, male or female. Femmes, drag queens, even male-to-female transsexuals: No one ever arrives at the point of being a real woman. ... Transsexuals are transsexuals before and after the long chemical treatments and surgical procedures, always on the way to a destination as impossible as the point of departure they leave behind.[29]

In a similar vein, the account of transsexualism provided by Parveen Adams in *The Emptiness of the Image* moves beyond the essentialist understanding of sexuality and the processes of sex change. Adams interprets the most frequent form of sex change, i.e. 'man-to-woman transsexualism', as a disavowal of sexual difference and a manifestation of a desire for both Woman and the 'secret of femininity' she keeps. The male-to-female transsexual is not satisfied with possessing the penis: he wants to become its idealised incarnation, the Phallus. From this perspective, Orlan's 'woman-to-woman transsexualism', coupled with her disentanglement of gender in both bodily practice and language ('Je suis *une homme* et *un femme*'[30]), splits open the fantasy of completeness and the desire for identity without difference. Queering/querying the notion of identity and the rigidity of cultural formations of gender, Orlan reveals that there is no essence, no Woman, behind the mask of her face: that an image of femininity is ultimately empty. In this way she replays the greatest mystery of femininity as masquerade, which Irigaray defines as 'the horror of nothing to see'. Interestingly, this fear of 'nothing to see' is for Burke the source of negative feeling in sublime experience. Even though the anxiety the sublime evokes in the self stems from the uncertain, unknown nature of the event which is about to take place, Barbara Claire Freeman argues that the origin of this fear can be traced back to the denial of sexual difference. It is precisely the enigma of woman, who is depicted as a labyrinth without a centre, that leads to a vertiginous, sublime sensation in the male observer: 'Rather than securing boundaries and limits', her body instils '"unsteadiness": this body does not provide a site where distinctions can be fixed but rather represents the point at which they come apart, and the observer, seeking a resting place, "slides giddily"'.[31]

Orlan does not attempt to make this 'unsteadiness' disappear. Instead of trying to cover up the gap between the image and its representations – and thus perform the masquerade 'in order to participate in man's desire, but at the cost of giving up [her] own'[32] – Orlan positions herself as the image, and thus collapses the active–passive dichotomy that regulates traditional aesthetics. Pursuing the strategy of mimicry, she reveals that the image which is to protect the 'enigma' of sexual difference and the fragility of its norm is ultimately empty.

> In this sense Orlan's work undoes the triumph of representation. During her operation Orlan's face begins to detach itself from her head. We are shocked at the destruction of our normal narcissistic fantasy that the face 'represents' something. Gradually the 'face' becomes pure exteriority. It no longer projects the illusion of depth. It becomes a mask without any relation of representation. In turn this disturbs a fundamental illusion concerning the inside and outside, that the outside provides a window onto what is represented. In this sense Orlan uses her head quite literally

to demonstrate an axiom of at least one strand of feminist thought: there is nothing behind the mask.[33]

Revealing the intrinsic lack at the core of identity, Orlan mixes art, medicine and technology to produce an image of the software-body: an aestheticised cyborg. The sublimity of her performances, which puts forward the intrinsic unpresentability of identity, collapses the distance between the subject of reason and the grand object which was maintained in traditional theories of the sublime. Intermixing pleasure with pain and life with death, Orlan's art challenges the immobilisation of the feminine body as performed by the Old Masters of the Western artistic tradition. Although her body, opened by the surgeon's scalpel, may be a source of vertiginous feeling, it does not conform to the image of the passive, 'frozen' feminine corpus that Burke praised so much in his theories of the sublime. As witnesses of her surgery, 'We are confronted with the horrifying spectacle of the rawness of the passion, of the jouissance of the body as such, the jubilation of meat'.[34] Orlan's body, contorted by the excess of beauty represented by the cultural masks she subsequently dons, is also a connected body. The cyborgian technology of networking, which allows Orlan to send faxes and transmit her surgery all over the world, sidesteps the distance between object and image.

> When lying on the surgical table, what she experiences is the overwhelming desire to communicate. Faxes flood in from Russia, Latvia, Canada and France. … She sets off on the highway of information. But the spectator is forced to tarry in this circus, in this staging of speech, to witness something else, the something else which insists.[35]

This 'something else which insists' could serve as another name for the sublime with its category of the unspeakable: i.e. something that defies recognition and verbal mastery. As Lyotard puts it, 'What can one say that is not given? It is not difficult to describe, but the description is as flat as a paraphrase. The best gloss consists of the question: what can one say? Or of the exclamation "Ah"'.[36] Orlan's display of the masks of femininity signifies a refusal to seal off the process of gender identification. But, according to Judith Butler, 'femininity is an ideal which everyone always and only "imitates"'.[37] If 'Gender itself might be understood in part as the "acting out" of unresolved grief',[38] Orlan's performance of gender performance, her 'acting out' of the loss of sexual difference, can be seen as a renegotiation of woman's relation to her Self, and as a positive embracing of identity de-formation. Orlan acknowledges that her modified grotesque body 'becomes a place of public debate'.[39] However, it is necessary to emphasise the open-endedness of her project, which involves the possibility of an accident and failure. And yet it is precisely in its openness towards the monstrous that Orlan's cyborgian aesthetics becomes intrinsically ethical.

> A future that would not be monstrous would not be a future; it would already be a predictable, calculable, and programmable tomorrow. All experience open to the future is prepared or prepares itself to welcome the monstrous arrivant, to welcome it, that is, to accord hospitality to that which is absolutely foreign or strange, but also, one must add, to try to domesticate it, that is, to make it part of the household.[40]

This brings me back to the ethics of the feminine sublime, based on the recognition of the irreducible alterity of the other. Instead of protecting itself against the unknown, the self extends an invite to the always already monstr-ous (in the sense of 'showing itself as something that is not yet shown') other, and thus recognises the necessary doubling – but also splitting – of identity. I thus perceive Orlan's carnal art as an ethical space in which this search for new forms of identification is performed from the position of openness and hospitality. The ethics of hospitality, a recurring thread in Derrida's work, is based on the disavowal of the subject–object distance upon which the traditional aesthetics of the sublime was founded: hospitality implies the possibility – and danger – of the intrusion of the unpresentable, of what we cannot yet know or name, into the confined territory of the self. As Orlan herself announces from her operating table, 'I is an other'.

> They say she wears 'different veils according to the historic period.' They say her 'original attributes and epithets were so numerous … in the hieroglyphics she is called "the many-named", "the thousand-named" … "the myriad-named".'[41]

In her mimicry of femininity Orlan not only detaches the face from the bodily corpus but also disembodies her voice: during the surgery the spectator's attention is shifted from the gory detail of liposuction to the recitation of Lemoine-Luccioni's *La Robe*: 'I have the skin … of a woman, but I'm a man; I never have the skin of what I am'.[42] Putting on the voice of male authority, high culture and presence beyond the mask, Orlan also creates a gap between the act of speaking and the meaning transmitted in this act. 'If this use of the voice works, it is because it divorces her from meaning and designates her. It is the hypnotic quality of the voice present, not absent; but we are still talking about the emptying out of the object.'[43] To develop Adams's argument further, Orlan's performance does not replace the body with disembodied voice, but rather reveals a scission between the signifier and its meaning. In her artistic intervention both the body and the voice are presented as, first, co-dependent, and, second, as challenging a signifying hierarchy which allows us to distinguish between the object and its representation and thus possess 'the real thing'. Orlan's 'queering' of identity does not just happen on the level of her flesh, but rather in the opening between flesh and voice. If meaning is always already connected with articulation, challenging the naturalness of the link between what the body 'is' and what it 'does' is one way of undoing the signifying system that rigidly distinguishes between men and women on the basis of their bodily mould.

The work of Laurie Anderson, an American multimedia artist, is another example of queering gender and its bodily inscriptions through what we could term 'voice-crossing'. The shock effect her performances produce allows me to situate Anderson's art in the realm of the sublime: it is so easy to be lulled into a sense of false relaxation by her music before being made to face the unexpected. The solace offered by Anderson's mesmerising voice and her masterfully digitalised tunes is always temporary. As Richard Kadrey and Larry McCaffery argue, in Anderson's performances there can be felt

> an undercurrent of minimalistic dread, alienation, and paranoia that wafts over you so gently, as you sit entering spreadsheets data on your laptop while sipping cocktails in the business class of a 747. Slowly it dawns on you that you're only seconds from impact, and the reassuring voice of the 'pilot' was only another recorded message, that the arms of the loved one gripping you in a last embrace are really automatic, electronic arms, that all those amazing chemical reactions going inside your body right now to protect you aren't going to mean a thing when this lumbering, gas-guzzling pile of metal plows into a Kansas cornfield at 600 MPH with you strapped inside like the meat puppet you are. Stand by.[44]

Laurie Anderson's work conveys a sense of imminence, of an unexpected arrival of the unknown, which leads to the fear of annihilation and death but which also promises infinite jubilation. Significantly, the feeling of terror in sublime experience does not relate to the actual event but rather to the moment 'before the event', i.e. the unexpectedness of its arrival and the uncertainty of what it may bring. Lyotard goes so far as to suggest that it is precisely the sense of imminence that is most disconcerting for the self. 'One feels that it is possible that soon nothing more will happen. What is sublime is the feeling that something will happen, despite everything, within this threatening void, that something will take "place" and will announce that everything is not over'.[45] The fear of the unknown can thus be relieved by the messianic belief that the awaited event will eventually arrive. And then, croons Anderson, 'everything's shaking with a strange delight' ('My eyes').

> You're out on the ocean and you get pulled down
> Freefall to the bottom
> Like when you're drowning or falling asleep
> You get turned around
> And when you think you're swimming to the surface
> You're swimming straight down.
> Down to the bottom. All the way to the bottom. ('Freefall')

> But if I open my mouth I'll fall to the ground. ('Speechless')

There is something Faustian about Anderson's fascination with the images of the fall and descent. Attentive to the impending arrival of the unknown, she describes herself as a spy, utilising the material around her to spin her dangerous web. Her spy-der's technique relies on the expansion of her body through different prostheses such as phones, mikes, voice boxes, filters and keyboards, from which point it seems impossible to decide if the 'bug' she becomes belongs to the natural or the technical world. It is precisely this blasphemous confusion – which both acknowledges the boundaries in place and traverses them – that allows Anderson's art to be perceived as a cyborgian feminist strategy. While Orlan reveals a gap between body and self by literally lifting layers of skin from her face, Anderson demonstrates that her voice is not really 'hers'. (She looks like a woman but sounds like a man; she puts on voices like costumes, sliding between different positions: between Minnie Mouse and John Wayne, or human and machine. Her voice seems delayed, echoed, as if detached from the 'real' person.) In his article 'Laurie Anderson: Myth, Management and Platitude', Sean Cubitt observes that 'The triumph of the signifier over the signified arrives not as the strength of formal technique, but as the distances between speaker and spoken, spoken and hearer, the tyranny of mediation'.[46] However, what Cubitt perceives as the 'tyranny of mediation' which enacts the 'estrangement of the voice from the body', can be read as a feminist strategy of revealing that this 'individuality' is also a dangerously restrictive myth which has been used to channel difference – including sexual difference – into externally policed forms and formulas. I am therefore more inclined to read Anderson's performance as the exposure of the fact that the signifier of 'unalienated humanness' has always been empty. Playing with her synthesisers in order to challenge the gendering of the voice and even its intrinsic 'humanness', the artist adopts the role of a 'rebellious replicant' for whom 'identity is easy to simulate and merely one of many programs to be run'.[47]

'The Ugly One With the Jewels' story, included on the artist's 1994 album which features her readings from 'the Nerve Bible', is one example of such simulation. Thanks to the insertion of a bit of technology into her body (Anderson describes the awe and fascination her contact lenses evoked among the Native American tribe Tzotzil), 'the ugly one' becomes beautiful, reflecting herself in the mirror of the other's gaze. Depicting beauty and ugliness as products of the other's astonished look, Anderson can be easily accused of perpetuating the history of the idealisation of native peoples. Even though she acknowledges the reciprocal gaze of 'the natives', the power of voice remains on the side of the artist. But the experience of otherness Anderson depicts in her songs and stories is bilateral. Not only does she recognise the unbridgeable difference between the self and the other – it is this that allows her to tell the story of the Tzotzil from the position of surprise, (mis)recognition and estrangement – but she also 'becomes' the other by connecting herself to the techno-logical network and transforming her voice and flesh through a series of bodily extensions. Her artistic politics of the spy, conducted from a situated, privileged Western position, reveals a cut, or gap, at the very heart of representation. In Anderson's art the self is always already split. Exposed to the gaze of the other who does not share Western aesthetic standards, the artist's 'Americanness' is revealed to be an equally 'bad fit', a mimicry of what it means to be a white, privileged, American woman in post-industrial late twentieth-century society. In this way Anderson exposes an indeterminacy, even fragility, which underlies identitarian thinking in the West. As Homi Bhabha remarks,

> The authority of that mode of colonial discourse that I have called mimicry is therefore stricken by indeterminacy: mimicry emerges as the representation of a difference that is itself a process of disavowal. Mimicry is, thus the sign of a double articulation; a complex strategy of reform, regulation and discipline, which 'appropriates' the Other as it visualises power. Mimicry is also the sign of the inappropriate, however, a differ-ence of recalcitrance which coheres the dominant strategic function of colonial power, intensifies surveillance, and poses an immanent threat to both 'normalised' knowledges and disciplinary powers.[48]

For Bhabha mimicry does not belong to either of the sides of the colonial divide. It is not only a strategy of appropriation and discipline but also a sign of the inappropriate, questioning the colonial authority and crossing the boundary line between the oppressor and the oppressed. Performing the intrinsic alterity of the self estranged by the gaze of 'the other', Laurie Anderson both repeats and unravels the colonial structuring of power. This is not to justify her use of the metaphor of 'the native' but rather to indicate what we could call the simultaneous deconstruction of oppression represented by colonial masks. Interestingly, Donna Haraway builds a link between her cyborgian consciousness – arguably part of the privileged American discourse of late capitalism, although one that is constructed with a view to opening up a discursive space for the marginal and the oppressed – and what she defines, after the Vietnamese-American theorist Trinh Minh-ha, as 'inappropriate/d others'.

> Designating the networks of multicultural, ethnic, racial, national, and sexual actors emerging since World War II, Trinh's phrase referred to the historical positioning of those who cannot adopt the mask of either 'self' or 'other' offered by previously dominant, modern, Western narratives of identity and politics. To be 'inappropriate/d' does not mean 'not to be in relation with' – i.e., to be in a special reservation, with the status of the authentic, the untouched, in the allochronic and allotopic condition of innocence. Rather to be an 'inappropriate/d other' means to be in critical, deconstructive relationality, in a diffracting rather than reflecting (ratio)nality – as the means of making potent connection that exceeds domination. To be inappropriate/d is not to fit in the taxon, to be dislocated from the available maps specifying kinds of actors and kinds of narratives, not to be originally fixed by difference.[49]

From this perspective cyborgian consciousness should not be seen as something Haraway constructs and then gives to the 'inappropriate/d'. Instead, it describes the processes of identity (de)formation and resistance which occur across the matrix of dominant discourses. The cyborg is inappropriate/d because it (she?) cannot be easily situated within what Bhabha calls '"normalised" knowledges and disciplinary powers'. Cyborgian aesthetics is thus a challenge for the Western model of representation: it mimics its rationality and visual certainty by diffracting rather than reflecting its standards of propriety. If bodies are the markers of taxonomic difference in the Western narratives of identity and politics, shifting the level of identification beyond the visual and into the aural creates the possibility of identity displacement and of new forms of identification. In this sense, Anderson's artistic politics of 'voice-crossing' can be seen as a cyborgian strategy of difference, displaying a gap, or cut, between the visual and the aural. Cubitt ironically remarks that 'the complex interplay of art and industry seems to make her, in some malicious sense, author of the archetypal yuppie album [i.e. *Big Science*, which includes the 'O Superman' number-one hit]'.[50] But Cubitt's 'bitter' conclusion merely indicates that no one 'owns' cyborgian consciousness, and that its oppositionality results from the fact that it is not guaranteed or protected by any special laws. In order to be able to challenge the dominant narratives of power, the cyborg needs first of all to be 'in relation with' them: a totally disconnected cyborg is nothing more than a utopian fantasy of linearly traceable post-feminism or post-colonialism.

> But hey, girls?
> We can take it and if we can't
> We're gonna fake it. ('Beautiful Red Dress')

Significantly, Cubitt recognises the power of Anderson's 'voice-bending', but remains suspicious about its ability to change anything: 'Making a noise, as Anderson does, and making a noise with her voice, not just, in the words of the old rock'n'roll song, in the kitchen rattling the pots and pans, challenges both subordination and weak subjectivity. But it cannot do so without profound ambivalence about what is to be achieved'.[51] However, ambivalence in this context signifies failure: not before long does Cubitt accuse Anderson of banality and 'the decay of individuality'. '[T]he estrangement of the voice from the body' is for him an indubitably bad thing. Any oppositionality that Anderson's performance might have produced is, according to Cubitt, absorbed by the capitalist machinery of the culture industry: she thus becomes yet another object of the yuppie's pleasure. This kind of reading of what Cubitt himself terms 'a cyborg reconstruction' is an interesting example of an appropriation of the figure of the cyborg by the dominant narrative of 'normalised knowledges and disciplinary powers'. In his account, the capitalist media network encompasses the revolutionary character of the artist's noise, which becomes one more tune in the perfect symphony of high capitalism. And yet, it is difficult not to conclude that it is Cubitt's fixed perception of the working of culture and power (which, paradoxically, still lets him retain the critical awareness he deprives Anderson of) that allows him to overlook the intrinsic ambiguity at work in the mimicry of the artist's performance. What Cubitt defines as 'the tyranny of mediation' in Anderson's performances can be seen as the enactment of what Derrida terms 'iterability' in speech, revealing that our voice is never ultimately ours but rather belongs to, and comes from, the other. It is only in this sense that 'estrangement' can bring a promise of an ethical opening, extending a welcoming gesture to the unknown and not-yet-domesticated (i.e. not yet a guest in our *domus*/home). As Derrida concludes in *Adieu to Emmanuel Levinas*,

> One should no doubt extend without limit the consequences of what Levinas asserts in a passage where he repeats and interprets the idea of infinity in the Cartesian *cogito*: 'It is not I, it is the other that can say yes'. ... [C]ould it not be argued that, without exonerating myself in the least, decision and responsibility are always of the other? They always come back or come down to the other, from the other, even if it is the other in me?[52]

Anderson's modulated vowels which challenge the idea of 'the real voice', her splitting of the process of identity formation into a series of 'events' and her dependence on technological prostheses that intrude into and displace the togetherness of the human, all contribute to the cyborgian ethics of welcome. This ethics differs from Chris Hables Gray's more 'positivist' ethics of cyborg embodiment, which is focused on the cyborg bill of rights and the recognition of, as well as respect for, the self *before* the other. The cyborgian ethics I propose and trace in the work of Orlan and Laurie Anderson is a technological version of the singular ethics of the feminine sublime which I develop in previous chapters, an ethics which does not rely on the clearly delineated subjectivity of its moral agents. With the impossibility of the separation of a discrete aesthetic realm and the failure of representation, the ethics of the feminine sublime embraces the irreducible alterity of the other which defies perception but none the less evokes desire. The ethical moment arises out of the renunciation of the urge to domesticate this alterity by either maintaining a proper distance from the other or by translating the unknown into the familiar. This ethics – in a similar vein to Derrida's ethics of hospitality which goes back to Levinas's ethics before ontology and before the ultimate 'freezing' of the self – stems from the disavowal of the desire for totality. Introducing 'femininity' as a sign of both irreducible difference and masquerade, it reveals an inherent lack in the Western phallogocentric discourse of representation. The hybridity of the cyborg foregrounds thus an irreducible alterity of the self and the other, with technology acting as both mediation and interference.

> Only by being out of place could we take intense pleasure in machines, and then with excuses that this was organic activity after all, appropriate to females. Cyborgs might consider more seriously the partial, fluid, sometimes aspect of sex and sexual embodiment.[53]

The cyborgian ethics of hospitality can be perceived as a feminist project because it challenges the conformity and knowability of the self *and* the other. It allows for the rewriting of the boundaries of the body, which are seen as 'the limits of the socially hegemonic'.[54] Cyborgs challenge the traditional separation between nature and technology, revealing a hiatus at the core of identity: the art of both Orlan and Laurie Anderson demonstrates that the image of selfhood is ultimately empty. Their performances by no means constitute a proposal for an easy feminist politics of donning a new costume of women's identity, just as Butler's idea of gender as performativity must not be reduced to an agent-driven theatrical performance, conducted by the pre-conceptualised self fully in control of the available material. What Orlan and Anderson do is precisely reveal the impossibility of such a volitional change, directed from an egological position. Their masquerade both challenges the dominant modes of representation and depends on them for their project. Their 'masks' share the register they challenge, making '"visible", by an effect of playful repetition, what was supposed to remain invisible: the cover-up of a possible operation of the feminine in language'.[55] As Butler concludes in *Gender Trouble*, 'The critical task for feminism is … to locate strategies of subversive repetition enabled by those constructions, to affirm the local possibilities of intervention through participating in precisely those practices of repetition that constitute identity and, therefore, present the immanent possibility of contesting them'.[56]

The repetition of the feminine performance, the enactment of identity as prescribed by the rigid rules of the gender matrix, is always already subversive. It reveals the intrinsic emptiness of identity and its dependence on repetition which assures continuity. In this sense, Orlan and Anderson present a double act, performing the performance of gender and thus displaying a gap between the Symbol and the Thing which is ultimately empty. It is not necessarily through art that fixed identity can be challenged, but artistic practices of this kind foreground the broadly enacted performativity of identity: every act of 'doing femininity' is always already its undoing. These performances result in the acquisition of critical consciousness and the elaboration of the script that will now also incorporate a feminist gloss. Butler's argument bears an affinity with Derrida's understanding of deconstruction as an 'event', always already occurring in the network of discourses which Western metaphysics tries to protect from undecidability. In this light, 'gender' (and 'sex', which Butler also sees as constructed) presents itself as an event which is permanently fraught with instability, its very enactment bearing a trace of ruin and loss. As Butler herself explains:

As a sedimented effect of a reiterative or ritual practice, sex acquires its naturalised effect, and, yet, it is also by virtue of this reiteration that gaps and fissures are opened up as the constitutive instabilities in such constructions, as that which escapes or exceeds the norm, as that which cannot be wholly defined or fixed by the repetitive labour of that norm. This instability is the deconstructing possibility in the very process of repetition, the power that undoes the very effects by which 'sex' is stabilised, the possibility to put the consolidation of the norms of 'sex' into a potentially productive crisis.[57]

Cyborgian ethics as the technological 'application' of the ethics of the feminine sublime is one way of not only recognising this undecidability of gender but also of opening oneself to the arrival of the other. It encourages us to extend a welcoming (prosthetic?) hand to what will appear (i.e. de-MONSTR-ate itself) before our eyes. But monstrosity here is situated beyond eighteenth- and nineteenth-century semi-scientific discourse.[58] For Rosi Braidotti, monstrosity is a new value in a world in which desire for close encounters has not been superseded by the fear of mutability and chaos. Today's monsters do not remain confined to the space of the deformed, oversexual, but nevertheless traceable, body. Inscribed in the matrix of cybernetic experiments and gender fluidities, they foreground both the threat *and* promise of technological change. The recognition of the experience of monstrosity as part and parcel of the everyday allows us to rethink the idea of the 'human', traditionally defined against expelled alterity (i.e. in the form of non-normative sexuality, skin colour, ethnicity, etc.). But the ethics of the feminine sublime I propose here does not celebrate the global transformation of the world by new technologies, instead focusing on singular events which take place in a local, minimal perspective. Contrarily to the great narratives of techno-logical progress *or* technological apocalypse, the feminine sublime reminds us that things change always differently.

Notes

1 Sadie Plant, *Zeros + Ones: Digital Women + the New Technoculture* (London: Fourth Estate, 1997), 11–12.
2 Donna Haraway, 'A Manifesto for Cyborgs: Science, Technology, and Socialist Feminism in the 1980s', in *Coming to Terms*, ed. Elizabeth Weed (New York and London: Routledge, 1989), 174.
3 Sadie Plant's work on cybernetic feminism gave impetus to the emergence of a wide number of texts investigating the relationship between women and new technologies and adopting the concept of the cyborg for a feminist agenda. For an interesting selection of writings on this subject see Jenny

Wolmark ed., *Cybersexualities: A Reader on Feminist Theory, Cyborgs and Cyberspace* (Edinburgh: Edinburgh University Press, 1999).

4 N. Katherine Hayles, 'The Life Cycle of Cyborgs: Writing the Posthuman', in *The Cyborg Handbook*, ed. Chris Hables Gray (New York and London: Routledge, 1995), 322.

5 I am aware of the debates in both the gay and lesbian and the feminist community concerning the expansion of the term 'queer', which some see as a welcome shift beyond the ghetto of identity politics while others perceive as a reappropriation of the homosexual discourse by some 'straight theorists' in search of 'sexy' jargon. Biddy Martin's article 'Sexualities Without Genders and Other Queer Utopias' in *Coming Out of Feminism*, eds Mandy Merck, Naomi Segal, Elizabeth Wright (Oxford: Blackwell, 1998) is an interesting attempt to 'reconnect' queerness to specific sexual practices. The way in which I use the idea of the queerness of identity in this chapter is thus not disconnected from the sexual aspect of being: queerness queries the normativity of what Butler describes as the heterosexual matrix. However, it should not be seen as a one-way shift from the norm of the hetero to the playful uncertainty of the homo. If this approach is to be read as a betrayal of the concept of queerness, let me just quote after Patrick D. Hopkins that '"Queers" – the name itself bespeaks curiosity, treachery, radical unidentifiability, the uncategorised, perverse entities, infectious otherness', 'Gender Treachery: Homophobia, Masculinity, and Threatened Identities', in *Race, Class, Gender, and Sexuality: The Big Question*, eds Naomi Zack et al. (Oxford: Blackwell, 1998), 184.

6 Haraway, 'A Manifesto for Cyborgs', 176, emphasis added. In her 'Manifesto', Haraway emphasises the uncertain ontology of the cyborg: 'The cyborg is a condensed image of both imagination and material reality, the two joined centres structuring any possibility of historical transformation' (174). It is only in some later projects based on her idea that the cyborg undergoes a process of 'literalisation', thus losing its ambiguous positioning between the material and the virtual, or object and metaphor.

7 Claudia Springer, 'The Pleasure of the Interface', in *Cybersexualities*, 35.

8 Andreas Huyssen, 'The Vamp and the Machine: Technology and Sexuality in Fritz Lang's Metropolis', *New German Critique*, 24:5 (1981–82), 226.

9 Ibid., 152.

10 Luce Irigaray, *This Sex Which Is Not One*, trans. Catherine Porter (Ithaca, New York: Cornell University Press, 1985), 76.

11 This suggestion comes from Judith Halberstam, who was a very supportive reviewer for one of my earlier projects on cyberfeminism and women's art.

12 Sadie Plant, 'The Future Looms: Weaving Women and Cybernetics', *Body and Society*, 1:3–4 (1995), 63.

13 The idea of femininity as masquerade was developed by Joan Riviere in her essay 'Womanliness as a Masquerade', which was first published in 1929 (in *Psychoanalysis and Female Sexuality*, ed. Hendrick M. Ruitenbeek (New Haven: College and University Press, 1966)). For a discussion of how this concept evolved in twentieth-century theories of sexuality see Mary Ann Doane, 'Film and the Masquerade: Theorising the Female Spectator' in *Writing on the Body*, eds Katie Conboy, Nadia Medina and Sarah Stanbury (New York: Columbia

University Press, 1997) and Judith Butler, 'Lacan, Riviere and the Strategies of Masquerade', in *Gender Trouble: Feminism and the Subversion of Identity* (New York and London: Routledge, 1990).

14 Jean-François Lyotard, *The Postmodern Condition: A Report on Knowledge*, trans. Geoff Bennington and Brian Massumi (Manchester: Manchester University Press, 1986), 81.

15 Jennifer González, 'Envisioning Cyborg Bodies: Notes from Current Research', in *Cybersexualities*, 268.

16 Sadie Plant, 'On the Matrix: Cyberfeminist Simulations', in *Cultures of Internet*, ed. Rob Shields (London, Thousand Oaks, New Delhi: Sage, 1996), 183.

17 Ibid., 170.

18 Haraway, 'A Manifesto for Cyborgs', 174, emphasis added.

19 However, Chris Hables Gray's article 'The Ethics and Politics of Cyborg Embodiment: Citizenship as Hypervalue', *Cultural Values*, 1:2 (1997) is promisingly radical in its extension of the issues of citizenship and ethics onto cyborgs. As Gray points out, the prosthetic transformations of bodies and identities provoke a whole new set of questions regarding ethics and politics in what he terms 'twenty-first century cyborg societies'.

20 Jill Marsden, 'Virtual Sexes and Feminist Futures: The Philosophy of "Cyberfeminism"', *Radical Philosophy*, 78:July/August (1996), 14.

21 Jacques Derrida, 'Passages – from Traumatism to Promise', in *Points … Interviews, 1974–1994*, Jacques Derrida, ed. Elizabeth Weber (Stanford: Stanford University Press, 1995), 386–7.

22 Ibid., 386.

23 Jacques Derrida, 'My Chances / Mes Chances: A Rendezvous with Some Epicurean Stereophonies', in *Taking Chances: Derrida, Psychoanalysis and Literature*, eds Joseph H. Smith and William Kerrigan (Baltimore and London: The Johns Hopkins University Press, 1984), 31.

24 González, 'Envisioning Cyborg Bodies', 272.

25 Michelle Hirschorn, 'Orlan: Artist in the Post-Human Age of Mechanical Reincarnation', in *Generations and Geographies in the Visual Arts: Feminist Readings*, ed. Griselda Pollock (London and New York: Routledge, 1996), 111–12. By early 2000, Orlan has not yet completed the initially designed cycle of her operations. She is now involved in a project called *Self-Hybridation*, which involves preparing a series of digitally mastered photographs of her face transformed by the aesthetics of Pre-Columbian America. For a detailed discussion of Orlan's current artistic engagements, see Robert Ayers, 'Serene and Happy and Distant: An Interview with Orlan', *Body and Society*, 5:2–3 (1999).

26 Sarah Wilson, '*L'histoire d'O*, Sacred and Profane', in *Orlan: This Is My Body… This Is My Software*, Orlan (London: Black Dog Publishing, 1996), 8.

27 Mary Russo, 'Female Grotesques: Carnival and Theory', in *Writing on the Body*, 318.

28 In his book *Second Skins: the Body Narratives of Transsexuality* (New York: Columbia University Press, 1998), Jay Prosser accuses Orlan of perpetuating the myth of transsexualism as only a skin-deep phenomenon. Allucquère Rosanne Stone, on the contrary, sees Orlan's work as offering a conceptual promise to rigid gender and sexual identities: '[H]er performances call into

question not only the way we ground identity in physical form but also ... force us to see how we collude in the destruction of our own human civilisation. The dislocation and revulsion at watching Orlan's operations is a reflection of the much deeper and more powerful revulsion of finding our own identities annihilated. Do you see the hope in this? I certainly do', 'Speaking of the Medium: Marshall McLuhan Interviews A. R. Stone', in *Orlan: This Is My Body...*, 49–50.

29 Plant, *Zeros + Ones*, 212.

30 Orlan, 'Conférence' in *Orlan: This Is My Body ...*, 85.

31 Barbara Claire Freeman, *The Feminine Sublime: Gender and Excess in Women's Fiction* (Berkeley, Los Angeles and London: University of California Press, 1995), 50. Freeman refers here to the following passage from Burke's *Enquiry*: 'Observe that a beautiful woman where she is perhaps the most beautiful, about the neck and breasts; the smoothness; the softness; the easy and insensible swell; the variety of the surface, which is never for the smallest space the same; the deceitful maze, through which the unsteady eye slides giddily, without knowing where to fix, or whither it is carried', quoted in Freeman, 50.

32 Irigaray quoted in Parveen Adams, *The Emptiness of the Image: Psychoanalysis and Sexual Difference* (London and New York: Routledge, 1996), 60. In 'Film and the Masquerade: Theorising the Female Spectator' Mary Ann Doane argues that 'It is precisely this opposition between proximity and distance, control of the image and its loss, which locates the possibilities of spectatorship within the problematic of sexual difference. For the female spectator there is a certain overpresence of the image – she is the image', in *Writing on the Body*, 181.

33 Adams, *Emptiness of the Image*, 145.

34 Ibid., 156.

35 Ibid., 154.

36 Jean-François Lyotard, *The Inhuman*, trans. Geoffrey Bennington and Rachel Bowlby (Cambridge: Polity Press, 1991), 150.

37 Judith Butler, *The Psychic Life of Power* (Stanford: Stanford University Press, 1997), 145.

38 Ibid., 146.

39 Orlan, 'Conférence', 88.

40 Derrida, 'Passages', 387.

41 Plant, *Zeros + Ones*, 59.

42 Orlan, 'Conférence', 88.

43 Adams, *The Emptiness of the Image*, 165.

44 Richard Kadrey and Larry McCaffery, 'Cyberpunk 101: A Schematic Guide to Storming the Reality Studio', in *Storming the Reality Studio: A Casebook of Cyberpunk and Postmodern Science Fiction*, ed. Larry McCaffery (Durham and London: Duke University Press, 1991), 25. The motifs of the fall, sudden turn of fate and impending catastrophe recur in a number of Laurie Anderson's songs. 'From the Air' featured on her 1982 *Big Science* album starts as follows: 'Good evening. This is your Captain. We are about to attempt a crash landing. Please extinguish all cigarettes.' Spiralling down the vocal tracks traced by the artist, we soon find out that 'There is no pilot. You are not alone. Standby. This is the time.'

45 Lyotard, *The Inhuman*, 84.
46 Sean Cubitt, 'Laurie Anderson: Myth, Management and Platitude', in *Art Has No History? The Making and Unmaking of Modern Art* (London and New York: Verso, 1994), 286.
47 Plant, *Zeros + Ones*, 95
48   Homi K. Bhabha, *The Location of Culture* (London and New York: Routledge, 1993), 86.
49 Donna Haraway, 'The Promises of Monsters: A Regenerative Politics for Inappropriate/d Others', in *Cybersexualities*, 319–20.
50 Cubitt, 'Laurie Anderson: Myth, Management and Platitude', 278.
51 Ibid., 282.
52 Jacques Derrida, *Adieu to Emmanuel Levinas*, trans. Pascale-Anne Brault and Michael Naas (Stanford: Stanford University Press, 1999), 23.
53 Haraway, 'A Manifesto for Cyborgs', 203.
54 Butler, *Gender Trouble*, 167.
55 Irigaray, *This Sex Which Is Not One*, 76.
56 Butler, *Gender Trouble*, 188.
57 Judith Butler, *Bodies That Matter: On the Discursive Limits of 'Sex'* (New York and London: Routledge, 1993), 10.
58 As Rosi Braidotti explains, monstrosity does not signify an abstract marker of difference. Instead, it should be seen as a historically produced political category which helped to organise the psycho-social universe and control what could potentially threaten its limits. In the eighteenth and nineteenth century, monsters were seen as figures of 'bad flesh', but they also provided an opening for the corporeal fascination which did not conform with what Judith Butler terms 'the heterosexual matrix', with its pre-defined spaces and objects of desire. 'The Greek etymology of the term [monster] … leaves us in no doubt as to what is at stake: *teras/teratos* refers to both a prodigy and to a demon. It is something which evokes both horror and fascination, aberration and adoration. It is simultaneously holy and hellish, sacred and profane. Again, this simultaneity of opposite effects is the trademark of the monstrous body. … A working definition of the term 'monster' has been available since the late eighteenth century, when Geoffroy de Saint Hilaire organised monsters in terms of excess, lack or displacement of his/her organs. There can be too many parts or too few; the right ones can be in the wrong places or duplicated at random on the surface of the body.' 'Signs of Wonder and Traces of Doubt: On Teratology and Embodied Differences', in *Between Monsters, Goddesses and Cyborgs: Feminist Confrontations with Science, Medicine and Cyberspace*, eds Nina Lykke and Rosi Braidotti (London and New Jersey: Zed Books, 1996), 136.

3 Micro-spaces of the everyday: 'the [feminine] sublime is here and now'

Minimal perspective

> I found it terrible and magnificent, this workaday world, with coffee pot and rolls and Marie's washed-out blue and white apron over her green dress, and it seemed to me that it was only women who took the workaday world as much for granted as their bodies. (Heinrich Böll, *The Clown*)

In this chapter I want to explore the possibility of the occurrence of the sublime in a minimal, local perspective, as opposed to the grandeur of scale which characterised the traditional sublime. The minimal perspective will be a guarantee of the singularity of an ethical event of the sublime and will prevent this event from being judged according to a pre-established moral code. Inspired by Wittgenstein's philosophy of ordinary language and the attitude of 'Critical Regionalism' in postmodern architecture, I intend to follow architectural metaphors to trace the limits of the sublime space. This will help me to elaborate the concept of the cybercity, which I will use as an example of a space in which the singular ethics of hospitality and respect I have developed here under the name of the feminine sublime can take place. Suspended between the excess of digital signs and spaces and the lack of a clearly traceable form, the cybercity transgresses the splendour of the modernist metropolis, with its underlying ideology of progress and mastery.

According to Jean-François Lyotard, it is precisely in the minimal perspective that the sublime can be encountered: 'What is sublime is the feeling that something will happen, despite everything, within this threatening void, that something will take "place" and will announce that everything is not over. That place is mere "here", the most minimal occurrence'.[1] Drawing attention to the uniqueness of every event, Lyotard advises respect towards the unpresentability of the sublime. This kind of attitude can be displayed by a mature self, one that is ready to take responsibility for the irreducible difference encountered in the sublime event instead of trying to subjugate it. In

this way, colonising fantasies are overcome by the desire of the wanderer, who is keen to learn as much as possible about new territories.

Such a respectful attitude towards the minimal and the local
corresponds to what Kenneth Frampton calls Critical Regionalism, a
term he uses to expound his theory of the architecture of resistance:

> The fundamental strategy of Critical Regionalism is to mediate the
> impact of universal civilisation with elements derived *indirectly* from
> the peculiarities of a particular place. It is clear from the above that
> Critical Regionalism depends upon maintaining a high level of
> critical self-consciousness. It may find its governing inspiration in
> such things as the range and quality of the local light, or in a *tectonic*
> derived from a peculiar structural mode, or in the topography of a
> given site.[2]

I would like to propose that every encounter with the other occurring
under the aegis of the feminine sublime be seen as a singular event,
immersed in the local perspective and defying the possibility of
comprehensive theorisation. It is the recognition of not only the
alterity of the other but also the specificity of the place in which the
encounter with the other is occurring that will grant this event an
ethical character. Respect for what Frampton calls 'the peculiarities of
a particular place' will result in both parties maintaining 'a high level
of critical consciousness'. This critical attitude and the recognition of
spatial detail save the ethics of the feminine sublime from being
confined to a generalised prescriptive formula. The ethics of the feminine sublime cannot be described as a sum of possibilities, as there
always remains an event which has not happened yet but is only on
the verge of taking place. However, this ethics is also haunted by the
fear of nothing happening at all. A participant in the event occurring
under its aegis can, nevertheless, find a way of relieving this tension
by concentrating on an illogical belief in the long-awaited arrival of
the other and the pleasure resulting from his or her potential
proximity. Due to its unstable positioning and uncertain occurrence,
the sublime event, which is not 'a major event in the media sense, not
even a small event, [j]ust an occurrence',[3] is thus characterised by
certain poverty, or what Lyotard refers to, after Burke, as privation.
Even though the everyday event of the sublime borders on nothingness, it does not reduce the gravity of the ethical duty. Its minimality
does not justify disrespect: it calls for a change of perspective.

In her book *Szczeliny istnienia* (The Crevices of Being), the Polish
thinker Jolanta Brach-Czaina accuses philosophers of disregarding the

particularity of existence. This results in their inability to hear Being speak to us, 'not as a totality, but through existential detail, or meaningful particulars. These can indeed evoke the voice of totality, but only when it is reverberating in the particles of being'.[4] The particles of being are, nevertheless, different from 'fragments of reality', which have been stained with violence and separation. According to Brach-Czaina, fragments have a cataclysmic nature; they remind us of wounds and evoke the physical and emotional pain of separation. 'The act of cutting fragments out of reality is a result of the mind's desperate struggle to find its place in the world. This struggle is conducted, nevertheless, in a way that does not allow us to listen to the world, but only to tear apart, crunch and hurriedly exploit the reality around us.'[5] The violent act of fragmentation silences what Brach-Czaina calls 'the voice of the world'. This is why she suggests we should let ourselves be attracted by the particles of being and, consequently, lend them attention. Approaching the particularity of existence as listeners rather than conquerors enables us to perform an ethical act towards every inconspicuous object in the world.

Such an attitude of respect does not seem groundless, given the effect everyday objects can have on us. A simple stone, too common to be noticed, can, in fact, be a source of fear 'when we think of our fragility compared with the impertinence of the stone's solidity'.[6] The flavour of a plain cherry can *under certain circumstances* paralyse our sense of well-being, offering more than we can accommodate into our conceptual or sensual spectrum. 'It is so complex that one cannot really describe in one word what it is like. Probably disturbing, first of all.'[7] Brach-Czaina constructs here a kind of 'inverted sublime', revealing the boundless residues of affect that can be triggered by the objects of everyday life. We can trample over them, ignoring their insistent call, and thus exerting physical power over them, but we can also open to the particles of being and listen to their story. Here, delight will always be combined with disappointment. The apparent familiarity of everyday objects will eventually disillusion the self that desires to accumulate complete knowledge about the world and systematise it into its own private encyclopaedia. The everyday transcends the traditional wisdom of the Book. It reveals more than can be housed in the mind of Experts and Philosophers, who refuse to accept the limitlessness of Being.

Wittgenstein's philosophy of ordinary language

> If our existence mainly takes place through commonplace experi-
> ence, among ordinary activities, then by denying them significance
> we negate ourselves. (Jolanta Brach-Czaina, *Szczeliny istnienia*)

Neither Experts nor Philosophers hold the key to the wisdom of the
world. If their scientific calculations, performed from a position of
distance, were to give way to the act of listening Brach-Czaina recommends, such a respectful attitude towards what we may call 'the
existential excess of the everyday' would have to result in the rejection of the position of mastery towards language. Michel de Certeau
notices that philosophers often believe in their privileged relationship
to meaning, while in fact they only '*think that they dominate it* so that
they can authorise themselves to deal with it'.[8] Subject to ordinary
language, and thus deprived of the critical distance they would like to
retain in relation to the object of their analysis, they are denied the
exclusive position they have claimed for themselves. As de Certeau
concludes:

> By being 'caught' within ordinary language, the philosopher no
> longer has his own (*propre*) appropriable place. Any position of mastery
> is denied him. The analysing discourse and the analysed 'object' are
> in the same situation: both are organised by the practical activity
> with which they are concerned, both are determined by rules they
> neither establish nor see clearly. ... Philosophical or scientific privi-
> lege disappears into the ordinary.[9]

Ludwig Wittgenstein's philosophy of ordinary language is opposed to
both specialised and technicised discourses of modern experts, and to
the nonsensical babble of the crowd. In his attempts to protect the
ordinary against the rhetorical brilliance of philosophers who only
manage to confirm their authority, Wittgenstein starts from the most
basic premise: 'The world is everything that is the case'. This proposition is further developed by means of the following statement: 'The
world is the totality of facts, not of things'.[10] In Wittgenstein's theory
of language, 'language consists of propositions which picture the
world. Propositions are the perceptible expressions of thoughts, and
thoughts are logical pictures of facts'.[11] The reduction of being to facts,
or possible states of affairs, makes volatile philosophical disputes
pointless from the very start: philosophy can only *describe* the world
and not explain it. The aim of this approach is not, however, to
discourage people from attempting to say the unsayable, but, first of

all, 'to protect the ethical from babbling'.[12] This seems to be the idea behind the whole of Wittgenstein's first major work, *Tractatus Logico-Philosphicus*, whose precise and almost geometrical structure illustrates the limits of language. Even though language will never be able to express the unspeakable, this should not stop people from trying to 'constantly run up against the limits of the language'. In this way, Wittgenstein opens a debate about the ethical and its duty.

Wittgenstein's thought is by no means opportunistic. Although in a world understood as a logical space, and whose reality consists of '[t]he existence and non-existence of atomic facts',[13] the advocated silence is the only possible way of dealing with the inexpressible, Wittgenstein does not deny the existence of what defies language and perception. 'There is indeed the inexpressible. This shows itself; it is the mystical.'[14] He recommends an attitude of humility towards such phenomena, which results from his awareness of the self's limitations. Recognising the boundaries of its world, the self abandons the mastering desire to say what cannot be said, and then to pass it for 'truth'. This is why absolute aesthetic and ethical utterances – even if pronounced in a voice of authority – are meaningless, as they remain outside the reach of language. Philosophy can only describe the world, but it cannot explain it to us, even though metaphysical pretence (i.e. belief in the ability to explain the principle of being), since Parmenides and Plato, has constituted its unspoken foundation. Again, this does not mean that Wittgenstein is not interested in ethical issues, even if he does challenge the traditional understanding of ethics and its tasks. As George Pitcher argues:

> Ethical propositions, as usually understood, do not state facts, do not state what happens to be the case. On the contrary, they say that certain situations are good or bad, ought or ought not to exist, and so on – they pass judgement on what happens to be the case. Ethical propositions thus purport to say something 'higher' than ordinary descriptive propositions, which merely state facts. But if the doctrines of the *Tractatus* are correct, such things cannot be said; descriptive propositions say all that can be said. Hence ethical propositions, as usually understood, do not exist any more than metaphysical ones do.[15]

Wittgenstein's whole project of tracing the boundaries of ordinary language can itself be seen as an ethical undertaking. Its 'rationale' springs from a desire to protect the inexpressible from being appropriated by the true/false discourse, whose truthfulness cannot be justified in language. In the *Tractatus* Wittgenstein calls for the recognition of the unnameable which should not be eliminated or forgotten. The necessity to constantly retrace the paths of language in search of possible significations, combined with the invitation to lend attention to the most minuscule detail, constitutes a singular ethical duty. The ultimate responsibility for meaning rests with the individual (or what Wittgenstein terms 'the empirical self'), who draws boundaries for the understanding of 'propositions', i.e. projections of all possible states of affairs. Meaning can thus be approached only from a singular, minimal position, expressed in the following declaration: 'I am my world. (The microcosm.)'.[16] However, Wittgenstein does not privilege individual experience as an irrefutable guarantee of transcendental meaning. On the contrary, the statement, 'I am my world. (The microcosm.)', expressed at the end of the *Tractatus*, illustrates his consent to remain silent about the things of which one cannot speak. This is an attitude of the self that does not situate itself above language and does not intend to confine inexpressible meanings to a coherent 'theory'.

In his book *Wittgenstein*, Robert J. Fogelin reveals Wittgenstein's fascination with Tolstoy's ethical ideal: 'one of simplicity, austerity, honesty, and humanity'.[17] Such an ideal manifests itself in simple stories and genuine narratives about the objects of everyday life. If the world 'is everything that is the case', the contemplation of each thing *as if it was the world* shifts the perspective from the universal to the particular which can *become* the whole world, provided it is given enough attention. Wittgenstein explains, 'If I have been contemplating the stove, and then am told: but now all you know is the stove, my result does indeed seem trivial. For this represents the matter as if I had studied the stove as one among the many things in the world. But if I was contemplating the stove *it* was my world, and everything else colourless by contrast with it.'[18] Diané Collinson explains that 'This is again consistent with traditional accounts of aesthetic contemplation where it is typically one in which the whole of consciousness is inhabited by the object contemplated'.[19]

Wittgenstein's immersion in the perceived object is akin to Burke's and Kant's fascination with sublime phenomena that for an instant *become* the whole world for the spectator. Nevertheless, while earlier theorists of the sublime focused on extraordinary phenomena which threatened the self physically and emotionally while also alluring it with their power, Wittgenstein is attracted to the power of the everyday. He postulates the *sub specie aeternitatis* (i.e. 'from the standpoint of eternity') way of perception, which he explains as follows: 'The usual way of looking at things sees objects as it were from the midst of them, the view *sub specie aeternitatis* from outside.'[20] This eternal perspective allows him to propose an equation between aesthetics and ethics. Collinson provides the following justification for this conclusion:

> The attitude that is common to ethics and aesthetics is the way of seeing. Any differences are between the objects to which the attitude is directed. Something seen from the standpoint of eternity is seen not 'from the midst of things' but, Wittgenstein says, 'from outside'. Here we have, as the phrase 'as it were' indicates, simile but as yet no deep puzzlement; rather, an account that is certainly familiar as a description of aesthetic perception, characterising it as a shift from the everyday, practical relationship with what is perceived so that the object is seen and known in a way which is at once more vivid and more detached that the everyday attitude. We are to think of the ethical as sharing this attitude.[21]

The contemplation of another person or object *as if they were the whole world* establishes the conditions of value for the metaphysical self. It seems to me that aesthetics and ethics are not only comparable in this context but that the aesthetic contemplation of greatness in fact gives way to ethical engagement. The standpoint of eternity, which envelops the aesthetic and ethical space, leads to the annulment of the distance maintained by the metaphysical self. Totality is breached here by the singular instance of ethical contemplation, in which the stove, the cherry Brach-Czaina refers to, or another human being *becomes the whole world*. It was this potential intrusion of the grand object into the separate domain of the self that Burke and Kant perceived as a danger in the contemplation of greatness. In their theories of the sublime, they tried to diminish this danger by insisting on the necessity of maintaining a proper distance between the self and the source of greatness. In this way, sublime immersion was superseded by an act of observing one's distance.

Wittgenstein wants to save the contemplation of the aesthetic and the ethical from totalisation, which is why he finds it impossible to write a book on ethics. (We have moved here from the traditional perception of ethics as a collection of propositions about values to the understanding of ethics as withdrawal of a desire to formulate such propositions, coupled with a conviction about the need to constantly retrace the boundaries of language and the propositions it allows us to make.) A book on ethics would 'with an explosion, destroy all the other books in the world'[22] and thus would turn the contemplation of inexpressible greatness (which is a description of, or even another name for, sublimity) into an act of violence. Instead, Wittgenstein argues this unspeakable greatness should be left in the form of a potential which would exceed the expressible, but which would not be materialised into a manual of ethics. When attempting to fix his mind on an absolute or ethical value, Wittgenstein concludes: 'And there, in my case, it always happens that the idea of one particular experience presents itself to me which therefore is, in a sense, my experience *par excellence* and this is the reason why, in talking to you now, I will use this experience as my first and foremost example. ... I believe the best way of describing it is to say that when I have it *I wonder at the existence of the world*'.[23]

To be considered ethical, the events that occur to us do not have to be 'major events in the media sense'. Their minimal character and local positioning do not deprive them of an ethical signification. Indeed, Wittgenstein has argued that it is only through the most minimal occurrences that any sort of 'truth' about the world can be revealed. Unable to draw the ultimate ethical proposal in a language which can only describe the world, I therefore resort to narration as one possible way of not only 'saving the ethical from babbling' but of also ascertaining that, despite everything, ethical questions will be raised. But the ethics of the feminine sublime which I am expounding in the book cannot be reduced to a list of prescriptions and regulations: it can only be described, and thus, necessarily, displaced. Perhaps it is not even a matter of remaining silent about the things we cannot authoritatively talk about, as Wittgenstein has concluded, but rather of recognising the dimension of undecidability in language (something his work testifies to in more than one way). This undecidability, or heterogeneity, of language makes the adequate representation of the world impossible. Contaminated by the virus of non-identity which continually entangles its multiple signifying threads, language is unable to raise itself above the world in order to tell a higher 'truth' about it.

In Wittgenstein's philosophy of ordinary language (delineated here, for lack of space, only in a most cursory way) I have found justification for my argument that the ethics of the feminine sublime I am sketching here cannot be confined to a code book consisting of prescriptions and regulations. Therefore, what is at issue in the feminine sublime is not its essence but the occurrences happening in its realm, the experience of which can lead to wonder and bewilderment. As I argue in chapter 2, the ethically predisposed self meets the other in his or her alterity. Demonstrating respect towards this alterity and opening to the amorous encounter, it is prepared to take delight in the fascinating, though also threatening, difference. In this way, a most commonplace event of meeting another being can turn the everyday into the extraordinary. The feminine sublime I develop in response to the tradition of the sublime could thus name the total immersion which characterises both aesthetic and ethical contemplation, and in which the dimension of distance and the subject–object separation are suspended. For Kant, the contemplation of greatness does occur *sub specie aeternitatis*, but – unlike for Wittgenstein – the blurring of the boundaries between aesthetics and ethics does not take place. The empirical self of aesthetic contemplation does not disappear either.[24] Instead, the contemplation of greatness confirms the boundaries of the metaphysical self, which is only able to wonder at its own greatness. It is worth mentioning, however, that the horizontal, everyday dimension is not explicitly rejected by Kant, as the following passage from the 'Analytic of the Sublime' reveals:

> Bold, overhanging, and, as it were, threatening rocks, thunderclouds piled up the vault of heaven, borne along with flashes and peals, volcanoes in all their violence of destruction, hurricanes leaving desolation in their track, the boundless ocean rising with rebellious force, the high waterfall of some mighty river, and the like, make our power of resistance of trifling moment in comparison with their might. But, provided our own position is secure, their aspect is all the more attractive for its fearfulness; and we readily call these objects sublime, because they raise the forces of the soul above the height of vulgar commonplace, and discover within us a power of resistance of quite another kind, which gives us courage to be able to measure ourselves against the seeming omnipotence of nature.[25]

Even though the self is temporarily threatened by the omnipotence of nature, its weakness is soon conquered by the power of reason. Where the senses fail due to their helplessness in the face of excessive height, reason comes to help with its ability to think what imagination cannot grasp. It is interesting to notice though that the battle between the faculties of one's mind takes place in two dimensions. On the vertical axis nature is superior because it poses a tangible threat to one's life.

Still, Kant introduces a horizontal dimension, represented by man establishing his secure position on earth, which is to assure his well-being and ultimate victory. Kant distinguishes here between 'the vulgar commonplace', not defined directly but opposed to the state of sublime elevation towards morality, and the security of man's situation on earth, which he does not valorise negatively. The horizontal perspective seems to have a double value – depending on its function it can either be despised as vulgar, and thus not worth the attention of a moral self, or found practical, if it assures the self's safety and its elevation towards morality.

The sublime and the uncanny

Wonder and astonishment, underpinned by the sense of novelty, are the first condition of the sublime, leading to the awakening of the feeling of respect. By drawing attention to an elevating aspect of the meeting with the other, Emmanuel Levinas – whose writings abound in sublime imagery – situates his ethics of respect for incalculable alterity on a vertical axis. When discussing the metaphysical (and thus impossible to fulfil) desire for the absolute alterity of the other, he claims: 'It is understood as the alterity of the Other and of the Most-High. The very dimension of height is opened up by metaphysical Desire. That this height is no longer the heavens but the Invisible is the very elevation of height and its nobility.'[26] We find ourselves again amidst the Kantian rhetoric of the sublime, where the unapproachable and the frightening is represented in the form of high mountains, water cascades and eddying clouds. Levinas clearly foregrounds the elevation and unattainability of the absolutely other, who is also described as 'the Most-High': 'To recognise the Other is to give. But it is to give to the master, to the lord, to him whom one approaches as "You" in a dimension of height'.[27]

The feminine sublime I propose here calls for a redefinition of spatial perspective. Re-evaluating 'the lowlands', it displaces the amorous meeting between the self and the other from the celestial level. In her philosophy of sexual difference Luce Irigaray takes a step down from the height of Levinasian face-to-face encounter with the other: she is more interested in a sensual pleasure resulting from this encounter than in the elevating spirituality Levinas emphasises. Irigaray contrasts man's respectful relation to corporeal exteriority against woman's indwelling in the materiality of bodily folds. Occupying a threshold position between inside and outside, fluidity and solidity, which is symbolised by mucous, woman laughs at men's delusion that erection is necessary in seduction and that seduction must necessarily come from outside. Her sexuality is not submitted to the rhythm of erection and detumescence, nor is her 'threshold' a limit. Thus, she responds to the provisionality of the masculine sublime, erect but necessarily finite, with her own economy of desire which is not bordered by the metaphysical limitations of presence and absence. The masculine economy is locked in a vertical position; it is centred around the erect signifier of passion which is supposed to regulate both the relationships of sameness (between men) and the encounters with the (sexually) other. For women, claims Irigaray, the vertical axis of the mother–daughter relationship crosses over the horizontal dimension referring to the relationships between women, or 'sisters'. Embracing both these dimensions, the feminine sublime does not exclusively refer to women's experiences, though it descends from the phallogocentric celestial realm constructed in opposition to the low-liness of the everyday. In our search for the sources of greatness and wonder it invites us to explore the folded surface of being, which is full of gaps, cracks and crevices. Alluring us with its gasping cuts and lumps, the world demands an attitude of openness and elicits a desire for immersion As Brach-Czaina puts it, 'Existential opening may indeed seem revolting, but those who, on seeing it, look away in disgust, defile all being. It is only when we are not repelled by the repulsive that we are ready to accept the world. Menace does not evoke fear in us if we go through it towards enchantment'.[28] To participate in the heterogeneity of being means to undertake a personal risk of both physical and existential pain. The feminine sublime demands from us an ethical decision to penetrate into the folds of the world and expose our bodies to the infinity of personal stories of love, desire and unfulfilment.

Instead of projecting one's fears into some external territories and cherishing fantasies about the possibility of taming the excessive and the frightening, the ethics of respect towards irreducible difference calls for the recognition of the strange as part of the everyday. The separation between the comfort of the familiar and the anxiety pro-voked by the unknown is precarious, as Freud's discussion of the phenomenon of the uncanny indicates. On the one hand, the uncanny 'is related to what is frightening – to what arouses dread and horror',[29] and thus should naturally correspond to the unknown. When exploring the etymology of the word uncanny (that is *'unheimlich'* in German), Freud discovers the term's double-coding:

> [A]mong its different shades of meaning the word 'heimlich' exhibits one which is identical with its opposite, *'unheimlich'*. What is *heimlich* thus comes to be *unheimlich*. ... [T]he word *'heimlich'* is not unambiguous, but belongs to two sets of ideas, which, without being contradictory, are yet very different: on the one hand it means what is familiar and agreeable, and on the other, what is concealed and kept out of sight.[30]

'Uncanny' can then be used to describe the phenomena that have been defamiliarised and have remained confined to external spaces, while in fact they return to light in one form or another, often haunting the legislators of order and the purity of thought. The relationship between the sublime and the uncanny seems uncanny itself, as it assumes their identity which, nevertheless, excludes sameness. Wendy Wheeler notices that the two terms, taken subsequently from an aesthetic and a psychoanalytic register, describe the situation when the institutions of modernity, such as the bourgeois family and the nation state, cease to be socially binding. 'In this event, two experiences (of the sublime, and of the uncanny), which are named or represented during Enlightenment as ways of formulating what has become formless (*das Unform* – the monstrous) or difficult to regulate with the demise of the sacred, may subsequently emerge in a closer affinity.'[31] The uncanny can be interpreted as the representation of anxiety at the heart of the modern world, with its conflicting feelings of technophilia and technophobia. It points to the shock effect evoked by the multiplicity of signs and spaces the self is exposed to in its everyday travels through the highly industrial, technicised landscape of modernity.

Metropolitan encounters

Where better to explore this uncanniness of modernity than in the busy metropolis, with its almost irresolvable clashes between wealth and poverty, technicity and nature, and art and commerce? Its everyday familiarity can always reveal 'what is concealed and kept out of sight' and therefore seems a fitting image for our analysis of the murky landscapes of the sublime and its ethical mappings. If the question of the self's identity can be perceived as a product of modernity,[32] then the concept of the modernist city can help us investigate the experience of identity and difference that is produced in urban space. Denying the possibility of delineating a coherent ethical proposal on its basis, the city only allows us to explore the boundaries of identity and selfhood through narrating the occurrences happening in it. The multiplicity of minimal events simultaneously occurring in the cityspace creates an opportunity for the emergence of the first condition of the sublime event: wonder. However, this multiplicity can also lead to the feeling of saturation and excess, exacerbating the conflict between the desire for immersion and connectivity and the fear of 'the loss of self'.

Political theorist Iris Marion Young shares this ambiguous feeling about modernism's triumphant constructions. In *Justice and the Politics of Difference*, she provides us with the following account of her use of the city metaphor in her political investigations: 'I propose to construct a normative ideal of city life as an alternative to both the ideal of community and the liberal individualism it criticises as asocial. By "city life" I mean a form of social relations which I define as being together of strangers'.[33] She defines the city as an 'openness to unassimilated otherness',[34] only to disclaim this perception as 'an unrealised social ideal'. However, by drawing attention to the 'connected' nature of city life, Young eroticises the city, but refuses to ethicise it, i.e. to perceive it as an ethical possibility. Her thinking is thus entrapped in the rigid opposition between the strange and the familiar. It prevents her from developing an ethical dimension of the city life: the unbridgeable gap between reality and ideality shifts the ethical impulse to the level of the impossible.

It is not surprising that the modernist ideal of the city as a symbol of civilisation and of man's triumphant victory over savage nature should be treated with suspicion. But, instead of relegating city imagery to the realm of the dream-wish, I want to pursue its uncanny structuring in search of 'the unthinkable'. At the same time, I intend to move beyond the idealised version of the modernist city and focus on its late twentieth-century offspring: the cybercity. The concept of the cybercity can help us to overcome what I perceive to be a false opposition between reality and ideality. Rather than dream of the construction of hospitable cities, as Young does, I want to explore the ethical possibility of the cybercity, with its openness towards unassimilated difference. The cybercity will thus be for me an illustration of ethical possibilities created by 'the being together of strangers'. But this possibility will not be congealed into an 'A–Z of City Ethics'. The infinite singularity of different events occurring in the cybercity, coupled with the uncertainty of its positioning or, indeed, occurrence and the minimality of scale, only allow me to treat the cybercity as one possible illustration – or perhaps 'enactment' – of the ethics of the feminine sublime.

Ethics in the cybercity

> Now, it seems to me that if I had a habitus ..., [it] would be much more like a cyberpunk novel, in which this room is not the grounding of a tradition but just another knot in the net. (Meaghan Morris, conference discussion, *Cultural Studies*)

The concept of the cybercity is parentless in its origin, its multiple influences going back to virtual reality games, cyberpunk fiction and the Internet. If the arcade, situated between the closure of the build-ing and the openness of the outdoor realm, symbolises the modern cityscape, the cybercity will be represented by the digital game arcade, mimicking the rational design of the modernist city without attempt-ing to allure us with any of its promises of social harmony and general well-being.[35] Cybercities are a product of multinational capitalism that enforces its power through hegemonic negotiation. But they should not be seen as *only* a sign of globalisation: they encapsulate, as well as generate, the intrinsic alterity of the selves that inhabit it. In fact, the question that concerns us here is not whether cybercities are real, but rather what one does in them; i.e. how one maps one's identity on to the cyberscape, and what kind of connections this mapping can produce. This is why the cybercity as I understand it is not a mere representation, or even a 'better copy', of reality: it is precisely its blurring of the boundaries between reality and imitation (or virtuality), work and play, light and darkness, and proximity and distance that have attracted me to this concept.

The cybercity can be seen as an attempt to trace a familiar form in (i.e. to insert a matrixial grid into) the disorienting density of cyber-space in order to establish, at least temporarily, a certain degree of order among its signs and spaces.[36] However, as M. Christine Boyer observes in *CyberCities*, 'The form of the matrix brings to the city a systemic order that hides its heterogeneous nature and the disjunctive positions we hold within it'.[37] The cybercity is thus a momentarily stabilised space, one which cannot be ultimately regulated and mastered. An attempt to order it only foregrounds the intrinsically hybrid, incommensurate nature of the spaces that constitute it. The cybercity presents itself as another (darker?) version of the modernist city whose rational organisation and traceable boundaries hide the squalor and darkness of what Boyer describes as 'the forgotten spaces' and 'the disavowed places'. Therefore, the main difference between the modernist city and the cybercity seems to me to consist in what I call a 'pedestrian attitude'. While the modernist city is often evoked with a certain aura of nostalgia for the past and for the order which perhaps was never present in the first place but was rather simulated by the rigid structuring of public places, the cybercity signifies the abandonment of the fantasy of the modernist city and the recognition of its intrinsic heterogeneity. Rather than being its total negation, the cybercity can be seen as a conceptual extension of the modernist metropolis, i.e. as an incorporation of the ideas of both city *and* jungle, or light *and* darkness. My perception of the cybercity, which is a useful concept for tracing the boundaries of the self when facing inaccommodable alterity, embraces both the material and the virtual. It thus overcomes Boyer's radical separation between the dirty, crime-ridden postmodern metropolis of the late twentieth century on the one hand, and its sanitised computer image of the cybercity which reflects a nostalgia for the certainties of modernism on the other.

The 'pedestrian attitude' towards the deeply missed, idealised modernist city manifests itself in social theories which set modernity against vaguely conceptualised, but none the less threatening, postmodernity. Boyer herself seems to be more comfortable in the grid of the modernist city than in what she defines as the jungle of the cybercity. For her, the cybercity is an illustration of the contemporary American megalopolis; it is a centre of crime, disease, unemployment and 'global urban disruption'. Claiming that 'our postmodern era appears to be decadent and devoid of social responsibility',[38] Boyer seems to be echoing Zygmunt Bauman's diagnosis of 'postmodernity' as 'life-as-strolling-in-the-shopping-mall'. This type of activity is described as disinterested and non-committed, leading in the end to 'the suppression of the moral impulse as well as disavowal and denigration of moral sentiments'.[39] Postmodernity also amounts here to the withdrawal of proximity and intimacy, resulting in what Boyer calls 'action at a distance' and what Bauman refers to as 'disengagement and commitment-avoidance'. It seems to me that the main problem with analyses of this type is that they rely on some idealised, but also extremely generalised, version of the past, in which 'modernity' serves as the last vestige of morality and humanity on the declining curve of Western civilisation. Postmodernity, in turn, is seen here as an unwelcome fragmentation of the past unity of all humans, coupled with a definitive loss of attachments which are not sustainable at present. That this loss of the alleged unity, which in itself can be quite a colonising and reductive concept, might actually facilitate a rethinking of what counts as proximity and ethical engagement escapes theorists like Boyer and Bauman, theorists who seem to use the term 'postmodernity' to allow themselves a nostalgic venture into the past. In his *Postmodern Ethics* Bauman does consider the possibility of a new ethics generated by what he sees as the changed circumstances of our postmodern era, but it is still primarily an attempt to come to terms with the fragmentation and loss we have supposedly experienced. His project is thus an attempt to 'rescue' both humanity and morality from the snares of postmodern life, without considering that perhaps what he describes as a 'loss' can in fact be the first condition of a new ethics, one not based on the totalisation of the past or on some generalised conclusions regarding the current state of humanity.

For me, in turn, the ontology of cybercities is uncertain (i.e. both metaphorical and material, always dependent on the reworking of the (un)reality of the modernist metropolis). This is why what we do in them depends on what I have described as the 'pedestrian attitude' we adopt. I am thus reluctant to agree with Boyer's dire conclusion that 'The city no longer evokes our involvement; it has become numbed, speechless, without a story to tell. We are unable to develop architectural forms that are engaged politically with the urban environment'.[40] Rather than merely symbolise the loss of the modernist harmony and the total disconnectedness of selves, for me cybercities foreground some new forms of proximity, in which the distinction between public and private spaces on the one hand and their inhabitants on the other is blurred. It is in this sense, I believe, that the cybercity can be seen as a politically engaged architectural form. It can serve as a paradigm for an ethics of hospitality, of proximity without engulfment, in which the self opens towards the other to produce what Haraway describes as 'disturbingly and pleasurably tight coupling'. Transgressing the distinctions between the material and the virtual, between human and machine, the inhabitants of cybercities, with their software-bodies, experience alterity and connectedness as an irreducible part of the self. Of course, there is no guarantee that such connectedness will be necessarily seen as ethical. The case of the French performance artist Orlan, who is undergoing a series of plastic surgeries in order to mimic the discourse of Western aesthetics with its rigid ideas of beauty and femininity, and thus raise a number of political and ethical questions in a most 'engaged' way, can also be (mis?)read as a disavowal of the physical and the atrophy of any political impulse. As Boyer argues in relation to Orlan's work, 'in these postmodern times we have failed so completely to arrive at a "politicisation of aesthetics" first outlined by Benjamin'.[41] To counter-act such accusations, in the previous chapter, *Webwords: from the spider's web to cyberspace*, I have attempted to demonstrate that it is possible to trace an ethical dimension in Orlan's work. However, I do not intend to 'remedy' Boyer's argument with a positivist rereading of cyborg couplings. Indeed, it is the fact that cyborgian connectivity generates the possibility of its multiple readings that opens up a non-prescribed ethical space in it. This degree of undecidability character-ising the projects in which the inhabitants of, and travellers through, cybercities are involved is a guarantee of their ethical dimension. This ethical dimension can be either embraced and explored from thé perspective of respect for their alterity or simply absorbed by the totalising logic which yearns for the undisturbed unity of the self without the other.

In a similar manner, the work of the Australian artist Stelarc – another traveller through the material–virtual landscapes of cyber-cities – raises a number of political and ethical questions. Stelarc has been extending his body through performance since 1960s to produce what he terms corporeal 'connectivity', which is facilitated by new technologies. Challenging the more traditional perception of cyber-space and the Internet as bodiless realms, Stelarc explains: 'The Inter-net does not hasten the disappearance of the body and the dissolution of the self – rather, it generates new collective physical couplings and a telematic scaling of subjectivity. What becomes important is not merely the body's identity, but its connectivity – not its mobility or location, but its interface'.[42] It is in this sense that the cybercity as one possible architectural formation in which sexuated city-surfers have replaced detached *flâneurs* can be seen as an extension of the modern-ist city project.

It was the abundance of the modernist city life that provided the *flâneur*, a key figure of the city, with the sense of his existence, offering consolation to approaching boredom. Perceived as a kaleidoscopic performance, the city, with its newly built arcades, elegant shops and gas-lamps, was a friendly place for those privileged members of society who chose it as a companion. As Walter Benjamin explains, 'The street becomes a dwelling for the *flâneur*; he is as much at home among the façades of houses as a citizen is in his four walls.'[43] The city, appropriated through the voyeur's gaze, was turned into a collection of frozen images: alluring, but safe. The cybercity-surfer, the heir of the modernist *flâneur*, is stripped off the fantasy of his or her special positioning in the world. The illusion of homeliness has been shattered by the irresolvable alterity and ambiguity: cyberspace is intrinsically *unheimlich*. The lazy stroll, which indicates the *flâneur*'s control of the system and of his own desire, has given way to an accelerated chase through the labyrinths of the inconceivable metropolis of the sort depicted by William Gibson in *Neuromancer*:

> Night City was like a deranged experiment in social Darwinism, designed by a bored researcher who kept one thumb permanently on the fast-forward button. Stop hustling and you sank without a trace, but move a little too swiftly and you'd break the fragile surface tension of the black market; either way, you were gone, with nothing left of you but some vague memory in the mind of a fixture like Ratz.[44]

While darkness and impermeability are the characteristic features of the cybercity, in the modern city '[i]nterpersonal relations ... are distinguished by a marked preponderance of the activity of the eye'.[45] The strolling *flâneur* takes his time to register the objects in which he is interested, directing the spectacle himself and inviting kindness with his complacent look. The surfer in the cybercity cannot enjoy a similar sense of control. Dazzled by the excess of signs and spaces, he or she traces the maze of the streets in search of other human beings. Direction-seeking takes place on the level of gestures, as the mastery of the eye recedes before the oncoming blindness which results from the constantly accelerated generation of signs, images and spaces. The experience of the cybercity is no longer visual, as the eye fails when faced with the palimpsest of the urban space. Its text-ure calls for total immersion, enticing with its mystery and the possibility of its solution. Kenneth Frampton, to whose concept of Critical Regionalism I referred earlier, emphasises that contemporary architecture appeals to multiple senses. 'The tactile resilience of the place-form and the capacity of the body to read the environment in terms other than those of sight alone suggest a potential strategy for resisting the domination of universal technology.'[46] Any event happening in the city space, uncanny in its deferral of the known and the production of both desire and anxiety, is first of all experienced on the level of the flesh. The skin becomes a screen on to which the external image can be projected; it is both an envelope that protects the self from the world and the means of communication with it.[47] The modern arcade recedes into the human body, and the openwork of its columns is replaced by the porous texture of the skin, which makes it, on the one hand, a filter for the inpouring signs, and, on the other, a channel tuned into the frequency of the city. The universal technology shunned by Frampton can be resisted by allowing micro-technologies to enter the bodily space. Explaining the reasoning behind his 'Stomach Sculpture' project, in which a dome capsule built of quality metals was inserted into his body and then arrayed with switches on the control box and documented by means of video endoscopy equipment, Stelarc calls for the radical opening of the bodily space:

> It is time to recolonise the body with MICROMINIATURISED ROBOTS to augment our bacterial population, to assist our immuno-logical system and to monitor the capillary and internal tracts of the body. ... SPECK-SIZED ROBOTS ARE EASILY SWALLOWED, AND MAY NOT EVEN BE SENSED! At a nanotechnology level, machines will inhabit cellular spaces and manipulate molecular structures.[48]

In the era of cyborgs, corporeal art and nanotechnology, the body can no more be seen as a sacrosanct realm, veiled for its protection by the layer of impenetrable skin. There is no room for the rural fantasies of purity and return to 'nature' any more: abjection has to be recognised as part and parcel of the everyday. Interestingly, Stelarc perceives this interpenetration between human and machine as a promise of some new forms of hospitality and intimacy: 'The body has been aug-mented, invaded and now becomes a host – not only for technology, but also for remote agents.'[49] These new forms of connectivity facili-tated by the Internet are not meant to, putting it crudely, replace sex with cybersex, or to erase any traces of proximity. Rather, they allow for a redefinition of the boundaries of the self as well as facilitating a broader scope of connections which transcend the closeness–distance opposition.

Stelarc's work is important for me in the context of an ethical possibility generated by cybercities because it allows for the redrafting of the relationship between the human and his or her environment. Exploring the new forms of proximity facilitated by the Internet,

Stelarc allows us to formulate a new set of questions regarding both aesthetics and ethics. I believe his artistic performances can thus be seen as a conceptual challenge to the claims about the aestheticisation of everyday life and the decline of the ethical impulse. Opening his body to the intrusion of technology and thus shifting the locus of human agency, Stelarc renounces the possibility of knowing the consequences of his connected performances in advance. By abandoning the desire to master the house of his own body and opening himself to the (perhaps hostile) intrusion of the guest, Stelarc performs the most ethical act of what Derrida terms 'unconditional hospitality': 'For unconditional hospitality to take place you have to accept the risk of the other coming and destroying the place, initiating a revolution, stealing everything or killing everyone. That is the risk of pure hospitality and pure gift'.[50] Unlike in traditional theories of the sublime, which relied on erecting barriers and boulders between the self and the source of alterity, in the feminine sublime the subject–object barrier is transformed into a welcoming embrace of the unknown (which, in fact, may not even arrive at all).

If, as Stelarc argues, 'The body becomes the landscape of machines, machines are no longer in the human horizon but within the human body itself',[51] it is not only the body that undergoes a transformation here: we are also experiencing the blurring of boundaries between the city and its inhabitants, or between landscape and flesh. The cybercity can thus serve as a model for an ethics of hospitality which calls for the opening of the self to the arrival of an incalculable and unpredictable alterity. Going back to Irigaray's ethics of sexual difference, we can conclude that this alterity is always already sexualised. If his or her otherness is to be acknowledged, the other – the encounter with whom still remains uncertain – has to be recognised as a sexuate being.

Love is in the air …

Where are 'things'? In amorous space, or in a mundane space?
(Roland Barthes, *A Lover's Discourse*)

Sexualisation is by no means an experience solely restricted to the cybercity. Henning Bech argues that this was already a characteristic feature of the *modern* city: 'sexualisation is generated in the spatial arrangements of the [Victorian] pub as a particular space of strangers. … Modern *being-in-the-world* is essentially *being-in-the-city* (and *being-in-the-telecity*), and *sexualisation* is an essential and inescapable basic *tuning* of being-in-the-city.'[52] Interestingly, it was precisely the sexual dimension of the modernist city that disturbed its otherwise transparent and clear architectonics. To diminish the fear associated with the unwanted, hidden aspects of the city, the source of this fear was represented by means of the image of femininity. The cinematic genre of *film noir* was one such mechanism through which the taming of the excess of modernity took place: as Boyer points out, the dangers of the city were presented as the dangers of sexual liaisons, and were further associated with the *femme fatale*. Using the arguments of Rosalyn Deutsche, Boyer claims that this approach has been now taken on by some contemporary theorists who adopt the role of 'detectives', attempting to arrive at the clear vision of postmodern landscapes and thus achieve mastery over them:

> By hiding the presence of women – making them either disappear or appear invisible – these critics desexualise the terrain of the postmodern city. Such criminal acts against women subsequently enable the same detectives to become the rational masculine subject who gives form and shape to or who controls what they consider to be indeterminate, characterless, and neutral feminine matter.[53]

Significantly, the association of the dangerous, untameable aspect of the city with women, who are then silenced and erased from the picture in one way or another, allows the male 'detective' to maintain a distance between himself and what he finds threatening. It also leads to a paradox: the detective can only perform his role well when he is detached from crime, which is seen as both an object of his enquiry and a distraction from this enquiry. The object of his investigation must, then, be disavowed and forgotten. As a result of this disavowal, concludes Boyer, 'the feminine is doubly encrypted: it has affected the manner in which space is conceptualised and theorised, yet it is simultaneously denied an appearance in that space'.[54] This manoeuvre is reminiscent of the retreat resorted to by the theorists of the sublime in their attempts to control the theoretical excess of the discourse they were developing. In both cases, the image of woman serves as a displacement of the excess that threatens the identity of the (male) subject.[55] The parallel between the discourse of the sublime and the discourse of the city is not groundless, as both these discourses are concerned with the construction and simultaneous destruction of the modern subject. While, as Peter de Bolla argues, the modern subject is a side product of the eighteenth-century discourse of the sublime and of the reflexivity it generates, it is elevated on precarious foundations, depending, in fact, on the annulment of sexual difference and the assertion of the self's totality and sameness. (I discuss the relationship between subjectivity and the sublime in chapters 1 and 2.) These precarious foundations of modern subjectivity are further threatened by modern (and postmodern) 'being-in-the-world'. Enlightenment rationality, celebrated through the Kantian elevation of reason in the discourse of the sublime and dependent on the confinement of women to the sphere of the pre-ethical, is constantly haunted by the spectre of sexual difference. Describing the threat the city poses to the subject in 'feminine' terms is intended to reduce this threat and reassert the self-sufficiency of the modernist *flâneur*. Femininity cannot be a 'real' danger if it is associated with, as Boyer writes, 'all the phantasmagoria and artifice of modernity – *in terms of images, styles, spectacles, and fictions* – as well as the destructive tendency of false promises and unfulfilled desires, and the melancholic loss of equilibrium and the emptying of experience. It captures the double nature of things, *being both the source of anxieties and the promise of pleasures*'.[56]

Interestingly, Boyer makes use of the rhetoric of the sublime to convey this ambiguity of the feminine used as an image of the city. She argues that the feminine aspect of the city, even though only evoked to reinforce the self-sufficiency and mastery of its male inhabitants and to ward off their fears of sexuality and difference, in fact points to the masquerading aspect of identity as such. Describing 'woman' as an artifice, merely a question of style, is a well-known strategy which is employed to diminish the fear of sexual difference and the inaccommodable sense of alterity it evokes.[57] But all these desperate attempts to 'seduce from a distance' and thus tame the 'woman' who threatens to undermine masculine identity with her playful tricks are futile: the belief that femininity can be reduced to a stepping stone for the erection of man's identity is only a fantasy. Taunting the philosophers who for centuries have relied on the image of 'woman' to assert their discursive control over space, time, identity and language, Derrida writes in *Spurs*:

> That which will not be pinned down by truth is, in truth – *feminine*. This should not, however, be hastily mistaken for a woman's femininity, for female sexuality, or for any other of those essentialising fetishes which might still tantalise the dogmatic philosopher, the impotent artist or the inexperienced seducer who has not yet escaped his foolish hopes of capture.[58]

These hopes of capture are deemed foolish because 'femininity as space' reveals its intrinsic ambiguity and in*essential*ity. Taking recourse to the image of woman's body (which in Western philosophy since Plato has been associated with a broader concept of space) only 'underscores an anxiety about this "entity" and the precariousness of its boundedness'.[59] Even though woman has been defined by man as his utensil and envelope, she can still claim an identity of her own from among the debris of representations which haven been forged for her. Irigaray argues that 'If after all this, she is still alive, she continually undoes his work – distinguishing herself from both the envelope and the thing, ceaselessly creating there some interval, game, something in motion and un-limited which disturbs his perspective, his world, and his/its limits'.[60] Developing Irigaray's ideas, Sue Best points out in her article 'Sexualising Space' that, according to Irigaray, 'one way to challenge philosophy's construction of woman is by using the very same tools that have inscribed the body of woman. ... This rewriting of metaphor as grounded in body-matter prevents philosophy from being able to recuperate metaphor or absorb it into the masculine side of the binary – the realm of ideas, the intelligible and ideality'.[61] This brings me back once again to the problematic of the feminine sublime and its occurrence in the minimal spaces of the everyday. As I have argued in the previous chapters, the feminine sublime is not a sexualised version of the traditional sublime. The discourse of the sublime has always relied on femininity as its foundation, but it has been a fantasised, stylised version of femininity, something that has allowed the male artist or philosopher to feel complete and undisturbed by the signs of alterity. My proposition for an ethics of the feminine sublime relies on the 'femininity' of the traditional discourse of the sublime. By using 'the very same tools that have inscribed the body of woman', the feminine sublime mimics the masculine discourse of ideas by foregrounding its rootedness in the materiality of the female body. It thus retraces the lost connection between materiality and ideality, or body and language. It also challenges the rigid structuring of the (feminine) space in the sublime event by collapsing the prescribed distance between the self and the source of its fear and desire. As a result, the feminine sublime facilitates the emergence of what Irigaray terms 'an ethics of the passions' and 'a relationship between two loving subjects of different sexes'.[62]

In order to enable this loving rapport between different sexes, we need to revisit the traditional economy of (anti)love which deprives woman of the possibility of being an active and desiring lover. We can approach this project by looking at the representations of 'woman' in the modernist city, which was one of the illustrations of the modern concept of identity. In the modernist imaginary the city itself is described as 'woman',[63] thus establishing its associations with artifice, commerce and lasciviousness. However, the chain of meanings which is produced by the signifier 'woman' is then linked, in a somewhat surprising and unexpected way, with the term 'prostitute'. This slide is yet another mechanism employed to control the excess produced by the city. This process of 'the displacement of woman', which turns the engagement with the other into a capitalist transaction and the sexualised 'other' who participates in it into a mere commodity, is intended to ward off any fears of incalculable alterity. As Boyer observes, 'the prostitute exemplifie[s] the unreality of any love object, as well as the impotency of the male to curb or alter the loss of the maternal body, of a real love object, and of aura. She [can] only be re-idealised and re-presented as a false simulation, as a fiction of style and artifice'.[64] In this way, a hierarchy of subordination based on the rules of an economic transaction is established as a foundation of the relationship between the sexes. Disabling the emergence of an ethics of the passions, this hierarchy is employed to control and restrain pleasure and to manage the space in which this pleasure could potentially occur. In his reading of Henning Bech's eroticisation of the modernist city space, Bauman recognises the temporary nature of encounters taking place in the city. Although such encounters are a source of an almost orgasmic pleasure, they always prevent the self's ultimate immersion in the other:

> If, in the city event, pleasure supersedes fear (which is an equally omnipresent component of the experience), it is only due to the keeping of the strangers in the state of strangeness, to the freezing of distance and the prevention of closeness. The biological feeling of mutual alienation is a source of ecstasy which is only known to wanderers. It is a kind of unconstrained pleasure, which is not impaired by anxiety over consequences, possible duties and potential obligations one will have to undertake in case something happens.[65]

'Life-in-the-modern-city' does not leave us with many alternatives. Bauman bemoans the glorification of temporary encounters, which are free from any sense of responsibility, but he seems unable to see beyond this kind of disinterested engagement. In the modern city, the self does recognise the alterity of the other, thus guaranteeing mutual attraction, but this recognition does not lead to the crossing of the boundaries of identity. The ethics of the wanderer is an ethics of solitude, combining solipsistic hedonism with the withdrawal of responsibility for the other I might make love to but never love.

The ethics of the feminine sublime, which perhaps can be an answer to Bauman's nostalgia, is more demanding, though it might create an impression of similar disinterestedness. The distance maintained in its encounters is not annulled by an increasing intimacy. This is where the difficulty of the amorous relationship lies: caring for the other and respecting his or her incalculable difference, the self has to abandon the fantasy of the ever-after union for the sake of a temporary event. Yet, the recognition of the uniqueness of every moment poses the self with a task of exploring them *ad infinitum* (every encounter as if becoming the whole world, which is experienced, in Wittgenstein's terms, *sub specie aeternitatis*). Instead of relying on the legal guarantee of intimacy, the self has to accept the horror of nothing happening at all, but it also has to attempt to overcome this horror for the sake of both partners' *jouissance*. It is a thin line between Bech's ethics of frozen distance and the paradoxical closeness which does not annul distance postulated by the ethics of the feminine sublime. The insignificant episode taking place in the modernist city, free from both past and future, gives way to the uniqueness of the amorous event, which for a while as if becomes the whole world. The feminine sublime does not promise eternal or even momentary happiness, and yet the provisionality of its conditions does not exempt the self from responsibility for the other. The local, minimal character of the surroundings adds to the specificity of each encounter, without reducing its significance. Paraphrasing Wittgenstein, in the everyday space of the feminine sublime 'the other is everything that is the case'.

Notes

1 Jean-François Lyotard, *The Inhuman*, trans. Geoffrey Bennington and Rachel Bowlby (Cambridge: Polity Press, 1991), 84.
2 Kenneth Frampton, 'Towards a Critical Regionalism: Six Points for an Architecture of Resistance', in *Postmodern Culture*, ed. Hal Foster (London: Pluto Press, 1983), 21.
3 Lyotard, *The Inhuman*, 90.
4 Jolanta Brach-Czaina, *Szczeliny istnienia* (Warsaw: PIW, 1992), 6, translation mine.

5   Ibid., 9–10, translation mine.
6   Ibid., 18, translation mine.
7   Ibid., 20, translation mine.
8   Michel de Certeau, *The Practice of Everyday Life*, trans. Steven Rendall (Berkeley, Los Angeles, London: University of California Press, 1988), 11.
9   Ibid., 11.
10 Anthony Kenny ed., *The Wittgenstein Reader* (Oxford: Blackwell, 1994), 3.
11 Anthony Kenny, *Wittgenstein* (Harmondsworth: Penguin, 1973), 4.
12 Robert J. Fogelin, *Wittgenstein* (London and New York: Routledge, 1987), 99.
13 Kenny ed., *The Wittgenstein Reader*, 4.
14 Ibid., 31.
15 George Pitcher, *The Philosophy of Wittgenstein* (Englewood Cliffs, N.J.: Prentice-Hall, 1964), 160.
16 Kenny ed., *The Wittgenstein Reader*, 25.
17 Fogelin, *Wittgenstein*, 99.
18 Wittgenstein, *Notebooks*. Quoted in Diané Collinson, 'Ethics and Aesthetics Are One', *British Journal of Aesthetics*, 25:3 (1985), 268.
19 Ibid., 268.
20 Quoted in Collinson, ibid., 267.
21 Ibid., 267.
22 Kenny ed., *The Wittgenstein Reader*, 291.
23 Ibid., 292.
24 As Collinson observes, 'In the case of the aesthetic object the empirical self disappears because the aesthetic object is one's whole world: there is no logical space for an empirical self. That is consistent with the typical aesthetic experience in which we seem to inhabit or become what is contemplated. In the case of the ethical the empirical self disappears in that it becomes just one among the facts of the world which are seen as a whole, so that there is no individuation of any particular empirical self. And that is consistent with the typically ethical attitude in which a special place is never given to oneself', 'Ethics and Aesthetics Are One', 269.
25 Immanuel Kant, *The Critique of Judgement*, trans. James Meredith (Oxford: Clarendon Press, 1952), 110–11.
26 Emmanuel Levinas, *Totality and Infinity*, trans. Alphonso Lingis (Dordrecht, Boston, London: Kluwers Academic Publishers, 1969), 34–5.
27 Ibid., 75.
28 Brach-Czaina, *Szczeliny istnienia*, 27, translation mine.
29 Sigmund Freud, 'The Uncanny', in *The Standard Edition of the Complete Psychological Works of Sigmund Freud* (London: The Hogarth Press and the Institute of Psychoanalysis, 1956/1978), Vol. 17, 219.
30 Ibid., 224.
31 Wendy Wheeler, 'From the Sublime to the Domestic', in *The Most Sublime Act*, eds David Jarrett, Tadeusz Rachwał and Tadeusz Sławek (London: University of North London Press, 1996), 63–4.
32 For a discussion of identity as a modern question see, for example, David Kolb, *The Critique of Pure Modernity* (Chicago: University of Chicago Press, 1998); Stuart Hall and Paul du Gay eds, *Questions of Cultural Identity*